**with a new introduction
by the author**

*José
Brunner*

$\mathcal{F}reud$ *and the*

$\mathcal{P}olitics$ *of*

$\mathcal{P}sychoanalysis$

Transaction Publishers
New Brunswick (U.S.A.) and London (U.K.)

New material this edition copyright © 2001 by Transaction Publishers, New Brunswick, New Jersey. Originally published in 1995 by Blackwell Publishers.

This book is printed on acid-free paper that meets the American National Standard for Permanence of Paper for Printed Library Materials.

Library of Congress Catalog Number: 00-046725
ISBN: 0-7658-0672-X
Printed in the United States of America

Library of Congress Cataloging-in-Publication Data

Brunner, José, 1954-
    Freud and the politics of psychoanalysis / José Brunner ; with a new introduction by the author.
        p. cm.
    Includes bibliographical references and index.
    ISBN 0-7658-0672-X (alk. paper)
    1. Freud, Sigmund, 1856-1939—Political and social views. 2. Psychoanalysis—Political aspects. 3. Psychoanalysis—Philosophy—History. 4. Psychoanalysis and culture—History. I. Title.

BF109 .F74 B77 2000
150.19'52'092—dc21   00-046725

Contents

Introduction to the Transaction Edition

Freud and the Politics of the Mind, 1900—2000[1]

This book aims to recover the dialectical complexity of Freud's work that is lost when psychoanalysis is reduced to either a causal science that examines the dynamics of the mind only in mechanical terms, or to a hermeneutics exclusively concerned with hidden intentions and meanings of mental acts and behaviour. For the last three decades or so, much of the debate on psychoanalysis has been framed in terms of the hermeneutics-or-science controversy. Time and again, the question has been posed, whether psychoanalysis is an intentional psychology, based on an art or craft of interpretation and constructing narratives, which focuses on hidden meanings and purposes, or whether it is a science that can explain feelings and acts in terms of non-experiential causes, such as mental energies, processes, forces, structures, and so on. In other words, one is asked to decide whether to treat psychoanalysis as part of the humanities, relying on literary skills and historical insights, creating stories and providing plausible interpretations, or to liken it to a natural science of the mind, which establishes causes, discovers processes, and formulates mechanical laws of the mind's forces.[2]

As I wish to show in this introduction, written five years after this book was originally published, I regard the dichotomizing phrasing of this question as a mistake and the framing of one's approach to psychoanalysis in its binary terms a non-starter. In my view, psychoanalysis necessarily combines causal and intentional talk in a dialectical and deconstructive interplay, where they are not simply complementary, but also undermine each other and point to each other's radical insufficiency. Moreover, I argue that the fusion of causality and meaning in psychoanalysis pervasively 'politicizes' its discourse. (Those looking for definitions of 'politics', 'the political' and 'power' will find them in the preface, but for the purpose of reading this introduction any more or less commonsense notion of these terms will do. Generally I use the terms 'psychoanalytic' and 'psychoanalysis' to refer to Freud's work only.)

Thus, instead of reducing psychoanalytic discourse to only one of its dimensions, as so many other commentators on Freud have done, I seek to show not only that hermeneutics and mechanics are inevitably intertwined in Freud's work, but also that his attempt to achieve such a fusion led him to adopt a plethora of political metaphors and analogies—which I regard as constitutive and structuring, rather than illustrative and embellishing—and to dissect the inner world of the psyche in parallel with the outer world of politics. Because politics is a sphere where hermeneutics is ineluctably enmeshed with mechanics, it offers itself as a convenient repertoire of terms to describe mental processes, which portray them from both a hermeneutic and a causal perspective. Political actors continuously bring into play both symbolic power and material resources, rhetoric and force, ideology and armed struggle, charismatic appeal and economic control.

I wish to allude to just two examples out of the many that are brought up in the course of the book, illustrating the way in which political reasoning structures Freud's discourse: first, he construes the mind as an arena of a conflict that is based on an economy of scarcity. The psyche's invisible protagonists, such as the ego, id or superego, are portrayed as involved in a struggle over the allocation and use of mental resources, that is, of mental assets that provide them with control over the meaning of expressions and symbols. In this context it is significant that Freud put references to energy quantities under the heading of economy, not mechanics. Such economic struggles are at the core of politics, but politics always also has to do with persuasions, doctrines, world-views, identities and so on, that is, with artifacts of meaning.

Second, Freud refers to the mind as an arena of 'representation'. He defines this term in the political sense, distinguishing it clearly from pictorial or symbolic representation. For Freud mental representatives stand for a force, a wish or desire in the way in which parliamentary representatives stand for the electoral wishes, parties or government. Again, the power of such wishes is always a result of the forces that propel and oppose it, and of the ability of the various sides to articulate their interests and needs.

By revealing the politics in Freud's discourse, I seek to make three interrelated arguments: first, I contend that rather than contradictory and inconsistent, Freud's discourse is internally complex but coherent. Second, I maintain that a political reading of Freud not only captures its complexity and coherence, but is also more fruitful, comprehensive, parsimonious, consistent and cogent than reductionist presentations that turn him either into a natural scientist of the mind or into a hermeneuticist. Third, I claim that the politics of race, class and gender are intrinsic to Freud's discourse and cannot be severed from it.

Though I argue that Freud's fusion of the hermeneutic with the causal turned psychoanalysis into a political discourse, I wish to avoid the *propter hoc* fallacy of claiming that this consequence also constituted his motivation. I do not assume that Freud joined meaning with mechanics in order to create a political discourse, but that this was a momentous outcome of his attempt to achieve a dialectical fusion of these two perspectives. Moreover, I argue that he combined interpretation with explanation not for the purpose of completeness, but in order to demonstrate imperfection, for he took the latter to be the distinguishing characteristic of science.

In the first section of this new introduction, I portray the dialectics of hermeneutics and mechanics leading to a political discourse in one paradigmatic example. In this fashion I hope to make somewhat more explicit one of the central arguments that underlie the entire book. Then, in the second section I show that Freud regarded the experience of power and powerlessness, which lies at the core of the political, as primary to humans. This is done to prove that a political reading of psychoanalysis is not only justifiable on the basis of its logic and language, but also on account of one of its substantive claims that puts politics at the core of the human condition. I developed this argument recently, in response to some of the criticisms that I received. It was argued that since Freud did not consider power and politics to be fundamental human experiences, to focus on the political aspects of his discourse, as I do, means to turn psychoanalysis into something foreign to itself.

Since the original publication of this book in 1995, much of the debate on Freud has been overshadowed by the Freud Wars, as the rather vehement but mainly American controversy on Freud and his work has come to be called. In this dispute Freud has been charged with being a liar and a fraud, and psychoanalysis has been accused of being harmful to its patients. In the third and last section I place my argument in the context of this recent controversy, which gained momentum only after the book's manuscript was completed. Like Freud's militant detractors, I also think that the debate on psychoanalysis should move beyond the science-or-hermeneutics issue, but, as will become evident, I wish to take it in a direction that is diametrically opposed to theirs.

1. Dialectics of Imperfection, or How Freud Fused Hermeneutics with Causal Explanation

For Freud, science had to avoid excessive systematization, since systematization necessitated a reductionist and one-dimensional discourse, as well as pretensions at completeness that were illusory and detracted from work that still had to be done. Science had to avoid closures and, by creating inner tensions, open avenues for further critical explorations.

Let me demonstrate the dialectics of imperfection in Freud's work by joining him on a walk. In August 1899, while working on his *magnum opus*, *The Interpretation of Dreams*, he wrote to Wilhelm Fliess that it was 'planned on the model of an imaginary walk'. 'At the beginning the dark forest of authors (who do not see the trees), hopelessly lost on wrong tracks. Then a concealed pass through which I lead the reader—my specimen dream with its peculiarities, details, indiscretions, bad jokes—and then suddenly the high ground and the question: which way do you wish to go now?'[3] In the opening sentences of the book's third chapter Freud uses the same vocabulary, but this time he likens the process of dream interpretation itself to such an imaginary walk:'When, after passing through a narrow defile, we suddenly emerge up on a piece of high ground, where the path divides and the finest prospects open up on every side, we may pause for a moment and consider in which direction we shall first turn our steps. Such is the case with us, now that we have surmounted the first interpretation of a dream. We find ourselves in the full daylight of a sudden discovery'.[4]

This passage follows directly on a declaration in the conclusion of the book's second chapter, where Freud states:'When the work of interpretation has been completed [*vollendet*], we perceive that a dream is the fulfillment of a wish [*lässt sich der Traum als eine Wunscherfüllung erkennen*]'.[5] In other words, at this stage Freud posits that dream interpretation can reach an ending or a completion, and—in the original German—he claims that this endpoint is marked by the dream's readiness to give in to the interpreter's efforts and to reveal itself as a wishfulfillment.

Some four hundred pages later, in the beginning of *The Interpretation of Dreams*, Freud formulates the basic principles underlying the production of dreams and of mental functioning in general. There again he takes up the metaphor of the journey into the unconscious. But he describes as illusory the sense of completion that is obtained by the sudden illumination of interpretation:

> It is only after we have disposed of everything that has to do with the work of interpretation that we can begin to realize the incompleteness of our psychology of dreams. . . . For it must be clearly understood that the easy and agreeable portion of our journey lies behind us. Hitherto, unless I am greatly mistaken, all the paths along which we have travelled have led us towards the light—towards elucidation [*Aufklärung*] and fuller understanding [*zum vollen Verständnis*]. But as soon as we endeavour to penetrate more fully into the mental process involved in dreaming, every path will end in darkness.[6]

This, then, is the scientific journey into the mind's secrets on which Freud takes us: we leave the dark wood through a narrow, concealed pass, ascend to the open high ground—only to progress into darkness. At the end of the book we discover that *The Interpretation of Dreams* has been radically incomplete all along. After several hundred pages of detailed discussion of hermeneutic techniques concerned with the condensation and displacement of meaning, symbolism and censorship, we find that psychoanalysis cannot be reduced to an interpretive practice. Rather than writing a conclusion in the seventh and last chapter, Freud transgresses the boundaries of hermeneutics by the insertion of causal hypotheses. By pointing to a new realm of causal speculation that lies beyond hermeneutics, he radically undermines hopes for hermeneutic perfection or closure.

In the seventh chapter Freud's book is no longer concerned with the hidden meaning which the dreamer expresses in pictures and symbols. Instead, Freud tries to establish the origins of the dream's signs, that is, he seeks to explain what causes them. For this purpose he refers to a different category of entities: to non-experiential mechanisms and systems, currents of psychic energy and mental agencies, which fall under the heading of 'metapsychology'. His comment, as well as many that he made later, indicates that he was aware that the referents of metapsychological formulations lie in the dark and that hypotheses concerning their nature and functioning must remain conjectural.[7]

While adding an explanatory layer to the interpretative chapters that precede it, the seventh chapter of *The Interpretation of Dreams* also subverts them, denying the possibility of a complete and self-enclosed hermeneutics. Freud took thinking that was enclosed in apparently complete systems to be necessarily opposed to scientific thought. Science, he wrote in the last of his *New Introductory Lectures*, 'is not all-comprehensive, it is too incomplete and makes no claim to being self-contained and to the construction of systems'[8]. Its evident incompleteness or imperfection was for Freud a crucial characteristic of science, which differentiated it from philosophy and religion, whose illusory stability and coherence aimed to soothe their followers, lulling them into a misleading sense of security.[9] Criticizing their paralyzing influence on their believers, Freud referred to comprehensive thought-systems as *Weltanschauungen*. For Freud, a *Weltanschauung* was 'an intellectual construction which solves all the problems of our existence uniformly on the basis of one overriding hypothesis, which, accordingly, leaves no question unanswered and in which everything that interests us finds its fixed place'.[10] And although Freud also referred to science as a *Weltanschauung,* he pointed out that contrary to its philosophical and religious counterparts, it did not really deserve this title, since it did not pretend to be able to answer all questions.

These provisos and stipulations have to be kept in mind when one considers Freud's famous declarations that 'psycho-analysis has a special right to speak for the scientific *Weltanschauung*' and that it 'is part of science and can adhere to the scientific *Weltanschauung*'.[11] For by themselves such utterances do not explicate what Freud meant by the terms 'science', 'scientific' and '*Weltanschauung*'. On one level at least, Freud used this term to denote a form of thinking that, though methodical, orderly and aiming at precision, always also involved metaphor, speculation, multidimensionality, and, above all, a keen awareness of its necessary but fruitful incompleteness. At the same time, the structure of Freud's *magnum opus* makes it evident that he assumed that a science of the mind had to include both interpretation and causal explanation. As I have pointed out above— and documented in detail in part II of this book—it was the attempt to both fuse hermeneutics and mechanics, and pitch them against each other that'politicized'Freud's discourse.

2. Dialectics of Otherness, or Where Politics Comes From

There are a great number of theories on what is supposed to be at stake in political conflicts. Some theorists trace the origins and structure of politics predominantly to national interests or nationalism, others to religious divisions, gender, ethnicity, race or class. Thus, though politics need not necessarily be located in the public sphere or seen as a matter of collectives only, it usually is regarded as a matter of adult life. And though Freud did not explicitly refer to the origins of the political and the search for power, it seems to me that his writings contain a discourse that traces the quest for power to the earliest stages of life. In other words, I contend that experiences of power and powerlessness appear in Freud's writings as basic to human life and decisive for the development from infant to adult. Thus, from this angle too, to show psychoanalysis to be political does not mean to introduce an extraneous element into Freud's discourse, but to bring out an element that hitherto may have been somewhat neglected by Freud's readers and commentators.

As is well known, for Freud the aim of nervous life in general was to master stimuli, to rid itself of all tensions and, were it feasible, to'maintain itself in an altogether unstimulated condition'.[12] According to him, stimuli reaching the mind from the subject's own body and from the outside world are experienced as disturbances of an original state of rest to which the human being wants to return by satisfying the needs to which they give rise. All of Freud's basic postulates, models and metaphors deal with one or another aspect of this homeostatic principle: with the sources, pressure and pathways of stimuli, with their effects on the mind and the means for their mastery as well as with problems encountered in the attempt to master them. According to the'pleasure principle', the achievement of this task, that is, the reduction of psychic tension, is experienced as pleasurable.[13]

I regard Freud's view of the earliest stages of life, where the infant seeks to avoid or get rid of stimuli, as referring to a kind of pre-political notion of power. By depicting the quest for the mastery or avoidance of stimuli as primary to life, Freud invokes an original notion of power as characteristic of a stage at which there still is no differentiated subject, and certainly not yet a vision of self-other relations that could provide the basis for categories of social power. According to Freud, there is no possibility of remaining in a condition of quiescence or of getting rid of stimuli as soon as they arise in order to return to the original condition. Infants are born into a world that they experience as a source of excitation with which they cannot cope, and from which they cannot escape. Thus, they experience themselves as powerless in the face of stimuli impinging on them both from the inside and outside. In reaction to this, they imagine themselves as omnipotent.

Freud made much of this original helplessness ('*Hilflosigkeit*') of human beings and of the fantasies sparked off in reaction to it, referring to them both on the level of individual development and in terms of his theory of the development of humankind as a whole. In *The Future of an Illusion* Freud explained religion and animism as a result of the helplessness of early humanity in the face of overwhelming natural forces. In other words, Freud claimed that magic and religion were illusions that served to relieve anxieties resulting from powerlessness. Embedding their origin in dialectics of powerlessness and fantasy, he argued that natural forces were endowed with human features, since such humanization meant that'[w]e can apply the same methods against those violent supermen [*gewalttätigen Übermenschen*] outside that we employ in our own society; we can try to adjure them, to appease them, to bribe them, and, by so influencing them, we may rob them of part of their power [*Macht*]'.[14] People in early tribal societies, Freud argued, believed in the magical power of their thoughts, which'has to serve the most varied purposes—it must subject [*unterwerfen*] natural phenomena to the will of man, it must protect the individual from his enemies and from dangers and it must give him the power [*Macht*] to injure his enemies'.[15] Again, focusing on the dynamics of power, he portrayed animism as a fantasy of omnipotence, which derived from the refusal to recognize the finitude and mortality of human beings, and from what he described as the'unshakable confidence in the possibility of controlling the world [*Weltbeherrschung*]'.[16]

Thus, Freud's discourse establishes a parallel between infancy and early humanity, infants and tribal societies, narcissism and animism. However speculative and questionable this parallel may be, there is no doubt that on both levels it embeds early development in an interplay of real powerlessness and illusions of power. Freud has no doubts that, soothing as they may be in the short term, in the long term such illusions must end in failure and frustration. Recurrent frustrations lead to a thorough reorganization of the mental processes, which brings infants—and early tribal people—to tolerate a basic level of excitation and expand their attention from a restricted orientation towards pleasure, to one that includes the outside world or reality in general, taking note of all perceptions and ideas, even if they happen to be unpleasurable.[17] Thus the'reality principle'emerges, and with it the attempt to control others not only in one's thoughts.

As we see, for Freud the quest for real social power derives from the attempt to avoid pain that comes from the outside. This leads to an ambivalence towards the existence of others, which is at the basis of social behaviour: others are necessary for one's physical and emotional survival since they provide one with the cooperation, protection, love, and satisfaction one seeks. But at the same time, one also experiences the existence of others as an ordeal, since they may constitute a threat or burden, imposing demands and limiting one's freedom. As Freud emphasized in *Civilization and Its Discontents*, utilitarian considerations of interest and expediency are not strong enough to overcome what he called the 'primary mutual hostility of human beings'.[18] For even though he admitted that people acquire value for one another by working together, he claimed that even 'the advantages of work in common, will not hold them together'.[19] In his words,

> The element of truth behind all this, which people are so ready to disavow, is that men are not gentle creatures who want to be loved, and who at most can defend themselves if they are attacked; they are, on the contrary, creatures among whose instinctual endowments is to be reckoned a powerful share of aggressiveness. As a result, their neighbour is for them not only a potential helper or sexual object, but also someone who tempts them to satisfy their aggressiveness on him, to exploit his capacity for work without compensation, to use him sexually without his consent, to seize his possessions, to humiliate him, to cause him pain, to torture and kill him. *Homo homini lupus*.[20]

This short summary and the few extracts from Freud's text have shown, I hope, that powerlessness is a primary experience for Freud. The pursuit of power, both by illusory and real means, appears in his writings as a deep-seated feature of human nature that he traces to the earliest stage of development, both on an individual and a historical level.

According to Freud, humans not only experience external others both as potential threats and objects of satisfactions, they are also haunted by an internal otherness. The order in the mind's inner world is threatened by the existence of a dynamic unconscious, which confronts the subject with the threatening fact that, as Freud famously put it, 'the ego is not master in its own house'.[21] From a psychoanalytic vantage point, what one regards as oneself, what self-consciousness or introspection have access to, is only part of the whole story or the picture. The other part of the mind is not only hidden, it is also highly influential and operates according to rules that are foreign to the conscious psyche. Freud styled himself as messenger of an inner otherness and explained much of the opposition to his theory by an unwillingness to acknowledge the lack of inner mastery. What is radical in Freud's message, then, is not simply the postulate of an unconscious mind, which—as Freud's critics never tire to point out—was a common feature of much of German Romanticism. Revolutionary in psychoanalysis was its postulate of the unconscious as a radical alterity, a strange mental domain whose rules are incommensurable with those of consciousness.[22]

On the one hand, Freud portrayed the unconscious as a sphere of absence, lacking categories that are essential to conscious thought and language—to which psychoanalysts refer as 'secondary processes'—such as time, space, logic, causality and grammar. On the other hand, he depicted it as filled with energy, ideas, memories and wishes, interacting among themselves and with the conscious part of the mind according to 'primary process' principles of displacement and condensation, as well as those of visual representation. Thus, he sought to understand the personality as constituted in a complex relationship between two irreducibly heterogeneous sets of psychic processes that are governed by different laws, but continuously interfere with each other.[23] He suggested that we extend the way we interpret mental processes in other people to our own mind, to seeing the unconscious as if it was another person, illustrating this view in *The Interpretation of Dreams* by drawing on a well-known fairy-tale:

> No doubt, a wish-fulfillment must bring pleasure; but the question then arises, 'To whom?' To the person who has the wish, of course. But as we know, a dreamer's relation to his wishes is a quite peculiar one. He repudiates them and censors them—in short, he doesn't like them. Their fulfillment can therefore give him no pleasure, but just the opposite; and experience shows that this opposite appears in the form of anxiety, something still to be explained. Thus, in relation to his dream-wishes, a dreamer can only be compared to an amalgamation of two separate people linked by some important common element. Instead of enlarging on this, I will remind you of a familiar fairy tale in which you will find the same solution repeated. A good fairy promises a poor married couple to fulfill their first three wishes. They are delighted, and make up their minds to choose their first three wishes carefully. But the woman lets herself be tempted by the odor of sausages being grilled in the cottage next door and wishes for a pair. In a flash they are there; this is the first wish-fulfillment. But the man is furious, and in his rage wishes that the sausages would hang from his wife's nose. This happens too; and the sausages are not to be dislodged from their new position. This is the second wish-fulfillment; but the wish is the man's, and its fulfillment is most disagreeable for his wife. You know the rest of the story. Since after all they are in fact one—man and wife—the third wish can only be that the sausages should be removed from the woman's nose.[24]

From a psychoanalytic perspective, then, the mind's central political question is: 'Who controls the wish, my (conscious) self or the (unconscious) other (which, of course, is also part of myself)?' In an additional twist of these Freudian dialectics of otherness, the unconscious is presented not only as the domain where I am a stranger to myself, but also where my innermost self is located; that is, where my earliest memories, greatest fantasies, deepest wishes and strongest desires are kept alive. My internal otherness is not only a part of myself that I cannot get rid of, it also is the part that shelters the secrets to myself. Thus, according to Freud, I am most myself where I am a stranger to myself, where I threaten myself. In fact, I may be my greatest threat. Moreover, while each of us has an internal part that remains foreign to him or her, this part is also involved in each and every one of our relationships with external others—and, ironically, the more intimate these relationships are, the more involved one's internal stranger may become in them. As Freud wrote to Fliess, 'I am accustoming myself to regarding every sexual act as a process in which four individuals are involved'.[25]

Much of psychoanalytic discourse focuses on the various strategies and tactics deployed by consciousness in order to contain such interferences and threats, as well as on the dialectics that are set in motion by them. Adopting a tactic that Freud called 'repression', consciousness or the ego may refuse to acknowledge certain wishes by imposing censorship and keeping them at bay. In another negative response to an objectionable wish, they may even seek out to do the precise opposite of what is wished for in the unconscious. Freud referred to this as 'reaction formation'. Alternatively, the ego may attempt to bring about all kinds of compromise formations, however precarious and problematic—and, ultimately, unpleasurable—they may be. These, of course, are the symptoms. Finally, by means of 'sublimation' it may allow wishes into consciousness, but redirect them at substitutes, if their direct satisfaction seems dangerous.

As we shall see, for Freud the problems of internal and external otherness are inextricably entangled. The dialectics of interpersonal relationships are not simply a derivative of internal otherness. Although the latter does influence our relations to external others, the necessary prior existence of two such others—our parents—for our existence is made to account for them.

Freud differs from other theorists in that he presents the child's early self as developing not only in relation to some generalized external other, but always in relation to at least two—or paradigmatically two—separate and bodily differentiated, but sexually and socially interrelated others, each of whom takes up a different position towards the emerging subject. As is well known, Freud's perspective envisions the social condition as fundamentally triangular or Oedipal: each human being enters a world in which there are 'always already' at least two others, related by social/sexual bonds, whose existence is a precondition for his or her very being.[26] This triangular constellation intensifies and complicates the fundamental ambivalence humans feel towards others.

As we have seen, Freud described human development as progressing on a political axis, whose core is constituted by power and its absence, and the ensuing threat of alterity. The less power humans have—both at the beginning of their lives as individuals and in prehistoric times of humanity—the more they resort to fantasies in which they control that which is strange and threatening. Ironically, the realization of limitations, forced upon both the child and tribal societies by repeated frustrations, allows them to gain real power and diminishes the need for further illusions of omnipotence. The more the power of humans grows in reality, the less they need to compensate for its absence in fantasy.

Therapeutic intervention in such a complex social and mental universe can only be conceived in terms that are also both political and dialectical. Since war is the continuation of politics by other, more stringent means, the realm of the military and war provides the largest arsenal of metaphors and analogies for Freud's depiction of the psychoanalytic practice—a topic that is explored in detail in the third part of this book.

3. Dialectics of Debunking, or How to Read Freud During (and After) the Freud Wars

When I submitted the original manuscript of this book for publication in 1994, a decade had passed since the publication of Jeffrey Moussaieff Masson's *The Assault on Truth: Freud's Suppression of the Seduction Theory*.[27] Masson denounced Freud's attempt to construct a conflictual model of our inner world, with drives, fantasies and unconscious desires, as an opportunistic and deceitful byproduct of his careerism. For Masson, psychoanalysis was born in a lie that served to cover up the truth of early child abuse, which Freud had accepted in his earlier seduction theory, but which he then rejected in order to be accepted by his peers. Masson's book created a scandal for a number of reasons.[28] One of them was that in contrast to earlier criticism of Freud's work, he did not dismiss it for being speculative, inexact, mistaken or unfalsifiable. Instead, he sought to expose it as a fraud that was rooted in evil intentions and propagated despite Freud's awareness of the facts.[29]

By 1994 the scandal around Masson had died down. Frederick Crews' bellicose criticism of Freud, published in November 1993 in the *New York Review of Books* under the title 'The Unknown Freud', rejected the specifics of Masson's argument—and the latter's support for the 'recovered memory' movement—but his attack on Freud had much of the pathos that had characterized Masson's.[30] Like Masson, Crews thrashed Freud for having been a liar and fabricator rather than a theorist and therapist. However, Crews' essay, ostensibly a review of four books, sparked off the largest number of letters to the editor of the *New York Review of Books* ever received by the journal in response to an article. It was followed by a two-part essay by Crews, 'The Revenge of the Repressed', published a year later.[31] Crews' texts and some of the exchanges that they had triggered off appeared as *The Memory Wars* in 1995.

In the same year the Library of Congress announced its plan to hold a major exhibit on Freud in 1996. This was a further occasion at which the campaign against Freud received much publicity. In July 1995 Peter Swales initiated an open letter to officials of the Library of Congress that was signed by forty-two scholars and intellectuals, by no means all of them fierce Freud debunkers. The petitioners argued that the exhibit's advisory committee was composed only of Freud partisans and that it was designed as a dated and uncritical acclamation of his work, which failed to take note of the more recent, critical revisionist historiography. The petition created an uproar and it seems that the controversy surrounding it led to the post-ponement of the exhibition, which opened only in October 1998—although this has been denied by the organizers.

Timed to appear with the delayed opening of the exhibit, Crews—by then the undisputed doyen of Freud's militant detractors—edited a com-pendium that included both more moderately critical and militantly de-bunking essays under the title *The Unorthodox Freud: Doubters Confront a Legend*. The publication of this anthology shows that by the end of the twentieth century contributions of individual authors, important as they may have been, became part of a discourse that brought home the message of Freud's fraudulence and the harmfulness of his therapeutic procedures.

When one examines this debunking discourse more closely, one finds that there was a dialectics of deflation at work; for even though it presented itself as unmasking a legend, it created a myth, or generated a counter-myth, as it were. It produced a kind of negative mirror image of the hagiographic biographies in which Freud was portrayed as a lone hero fighting against all odds to bring humanity unpleasant truths about the inner world that would allow it to heal many of its ills.[32] As Richard Skues put it, 'it is increasingly the case that bad history written by Freudians is not being challenged by good historiography, but by bad history written by anti-Freudians'.[33]

The verbal violence and combativeness with which Freud's radical de-tractors approached him, was made unmistakably plain in the titles of their books that appeared at short intervals throughout the last decade of the twentieth century. A by no means exhaustive list includes works such as E. Fuller Torrey's *Freudian Fraud: The Malignant Effect of Freud's Theory on American Culture and Society*, which was published in 1992. Alan Esterson's *Seductive Mirage: An Exploration of the Work of Sigmund Freud* from 1993, and Robert Willcocks' *Maelzel's Chess Player: Freud and the Rhetoric of Deceit* from 1994. In 1996 the prestigious British medical journal *Lancet* published Raymond Tallis' provocative 'Burying Freud', leading to the establishment of a web site under the same name, where Freud's detractors and defenders cross verbal swords. Edward Dolnick's *Madness on the Couch: Blaming the Victim in the Heyday of Psychoanalysis* was published in 1998, and in 1999 Ethan Watters and Richard Ofshe brought out *Therapy's Delusions: The Myth of the Unconscious and the Exploitation of Today's Walking Worried*.

Other authors could be added, showing that throughout the 1990s not a year passed without at least one comprehensive and definitive deflation of Freud, psychoanalysis, or all psychotherapeutic practices that rely on the assumption of a dynamic unconscious. These unmasking exercises were designed to show the world once and for all—but also again and again—that psychoanalysis was not only bunk, but also dangerous. By associating in their titles Freud and psychoanalysis with exploitation, seduction, fraud, deceit, malignancy and victim blaming, these books produced a resounding indictment of Freud as a person and of his work. As a whole, the anti-Freudian discourse told a dramatic story of the endless deviousness of one man, whose seductive words allowed him to cast a magic spell across decades and oceans, implanting in the minds of many one of the most extraordinary chimeras of the modern world, thereby causing severe harm to patients.

I hold a political reading of Freud to be particularly pertinent during and after the Freud Wars; for even though the aim of Freud's militant detractors was to depoliticize the mind, their discourse conjured up a political myth. The mythical features of this discourse come clearly to the fore when its overarching argument is divided into six interrelated claims, which, though not necessarily held by each of Freud's debunkers, nevertheless form the building blocks of the current derogatory discourse on Freud.

Claim 1: *There is no scientific truth in psychoanalysis.* Already before the nineties a number of widely read authors flunked Freud as a scientist, arguing that psychoanalysis either could not be tested according to empiricist standards or that its basic tenets were falsified if subjected to them. Adolf Grünbaum was one of the main contributors to this presentation of psychoanalysis as a science *manqué*. He made his major contribution to the condemnatory scrutiny of the scientific credibility of psychoanalysis in 1984 with *The Foundations of Psychoanalysis: A Philosophical Critique,* but his work continued throughout the nineties, including a collection of articles, which appeared in 1993 under the title *Validation in the Clinical Theory of Psychoanalysis: A Study in the Philosophy of Psychoanalysis.* Malcolm Macmillan's *Freud Evaluated: The Completed Arc* was published twice during the nineties, first in 1991 with a less well-known publisher, and then in 1997 with the more prestigious MIT Press. A year earlier MIT also brought out Edward Erwin's *A Final Accounting: Philosophical and Empirical Issues in Freudian Psychology,* which declared, 'More than 1,500 Freudian experiments have been done . . . many reflecting great ingenuity and immense labor. Yet the amount of confirmation of distinctively Freudian hypotheses is close to zero'.[34] At the same time, Erwin admitted that 'devising experiments that would really test Freudian theory, and not merely some pale commonsense reflection of it, is extremely difficult'.[35] Thus, his final verdict was not only that the effectiveness of Freudian therapy had not been empirically established and that his theory had not been confirmed, but also that this situation will not change in the future.[36]

This claim seems true. I share it with Freud's detractors, with some of his more circumspect recent critics, and with all those psychoanalysts and philosophers who regard Freud's work as hermeneutic rather than fitting into a natural-science paradigm. Thus, the first claim of Freud's detractors causes problems mainly to those who espouse a medical model of psychoanalysis.

Claim 2: *Psychoanalysis is a fraud.* A number of possible explanations can be given to account for the fact that Freud's work does not conform to empiricist standards. One may argue, as I do, that his science was never designed to be confined within the limits of a natural science or medical model and that therefore Freud allowed himself to make claims that are untestable according to its principles—as do most psychologists, sociologists, political scientists, historians, and many other researchers and academics whose work is accepted as scholarly. Alternatively one may claim, as Grünbaum seemed to do, that Freud intended psychoanalysis to match empiricist standards, but blundered. In such portrayals Freud appears as a thinker whose theories and practice contain uncorroborated and even falsified hypotheses, unwarranted conclusions and other errors or mistakes. These, then, might be explained as a result of theoretical and personal blind spots or oversights, as well as historical limitations. One could even speculate that Freud did not notice his blunders because he was blinded by the ambition and the single-mindedness of an intellectual conquistador, who simply could not conceive that reality would not confirm his daring thoughts.

Such a view of Freud would expose him as weak and in some ways limited. Typically, Freud's contemporary debunkers did not adopt this perspective; instead, they depicted him as powerful and insidious. They were by no means the first to do so. Already in 1973 Frank Cioffi gave a radio talk under the title 'Was Freud a Liar?'.[37] In the footsteps of Cioffi and Masson, Crews called Freud 'endlessly calculating'.[38] He spoke of a 'notably willful and opportunistic Freud',[39] as well as of the 'fanatical, self-inflated, ruthless, myopic, yet intricately devious Freud who has been unearthed by the independent scholarship of the past generation'.[40] In *Unauthorized Freud* he referred to Freud's 'want of candor' to explain some of the flaws of psychoanalysis,[41] and claimed that '... [Freud] was lying',[42] likening him to 'an overeager salesman' who was 'concealing his doubts about questionable merchandise while privately casting about for something better'.[43]

Claim 3: *Psychoanalysis is the greatest fraud ever.* Needless to say, this claim only makes sense, if the second claim is granted. In making this assertion Freud's detractors augmented the feat achieved by their deflationary exercise. They sought to show that debunking Freud meant slaying a scientific dragon or felling an intellectual Goliath. Only if Freud was an almost omniscient, towering villain, only if his fraud was of world historical proportions, could a victory over Freud be glorious and bring fame to those struggling against him.

Again, Freud's contemporary detractors were not the first to make extravagant pronouncements against him. Peter Medawar declared already in 1975 that 'psychoanalytic theory is the most stupendous intellectual confidence trick of the twentieth century '.[44] In contrast to the seventies, however, in the nineties such immoderate declarations became commonplace among some of Freud's critics.

Allan Esterson speculated that one day psychoanalysis may be seen 'as one of the most extraordinary aberrations in the history of Western thought'.[45] According to Frederick Crews, 'we are learning that Freud has been the most overrated figure in the entire history of science and medicine—one who wrought immense harm through the propagation of false etiologies, mistaken diagnoses and fruitless lines of inquiry'.[46] Commenting on one of Freud's widely discussed interpretations of a 'Freudian' slip, Peter Swales condemned it in an open letter addressed to James Billington, the head of the Library of Congress, as 'a pure fabrication, indeed, perhaps one of the most influential and insidious frauds in the whole history of twentieth century science'.[47] Even if one assumes, for the sake of argument, that Swales does have documentation that plausibly attests that Freud did lie in this instance, he does seem a bit hyperbolic.

Claim 4: *Psychoanalysis seduces.* Why did the twentieth century fall victim to Freud's pernicious lies? How come he managed to cheat so many for so long? Again, the possibility of raising questions such as these hinges on the prior acceptance of the first three claims. If some grains of truth were granted to psychoanalysis, it could be argued, for instance, that its partial truth brought Freud's followers and patients to accept additional, erroneous assertions. Only if all veracity is denied to psychoanalysis does one need to maintain, as Freud's militant detractors did, that he used devious means to trick generations of medical doctors, psychologists, researchers, scholars and patients all over the world. Freud's derogators invoked the image of Freud as a figure of power and as an abuser of his power over his patients. John Forrester has pointed out that at least part of the deep mistrust of psychoanalysis that characterizes Freud's militant detractors seems to stem from their 'view that the power of the psychoanalyst is so great, because of the relationship of power . . . that he exerts over the patient and, by extension, over the whole of twentieth-century culture'.[48]

However, Freud's detractors provided rather weak accounts of the way in which Freud's spirit is supposed to exercise its power until today. Often they attributed the impact of psychoanalysis to rhetoric. As Raymond Tallis put it, 'the sheer crankiness of Freud's ideas was concealed by his marvelous prose'.[49] Crews referred to Freud as a 'literary magician', whose every sentence 'amounts to an act of cunning self-dramatization'.[50] Similarly, he wrote of 'Freud's genius for rhetoric' that is said to have covered 'a therapeutic and scientific fiasco'.[51] Esterson attributed Freud's success mostly to 'an extensive and ingenious use of psychological concepts (many of which were previously posited by others) within an explanatory mode of discourse of almost infinite adaptability; voluminous writings in which he presented his ideas persuasively to a wide public; an exceptional literary skill, which included the talents of a great propagandist . . .'[52]

In my view, this point in the attack against Freud contains an important truth about psychoanalysis, though it is presented in a somewhat distorted form. Freud's radical detractors are right when they depict Freud's theory of the psyche as a rhetorical construction. One cannot observe the mind, one can only imagine its processes and structures by extrapolating from accessible phenomena in the outside world. As Freud knew and acknowledged, he hypothesized the psyche's causally active components on the basis of interpretation and formulated their processes by means of metaphors. By pointing to the literary, poetic quality of psychoanalysis, Freud's radical critics reminded psychoanalysts and other guardians of psychoanalysis of something they sought to forget: the aesthetic, artistic, creative and imaginative origins of psychoanalytic theory. As Nietzsche put it:

> Only by forgetting that primitive metaphor-world, only by the hardening and rigidification of the mass of images that originally gushed forward as hot magma out of the primeval faculty of human fantasy . . . only insofar as man forgets himself as . . . an *artistically creative* subject, does he live with some calm, security and consistency. If he could even for one moment escape from the prison walls of his belief, then his high opinion of himself would be dashed immediately.[53]

It seems to me that much of the psychoanalytic establishment's high opinion of itself as well as its intellectual prison walls were the product of its forgetting that the core of its theory of mind was metaphorical. Even though I do not share Nietzsche's perspectivist concept of truth as a general epistemological approach, in my view the truth about an invisible domain such as the mind cannnot but be 'a mobile army of metaphors, metonyms, antropomorphisms, in short, a sum of human relations which were poetically and rhetorically heightened, transferred and adorned, and after long use seem solid, canonical, and binding . . .'[54]

Claim 5: *Psychoanalytic seduction is harmful.* Earlier critics of psychoanalysis portrayed analysands as wasting their time on the couch and pointed to high expenses involved that could not be justified by the low or unproven effectiveness of analytic practice. In contrast, the discourse of Freud's debunkers turned psychoanalysis into a most dangerous seductress, whose magical spell could be perilous. Tallis accused psychoanalysts of attributing serious bodily illnesses to psychological causes, thus diverting attention from their actual organic origins. According to him, this practice had 'often fatal consequences'.[55] Moreover, even 'where [psychoanalysts] are not medically incompetent, their peculiar ideas often confuse and further undermine desperately vulnerable individuals'.[56] E. Fuller Torrey referred to 'the sad spectacle of approximately 200,000 untreated mentally ill individuals among the nation's homeless population', reaching the conclusion that 'the scene is one more legacy of Freudian theory'.[57] According to Crews, an estimated number of one million patients were persuaded by their therapists that they had been victims of molestation, but, he pointed out '[t]he number *affected* is of course vastly higher, since, as all parties acknowledge, virtually every case sows dissension and sorrow throughout a family'.[58] Freud was blamed for the innumerable victims of 'recovered memory' therapy. According to Crews, 'every feature of the recovered memory therapy, even the crudest, was pioneered by Freud . . . the recovered memory movement would have been inconceivable without our society's more diffuse allegiance to the Freudian psychodynamic paradigm'.[59]

Logically, this fifth claim is independent of the three preceding ones. Psychoanalysis could be equally harmful even if it were based on mistakes or blindness and not, as is alleged, on deception. However, the attribution of damaging effects to psychoanalytic practice made its alleged deceptiveness appear to be particularly devious. Moreover, in terms of the facts that they described, though not the causality they invoked, the statements of Freud's detractors were accurate. Psychoanalysis does attribute symptoms to psychological causes, there are a great number of seriously mentally ill among the homeless, while the main *clientèle* of psychoanalysts is made up of neurotics who by and large are functional and belong to the educated middle class. Finally, 'recovered memory' therapists did avail themselves of ideas promoted by Freud, such as the repression of early memories, especially of a sexual nature, and the importance of unconscious memories for later life. It seems disingenuous, therefore, to contend, as some of Crews' interlocutors did, that Freud's work had nothing to do with 'recovered memory' therapy.

However, the assertions made by Tallis, Fuller and Crews were paradigmatic of the way in which some of Freud's detractors inflated a kernel of truth into mythical proportions in order to deflate psychoanalysis. Crews failed to pay much attention to the fact that even though 'recovered memory' therapies did take some of their inspiration from Freud, when they gained ground, they presented this as a victory over Freud's approach and contemporary psychoanalysis, since both were identified with the refusal to acknowledge the patients' stories of early abuse as factual accounts. In order to understand the success of these therapies in the early eighties it simply is not enough to point one's finger at Freud. One has to explain what is it that made contemporary American non-analytic therapists return to a hypothesis that Freud maintained for only a few months in late nineteenth-centuryVienna, but then explicitly rejected. One has to spell out why and how these therapies completely abandoned the Freudian notion of a dynamic unconscious, into which memories are not only supposed to be repressed, and where they are not only said to be maintained, but also transformed under the influence of internal forces, such as desires or drives, so that they are bound to return into consciousness in a highly distorted form. In other words, in order to come to terms with the flourishing of the 'recovered memory' therapies in the eighties, one has to establish why and how American psychotherapists—but not psychoanalysts—produced a caricature of psychoanalytic treatment, by eliminating its core concept and stripping it of the therapeutic safeguards that Freud and his followers had introduced.[60]

Without inquiring into the cultural, social, legal and institutional dynamics underlying the rise of 'recovered memory' therapies, Crews' argument was about as plausible and subtle as the by now rather disreputable cold war literature that blamed Nazism on Martin Luther, G.W. F. Hegel or Friedrich Nietzsche, Stalinism on Karl Marx, and the terror regime in the wake of the French Revolution on Jean-Jacques Rousseau. All these thinkers created a theoretical frame of reference that could be deployed to legitimize atrocious practices of later generations. Nevertheless, social practices—both political and therapeutic—cannot simply be explained by the existence of texts that preceded them; theory does not translate itself into practice on its own. Moreover, in all the above cases the thinkers blamed for actions of later generations also expressly opposed and denounced in their writings some of the practices that later were said to derive from their work—just as Freud warned not to accept at face value childhood memories that emerged in the therapeutic setting.[61]

How many psychoanalysts were charged with the construction of false memories in therapy? Were there any at all? Crews did not say, for such simple facts did not matter to his wild argumentation. Similarly, Tallis stated that psychoanalysis 'often'—how often is often?—had fatal consequences for patients whose organic illnesses were misdiagnosed as mental symptoms, but he did not substantiate his assertion with any documentation. Needless to say, in order to single out psychoanalysis for condemnation, he also would have had to show that fatal incompetence was more frequent than among other psychotherapists or general practitioners. One wonders also why Fuller Torrey chose to blame primarily psychoanalysis for the high numbers of mentally ill people among the homeless, rather than criticizing monetary policies, misguided ideologies of community welfare, insufficient social welfare policies and popular indifference. Ironically, neither Tallis', nor Crews', nor Torrey's arguments lived up to the empirical standards that Freud's detractors demanded of psychoanalysis. The purpose of their thin, biased, idealist and monocausal accounts was not to explain or understand social phenomena. They sought to accuse and inculpate, hence they offered simple categories and a culprit; in other words, they created a myth or, as I pointed out above, a counter-myth, which they opposed to that which psychoanalytic hagiography had spun around Freud.

Claim 6: *Getting rid of psychoanalysis is liberating.* It is the aim of mythical stories to single out a villain—in this case Freud, the swindler—whose ruin promises happiness for us all. In this fashion, Freud's detractors presented the purging of the contemporary intellectual scene of remnants of psychoanalytic contamination as an enlightening, emancipatory activity.[62] It is ironic that Freud's detractors promoted their critique of psychoanalysis very much in the spirit in which Freud fought religion. Like him, they were greatly concerned with the effects of a belief system over the minds of those who succumbed to its absurdities. Their aim was to remove a powerful but damaging magic from the scene—to unmask false consciousness, as it used to be called in the old days. Since they sought to promote liberation from a powerful but devious and harmful ideology, I consider their myth to be political.

Moreover, the momentum that this discourse has gained during the nineties also has to be explained politically, that is, as part of a politics of culture and institutions, as well as a result of the post-Reagan political climate in the U.S. I agree with Forrester, who argued that 'the political side of this hatred of Freud is connected to the death of American liberalism of the universalistic, New Deal variety. The identity politics of autonomy and difference is fundamentally antithetical to the universalizing claims of a discipline that puts in doubt the very concept of autonomy'.[63] Similarly, Joel Whitebook has stressed that the Reagan revolution and deregulated capitalism have not been 'conducive to self-reflection. After the intermezzo of the sixties, outward-directed values, that is, moneymaking and the pursuit of status and celebrity, have been largely reinstated as the highest goods'.[64] Ely Zaretzky, too, saw the attack on Freud as 'continuous with the attacks on the Left that began in 1968 . . . and are of a piece with the recent attacks on women's and African-American studies and on "political correctness."'[65] As we see, all of those who sought to place the Freud Wars in a wider, cultural and social perspective, such as Forrester, Whitebook, Zaretzky and Jonathan Lear rightly stressed that these verbal wars were part of a broader political trend and that more was at stake than Freud's reputation and legacy.

What, then, were the Freud wars all about? In addition to their political gist, it seems evident that—as has been pointed out by all the above quoted authors who wrote in defense of Freud—the Freud Wars were 'a fight about human nature'.[66] Jonathan Lear has also stressed that they focused on 'the very idea that humans have unconscious motivation. A battle may be fought over Freud, but the war is over our culture's image of the human soul'.[67] If Freud's radical detractors accept any psychology at all, it is fairly evident that they do allow for a dynamic unconscious of the Freudian kind, that is, for an inner, threatening alterity or strangeness that limits and disturbs, and has to be negotiated by consciousness. Therefore it is not surprising that Peter Swales resolutely denied the existence of a psychoanalytic unconscious, when pressed on this point by Joel Whitebook.[68] Explicitly or implicitly, Freud's detractors supplant the political model of the psyche—which, as I argue, forms the core of psychoanalytic discourse—by a fundamentally non-politically conception, where treatment and change are technologically engineered, perhaps by medication instead of social interaction.

Finally, the Freud Wars were about conceptions of knowledge. Freud's debunkers denied his status as scientist from the vantage point of a most narrow empiricism that, if it were accepted, would not allow the development of any theories in any discipline of the humanities and the social sciences.[69] Much of the Freud Wars seem to be against theory and against a particular form of critical thinking and destabilizing, subversive inquiry.[70]

There are many reasons why the Freud Wars managed to embarrass psychoanalysts as well as scholars sympathetic to Freud's work. In my view, some of these reasons have to do with the truths that can be found in the attacks on Freud, despite their mythical quality. First, as I have mentioned above, Freud's detractors stressed the literary nature of psychoanalytic theory. This is highly problematic for all those who wish to see psychoanalysis as an empiricist, natural science type enterprise. Second, Freud's radical critics rightly pointed to some rather reprehensible politics that were typical of the Freudian camp. For years many in the psychoanalytic community had accepted hero worship, secrecy and censorship, the slander of opponents, critics and dissenters, as well as unsubstantiated claims concerning therapeutic efficacy. Third, it seems that much of what they said about Freud as a person was right: he was not a caring human being or a flawless scientist, but an autocratic, self-centered patriarch who expelled from the movement those who dared to think too much on their own.

Starting with factual assertions that tended to be both truthful and critical of a small orthodoxy, Freud's detractors justifiably gained the sympathies of their readers. However, as I have shown, they used these facts as building blocks for a series of unwarranted and overstated causal claims and unsubstantiated warnings about the dire consequences of psychoanalysis. In my view, the lack of proportion of their rhetoric was a further reason for the strong impact of Freud's detractors. It created a dilemma for their interlocutors. How were they to respond to an overwrought belligerent discourse? War leaves little room for detachment and differentiation; one is either friend or foe. Since this was an intellectual war, one had to choose not only to which side one belonged, but also what tone one spoke in. If one replicated the savage tone of Freud's derogators, one played into their hands by accepting an embarrassingly coarse form of discourse as appropriate for a debate on Freud's work and psychoanalysis in general. Alternatively, if one ignored the high jinx of Freud's vociferous detractors, one could easily appear obtuse or overwhelmed.

Finally, for a variety of cultural and social reasons, Freud's detractors caught the psychoanalytic establishment at a moment in which it was weakened institutionally. Changing insurance policies and the contracting welfare state meant that psychoanalysts lost potential patients and students alike. A return to positivist and naturalist visions of the mind, combined with the apparent speedy effectiveness of psychopharmaceutics led to serious questions concerning any further use for talking cures. Leading positions in major psychiatric research and treatment centers were no longer predominantly in the hands of psychoanalysts, as used to be the case a few decades earlier.

In fact, much of American psychoanalysis was already in disarray when the Freud Wars started. A great proliferation of schools—some of which maintained a rigid conservatism while others adopted a shallow eclecticism—as well as uncertainty as to where psychoanalysis was heading in a postmodern age, led to deep insecurities. In March 1998 the *New York Times* reported at the occasion of a meeting at Manhattan's Mt. Sinai Hospital that under the influence of postmodern critiques from within their own ranks, many psychoanalysts had 'become obsessed with what they know and don't know, how they know and don't know it, and what their patients think they know and don't know'.[71]

Perhaps, the Freud Wars and the present crisis of psychoanalysis will lead to a more serious reconsideration of what Freud's work is all about. In any case, by now it may be evident that psychoanalysis should not and cannot be reduced to a medicalized and scientized discourse. At the same time, I suggest, it is not a hermeneutics concerned with the construction of healing narratives. Rather, Freud ought to be read as offering a theory of the mind, family, therapy and society that is deeply political. Political theories entail practices, and a political theory of the mind necessitates a therapeutic practice. However, such theories and practices cannot be tested in the laboratory, and empirical research can, at best, offer circumstantial evidence, whose meaning and relevance can always be seen in various ways. In the social sciences only extremely simple and rather trivial hypotheses are subject to unequivocal empirical corroboration.[72] Mostly, empirical evidence is open to a wide range of interpretations. What would be a valid test to establish why unemployed workers in the West tend to vote more for right-wing parties than their employed colleagues? How can empirical evidence by itself solve the debate between utilitarians and Kantians on principles that are to guide public policy, and how can it adjudicate the claims of rule-utilitarians against those of act-utilitarians? What empirical proof—in the terms acceptable to, say, a Grünbaum or Macmillan—is there for the political efficiency or cogency of one welfare policy as opposed to another, or for one feminist strategy against another? And yet, in all these questions there is theory and there is practice, and there is more or less reasoned debate, which always includes speculation, empirical evidence, interpretation and causal hypotheses.

I read Freud in a similar fashion, as proposing a model of the mind's inner order, on the same level as theories that seek to provide perspectives on external society, such as those developed by John Stuart Mill, Karl Marx, Friedrich Hayek, or Hannah Arendt. Similar to them, Freud also suggests practical procedures to restore the mind's order when it has become disturbed. Their scope is limited, for they do not seem to be capable of dealing with severe disturbances, and even in the best of cases, their success is always contestable, like that of any social policy. And as in political discourses on the external, public sphere, much must remain tentative and precarious, and much depends on the metaphoric lenses used in portraying the complex interplay of forces and interests involved.[73]

Even though Freud did not create a kind of natural science of the mind, this does not condemn psychoanalytic discourse to become a repository of vague philosophical truths about human beings, which, as Crews likes to state, could'be credited as easily to Shakespeare, Dostoevsky, or Nietzsche—if not indeed to Jesus or St. Paul'.[74] Of course, Freud was not the first thinker to use political metaphors for the mind. On the contrary, he used the perhaps oldest repertoire of metaphors, made famous already by Plato in *The Republic*. However, as this book shows, although Plato can be considered as one of Freud's predecessors and one of his inspirations—together with Shakespeare, Dostoevsky and Nietzsche—Freud cannot be reduced to either or all of them.

Pace Crews and Freud's other debunkers, this book shows that Freud did make an original, fruitful and substantial contribution to Western thought on the mind and its dynamics—though, like all grand theories, it is not without its blind spots, contradictions and shortcomings. His contribution belongs to a tradition of thought, but it also takes that tradition one significant step further.

Notes

Sources used in this introduction are not necessarily listed in the bibliography at the end of the book. All references which indicate only year of publication, volume (in Roman numbers) and page (in Latin numbers), are to Freud's books and articles in *The Standard Edition of the Complete Psychological Works of Sigmund Freud*, 24 vols., ed. J. Strachey (London: The Hogarth Press, 1953-74). All titles of items from the *Standard Edition* can be found in the list of'References to the Standard Edition'at the end of the book.

1. Earlier versions were presented at the international conference"Freud at the Threshold of the Twenty-First Century" in Jerusalem, December 1999, and at the Zürich Psychoanalytic Seminar, in January 2000. I am grateful for the comments that I received at these occasions. As always I am deeply indebted to Arnona Zahavi's careful and critical readings of my drafts.
2. For a good survey of the various positions see C. Strenger, *Between Hermeneutics and Science* (New York: International Universities Press, 1991).
3. S. Freud, *The Complete Letters of Sigmund Freud to Wilhelm Fliess, 1887-1904*, ed. and tr. J. M. Masson (Cambridge, Mass.: Harvard University Press, 1985), p. 365.
4. 1900a, IV:122
5. Ibid., IV:121.
6. Ibid., V:511.
7. See also 1916-17, XV:67.
8. 1933a, XXII: 182.
9. Ibid., XXII:160-61.
10. Ibid., XXII:158
11. Ibid., XXII:158, 181; see also 1940a, XXIII:158; 1940b, XXIII:282
12. 1915a, XIV:120.
13. 1916-17, XVI:356.
14. 1927c, XXI:17.
15. 1912-13, XIII:78-79.
16. 1912-23, XIII:91.
17. 1900a, V:565-66.
17. 1930a, XXI:112.
18. Ibid., 122.
19. Ibid., 111.
21. 1916-17, XVI:285.
22. D. Archard, *Consciousness and Unconsciousness* (London: Hutchinson, 1984), p. 24.
23. Ibid., p. 24.
24. 1900a, V:580-81n.
25. Freud, *The Complete Letters of Sigmund Freud to Wilhelm Fliess*, p. 364.
26. I have discussed this in more detail in 'Oedipus Politicus: Freud's paradigm of social relations', in M. S. Roth (ed.) *Freud: Conflict and Culture* (New York: Alfred A. Knopf, 1998).
27. J. M. Masson, *The Assault on Truth: Freud's Suppression of the Seduction Theory* (New York, Farrar Straus and Giroux, 1984).
28. For a detailed account see J. Malcolm, *In the Freud Archives* (New York: Random House, 1985).
29. For a more detailed discussion of Masson's claims, see pp. 37-40 in this book.
30. F.C. Crews, 'The unknown Freud', *New York Review of Books*, November 18, 1993, pp. 55-66.
31. F.C. Crews, 'The revenge of the repressed', *New York Review of Books*, November 17 and December 1, 1994.
32. Frank Sulloway has catalogued twenty-six different myths of what used to be the official psychoanalytic version of things. 'Over the years', he says 'psychoanalytic devotees have cultivated a complex and politically expedient mythology about their collective past'. F.J. Sulloway, *Freud, Biologist of the Mind: Beyond the Psychoanalytic Legend*. (London: Burnett/ André Deutsch, 1979), p. 5; see ibid., pp. 445-495.

33. R. Skues, 'The first casualty: the war over psychoanalysis and the poverty of historiography', *History of Psychiatry* 9 (1998): 175.

34. E. Erwin, *A Final Accounting: Philosophical and empirical Issues in Freudian Psychology* (Cambridge, Mass.: MIT Press, 1997), p. 294.

35. Ibid., p. 294.

36. Ibid., p. 296.

37. F. Cioffi, 'Freud as a liar', in F. Crews (ed.), *The Unauthorized Freud: Doubters Confront a Legend* (New York: Viking Penguin, 1998).

38. F.C. Crews, 'Introduction', *The Memory Wars: Freud's Legacy in Dispute* (New York: New York Review of Books, 1995), p. 12.

39. Crews, 'The unknown Freud', in *Memory Wars*, p. 35 (originally published in the *New York Review of Books*, November 18, 1993)

40. F. C. Crews, 'Unconscious deeps and empirical shallows', *Philosophy and Literature* 22 (1998): 272.

41. F.C. Crews, *Unauthorized Freud: Doubters Confront a Legend*, p. 44.

42. Ibid., p. 144.

43. Ibid., p. 71.

44. P. Medawar, *Pluto's Republic* (Oxford: Oxford University Press, 1984), p. 140.

45. A. Esterson, *Seductive Mirage: An Exploration of the Work of Sigmund Freud* (Peru, Ill.: Open Court Publishing House, 1993), p. 254.

46. F.C. Crews, 'Confessions of a Freud basher', in *Memory Wars*, p. 298 (originally published as 'Cheerful assassin defies analysis', in the *Times Higher Education Supplement*, March 3, 1995).

47. Letter of September 23, 1998, www.shamsdasani.u-net.com/freudexhibition.

48. J. Forrester, *Dispatches from the Freud Wars: Psychoanalysis and Its Passions* Cambridge, Mass.: Harvard University Press, 1997), p. 222.

49. R. C. Tallis, 'Burying Freud', *The Lancet* 347 (1996): 670.

50. F.C. Crews, 'Unconscious deeps and empirical shallows', p. 282.

51. F. C. Crews, 'Introduction' in *Unauthorized Freud*, p. xxxi.

52. Esterson, *Seductive Mirage*, p. 248.

53. F. Nietzsche, 'On truth and lying in an extra-moral sense', in S.L. Gilman, C. Blair and D.J. Parent (eds.), *Frierich Nietzsche on Rhetoric and Language*. New York and Oxford: Oxford University Press, 1989, p. 252. Original emphasis.

54. Ibid., p. 250.

55. Tallis, 'Burying Freud', p. 670.

56. Ibid., p. 670.

57. E. Fuller Torrey, *Freudian Fraud: The Malignant Effect of Freud's Theory on American Thought and Culture* (New York: HarperCollins, 1992), p. 252.

58. Crews, 'The revenge of the repressed', in *Memory Wars*, p. 160 (originally published in the *New York Review of Books*, November 17, 1994).

59. F.C. Crews, 'Preface', in *Unauthorized Freud*, p. xi.

60. E. Zaretzky, 'Freud's hatchet man in an age of deidealization', *American Imago* 53 (1996): 397-398.

61. See J. Lear, 'On killing Freud (again)', in *Open Minded: Working Out the Logic of the Soul* (Cambridge, Mass.: Harvard University Press, 1998), pp. 22-23 (originally published as 'The shrink is in', in the *New Republic*, December 25, 1995).

62. E.g. Tallis, 'Burying Freud', p. 671.

63. Forrester, *Dispatches from the Freud Wars*, p. 226.

64. J. Whitebook, 'Psychoanalysis and democracy', www.igc.org/dissent/archive/spring99/whitebook.html (originally published in *Dissent*, Spring 1999, 46 (2).

65. E. Zaretzky, 'The attack on Freud', *Tikkun* 9 (3): 67. See also Zaretzky, 'Freud's hatchet man in an age of deidealization', p. 390.

66. J. Whitebook, 'Psychoanalysis and democracy'.

67. Lear, 'On killing Freud (again)', p. 27.

68. Whitebook 'Psychoanalysis and Democracy'.

69. See Zaretzky, 'Freud's hatchet man in an age of deidealization', p. 394.

70. Zaretzky, 'The attack on Freud', p. 70.

71. *New York Times*, March 14, 1998.

72. C. Taylor, 'Neutrality in political science' in P. Laslett (ed.), *Philosophy, Politics and Society*, Third Series (Oxford: Blackwell, 1969).

73. E. F. Miller, 'Metaphor and political knowledge', *American Political Science Review* 73 (1979): 155-169. E. Zashin and P. C. Chapman, 'The uses of metaphor and analogy: Toward a renewal of political language', *Journal of Politics* (1974): 290-326.

74. Crews, 'Confessions of a Freud basher', in *Memory Wars*, p. 295.

Preface

In this book I chart the development of Freud's theory and practice in a dual – textual and contextual – approach in order to provide a comprehensive and historically anchored picture of the politics of psychoanalysis. Let me make clear at the very outset that throughout this book the terms 'psychoanalytic' and 'psychoanalysis' refer exclusively to Freud's work (unless their context clearly indicates something different). I return to Freud's texts in order to show more emphatically and radically than has been done hitherto that psychoanalysis is political in its medical origins, linguistic style, the logic of its models, the historical development and internal structure of its therapeutic practice, as well as in its analysis of culture, religion, history and society.

However, over the years, when I told students, friends and colleagues that I was writing on the political content and context of Freud's work, their most frequent response was a half-astonished, half-dismissive: 'Is there any?' On the one hand, this retort reflects the conventional view of Freud as a medical doctor and scientist concerned with mental illness, who primarily dealt with the private realm; that is, the family, sexuality, the analytic setting and the internal world of the psyche. On the other hand, it expresses a widespread but narrow conception of politics. Politics, most people assume, takes place only in specifically designed institutions, such as the cabinet, parliament, parties, and the judiciary, which all have to do with the state and the practice of government.

Therefore, most orthodox analysts neglect or reject political readings of psychoanalysis. Nevertheless, a number of authors have focused on political aspects of Freud's private life, dreams and letters.[1] Others have examined the institutional politics of psychoanalysis, such as the internecine disputes and struggles among Freud, his followers and their different schools.[2] In a third group one might place writers who apply or criticize psychoanalysis as a tool for the explanation of social and political processes, theories and actions.[3] Marxist Freudians, for example, tend to transform psychoanalytic concepts and appropriate them for their theoretical framework.[4] Cultural critics and historians have traced the politics of the reception of psychoanalysis, or assessed the ideological impact of Freud's work on the social ethos in the second half of the twentieth century.[5] In particular, an impressive and steadily growing body of feminist scholarship deals extensively with the gender-biased nature of psychoanalytic discourse.[6]

In all these groups there are some who present psychoanalytic discourse not only as related to political thinking or affected by it, but as constituting in itself a type of social or political theory. Authors who share this basic fundamental assumption – but differ from one another significantly in many other respects – include Jürgen Habermas, Russel Jacoby, Herbert Marcuse, Philip Rieff and Paul Roazen, and more recently also Jeffrey Abramson, Stephen Frosh, Yiannis Gabriel and Victor Wolfenstein.[7] It is with their work that my own argument has most in common.

However, before turning to a short outline of my argument, let me explain what I mean when I refer to something as 'political'. Robert Dahl, one of the most prominent representatives of contemporary political science, has stated that 'a political system is any persistent pattern of human relationships that involves to a significant extent, power, rule, authority'.[8] Indeed, students of politics from Plato to Foucault have not only been concerned with the public or governmental face of rule and domination, but with *all* social domains which involve power and domination. Moreover, during the last two decades feminist scholarship has done much to reveal ideological reasons and consequences of confining the political to the public. After the personal has so convincingly been unmasked as political, it is obvious that one cannot limit political discourse solely to questions referring to the state and public matters. Thus, I regard everything which has to do with the exercise of power as political.

What, then, is power, and what is involved in its exercise? In the sense in which I use it, the concept of power can be defined as the capacity of a social agent – an individual or a group – to intentionally affect the actions or attitudes of other agents.[9] It always denotes the power of a social agent *over* others; that is, a form of rule, control, influence or domination. However, it also is in the nature of all power relations that even those who are in a subordinate position could have acted differently; for we can only speak of political power within social relationships which do not completely deprive their members of their status as subjects. Where human beings are reduced to objects, by physical force or violence, for instance, we do not usually speak of political power. Thus, the exercise of power by one agent over another does not entail direct and complete physical control of the former over the latter. On the contrary, politics and power involve relationships among two or more social agents, who are able – in principle, at least – to resist the will of one another; but where one agent nevertheless has the capacity to bring others to adopt an attitude or to act in a way which they would not have done otherwise.

Yet, despite everything that has been said so far, one cannot speak of politics without bringing the state and government back into the discussion. Though power can be exercised in all social spheres, one also has to take note of the fact that its distribution is always in some way interdependent with the distribution and exercise of power by the state. On the one hand, one's possibilities and rights at the workplace, in school, on the road, on the sports ground, in the family and in therapy are affected by governmental decisions, whose effects obviously are not confined to the corridors of power in which they take place. War and peace, hunger and subsistence, wealth and poverty, work and unemployment, knowledge and ignorance, are all the result of governmental decisions. Moreover, government regulates – and, recently, more often deregulates – educational institutions, health care, the monetary system, scientific research, means of public and private transport, leisure activities and the mass media.

However, governmental decisions neither constitute the ultimate foundation of political processes nor an underlying basic substratum of power. As a rule they are affected by extra-governmental resources and interests, such as those of the military, industry, Church or labour. They reflect the level of economic and technological development, the distribution of private property, and conflicts among voluntary and ascriptive social groups. They represent prevalent ideologies and are formulated in terms of – or against – traditional notions of race, class, gender, family, health and religion. Such resources and interests play a political role to the extent that they either affect governmental practices or are affected by them.

Thus, there are two kinds of transgressions between the state and apparently non-political spheres: they may be material, when they involve money, labour power, technology, arms or territories; and/or they can be symbolic, when they appropriate language, images and gestures from one sphere and turn them into assets of power in another sphere. Often these two aspects are intertwined with one another; that is, territory can have symbolic as well as material value for government or for a particular social group, and the ability to impose a certain form of language or cultural form on a social group usually is contingent upon the possession of material assets.

Finally, the exercise of power also gives rise to a discourse in which social agents interpret, conceptualize and articulate the social processes which take place. Obviously, the ascription of meaning to, and representation of, such processes is itself a political act. For instance, a political terminology can depict certain social agents as perpetrators and others as victims, oppose them to one another as exploiters and exploited, or join them as equal and free partners. Such language can legitimize certain social practices and institutions and delegitimize others; it may be designed to deny, distort or disguise certain aspects of power, or to unmask and reveal hidden forms in which power is exercised. Moreover, social conceptualizations such as those of the feminine and masculine, childhood and family, class and ethnicity, law and government, can emphasize links among different social domains and uncover connections and causalities – or they can isolate these domains from one another and detract attention from the way in which different social practices form part of a larger whole. When they make causalities, links and meanings transparent, such discourses can emancipate social agents to new forms of social action; but when they obscure significances and connections they narrow the range of possible social action and fulfil a constricting function.

Hence, in my view, research into the politics of a particular social domain has to focus on three issues: (a) the distribution and exercise of power in this domain; (b) the various transgressions in which its dynamics of power are involved, that is, ways in which they affect and/or are affected by the distribution of material and symbolic resources in other social domains, especially in the state; and (c) ways in which the dominant vocabulary of the domain in question represents the dynamics of power, and the ramifications which such forms of representation have for further political action.

In the course of this study I discuss the politics of psychoanalysis from these three angles. However, in each stage of my argument I put the notion of 'politics' to a somewhat different use, depending on the topic on which I focus. In the first part the notion of 'politics' designates the relationship between Freud's early work and its ideological context; that is, it refers to the way in which Freud's writings on hysteria ignored, criticized or undermined bourgeois values, nationalist ideologies and racial prejudices which dominated medical and political thinking in the end of the nineteenth century. I contend that in this period the approaches of medical practitioners and government to nervous diseases reinforced and complemented one another in a way which makes it necessary to see them as two dimensions of a mixed medico-political discourse. By placing Freud's early writings on hysteria in this context, I aim to assess the various ways in which Freud's utterances and silences on the relationship between hysteria, heredity and ethnicity departed from the prevailing medico-political discourse.

In part II, the term 'politics' refers to the way in which Freud's metapsychology applies the language and logic of political discourse to the psyche. As I show in a detailed textual study of Freud's models of the mind, they transpose the vocabulary of imperial court procedures and evidently political practices – such as representation, censorship and elections – into the mind's internal world. By portraying the mind as a microcosm in analogy to the state's macrocosm, Freud depicts the former as a domain of conflict, power and control, and extends the dynamics of dominance and subjugation into the very depth of the unconscious. Thus, his metapsychology 'politicizes' the mind. Moreover, I show that even where Freud's discourse on the mind appears to be non-political, such as where it invokes hydraulic metaphors, it not only fails to conform to principles of mechanics, but also reveals an implicit political logic.

In the beginning of part III I take again a historical, contextual approach. Here 'politics' denotes the role which extraneous factors such as class, money, education and professional status played in the origins and constitution of the clinical setting of psychoanalysis. First, I discuss the way in which these factors influenced Freud's way of relating to his patients in the early days of his therapeutic practice. Then I scrutinize the activity of psychoanalysts during the First World War, where conscription, military hierarchy, nationalism and governmental interest intruded into the work of medical practitioners.

Finally, in the second half of part III 'politics' refers to the internal dynamics of authority and power in the analytic setting. In a study of the language and logic of Freud's depiction of the therapeutic practice of psychoanalysis, I present the latter as an emancipatory practice in the private realm. I show how this emancipation is made possible by the fact that analyst and analysand enter into a dual relationship, in which they meet both as allies and antagonists who are involved with each other in a dialectical interplay of contractual cooperation and conflictual opposition.

In part IV I discuss the ideological ramifications of the way in which Freud applied his notion of the Oedipus complex to all manifestations of authority and obedience, both within the family and large-scale social institutions. First I show that Freud presented an explicitly political portrayal of early childhood sexuality. He 'politicized' the family by construing its intergenerational conflict in terms of power struggles which are akin to those in the state and contain processes of submission, legitimation and liberation. Then I discuss Freud's conception of society as a family writ large, and his use of Oedipal categories as a prism for the representation of the dialectics of authority and obedience in a mythical primeval period and contemporary crowds. I argue that by depicting rulers and leaders as father figures whose dominance and authority are necessary to keep society together, Freud's Oedipal perspective advocates and legitimizes patriarchy and authoritarianism.

Thus, I employ the notion of 'politics' as a polymorphous concept, which may acquire a variety of meanings. What the various uses of the notion have in common, though, is that they always have to do with the way psychoanalytic theory and practice structure, influence and represent the distribution and exercise of power, and/or refer to the relationship between psychoanalytic theory and practice on the one hand, and explicitly political practices – especially governmental practices – on the other.

The various strands of my argument lead to the conclusion that psychoanalysis is political in its logical structure, language and categories as well as in its presuppositions, values and implications. They show that Freud's methodological innovations and practical applications carried a political significance within their scientific, therapeutic and social context. As a result, I claim that not only Freud's cultural, historical and social analyses – which are often seen as marginal to psychoanalystic discourse – have to do with politics. As I demonstrate, also the most fundamental categories of psychoanalysis, which refer to the mind, mental illness, therapy, sexuality and the family, belong by their very nature to modern political discourse.

* * *

What I believe to know about psychoanalysis, I learnt not only by struggling with texts written by Freud, his followers, critics, interpreters, and other authors, but also from personal contacts and conversations with analysts, teachers, students and friends in England, Israel and Switzerland. Indeed, it would have been impossible for me to master the learning process involved in writing this book – which has its origins in my doctoral dissertation – without the reflection which is provoked through dialogue. I have benefitted greatly from the suggestions, questions and objections of my interlocutors, though it is not possible to acknowledge all of them here. Nevertheless, some of them deserve special thanks.

It was a great pleasure and privilege to be supervised by Leszek Kolakowski during my years as a doctoral student at St. Antony's College, Oxford. It was indeed a great gift to have a supervisor on whose help and judgement I could rely with confidence. Ernest Gellner and Gerald Cohen – my examiners – proved that a doctoral defence can be both thought-provoking and enjoyable, and provided me with useful and encouraging criticisms. John Forrester read my thesis for Blackwell. From his comments I learnt how much work I still had before me, and his many pages of close questioning helped to transform the dissertation into this book. Joseph Sandler's graduate seminar at the Department of Psychology of the Hebrew University in Jerusalem allowed me to gain important insights into the development of psychoanalytic concepts and the thinking of practitioners.

Ilana Bet-El, Eva Illouz, Yagil Levy and David Vital commented on various parts of my drafts. Yael-Janette Zupnik was as rigorous in her critique of the logic and structure of my arguments as she was of their style and syntax. Naomi Alon assisted me in the arduous task of checking and double-checking notes and references. Stephan Chambers showed an extraordinary patience with an author incapable of keeping to deadlines.

However, this book would never have become what it is now, without the frank and pertinent responses which I received throughout my work from Leah Rosen, Yoav Peled and Daniel Strassberg. The impact which the continuously challenging and stimulating exchanges with them had on my thinking can hardly be overstated here. Most of all, however, they were friends and companions in what remains – despite dialogues and debates – essentially a lonely task.

Finally, I owe a singular debt of gratitude to Arnona Zahavi. She not only gave me the understanding, support and advice I needed when I was stuck with seemingly unresolvable questions, but also read the entire final draft with great care and a sharp eye for inaccuracies and unclarities.

* * *

I am grateful for the permission to include material which I previously published in 'On the political rhetoric of Freud's individual psychology', *History of Political Thought* 5 (1984): 315–32; 'The (ir)relevance of Freud's Jewish identity to the origins of psychoanalysis', *Psychoanalysis and Contemporary Thought* 14 (1991): 655–84; 'Psychoanalysis, psychiatry and politics in the First World War', *Journal of the History of the Behavioral Sciences* 27 (1991): 323–36; ' "Every path will end in darkness" or, why psychoanalysis needs metapsychology', *Science in Context* 7 (1994): 83–101.

Excerpts of about 870 words from *The Interpretation of Dreams* by Sigmund Freud. Translated from the German and edited by James Strachey. Published in the United States by Basic Books, Inc., 1956 by arrangement with George Allen & Unwin, Ltd. and the Hogarth Press, Ltd. Reprinted by permission of Basic Books, a division of HarperCollins Publishers Inc. Quotations from Sigmund Freud, *The Interpretation of Dreams* (vols IV/V of *The Standard Edition of the Complete Psychological Works of Sigmund Freud*, translated and edited by James Strachey) are also reprinted with permission of International Thomson Publishing Services Ltd. Quotations from Sigmund Freud, *Introductory Lectures on Psycho-Analysis*, translated from the German by James Strachey, are reprinted with the permission of Liveright Publishing Corporation. Copyright 1920, 1935 by Edward L. Bernays. Copyright 1963, 1964, 1965, by James Strachey. All rights reserved. Permission to quote from *The Standard Edition of the Complete Psychological Works of Sigmund Freud*, translated and edited by James Strachey, has also been granted by Sigmund Freud Copyrights, the Institute of Psycho-Analysis and the Hogarth Press.

Part I

Nervousness and Nationalism: Medical Politics and the Origins of Psychoanalysis

When Freud entered the medical discourse on nervous diseases in the late nineteenth century with his early publications on hysteria, he joined a controversy carrying strong political connotations. The way in which medical theories explained nervous diseases such as hysteria by the concept of 'degeneracy' both reflected and reinforced bourgeois values, nationalist ideologies and widespread fears in the face of rapid urbanization and industrialization. Thus, medical discourse was never only factual and descriptive; it always also contained an evaluative moral and political dimension. Moreover, although divided over hysteria's exact nature, Wilhelmine doctors – who at the time set the tone in Austria as well – were by and large in agreement not only on the organic origins but also on the geographic and national distribution of the illness. Thus, nervousness and nationalism were interrelated by attributing a special nervousness to certain nations and the concept of degeneracy became a major ingredient of a nationalist rhetoric, which focused on the biological potential and purity of the race. The message of this discourse was always the same: weakness in the face of vice, debauchery and decadence embodied in drink, sex and crime, could be transmitted by heredity. It could gain a biological momentum, work as a negative mechanism of selection and produce criminal madmen, degenerate assassins and prostitutes. Differences existed only in the way in which these components were put together into a causal chain.

Following in the methodological footsteps of Quentin Skinner, I wish to examine in part I the extent to which Freud's early work did conform to, oppose, ignore or undermine commonly accepted assumptions and conventions of this medico-political discourse.[1] I seek to uncover the motives and intentions which underlaid Freud's position, and to establish whether they have to be sought in his clinical practice or whether they were determined by political (that is, extraneous) factors. Finally, I assess the effects of Freud's medical position in terms of the moral and political issues of his period. In order to discuss these issues I provide at first a detailed picture of the medico-political background of Freud's work. This allows me later on to place Freud's early writings on hysteria in their historical context, and to inquire into their political significance.

1 Hereditary Vices

In the second half of the nineteenth century medical discourse inter-twined etiologies of nervous diseases with political concerns by con-necting such maladies to nationality and ethnicity or, as practically all European physicians put it then, to 'race'. Above all, this link was established by the concept of 'mental degeneracy', introduced into European medicine in 1857 by Bénédict-Augustin Morel.[1] Degeneracy was generally understood to constitute a long-term effect of modern-ity – especially urbanization and industrialization – whose vices, pressures, demands, speed and noise were said to impose an inordin-ate burden on the nervous system, lead to fatigue and bring people to seek consolation in drink, sexual perversion or crime. Such decadence was assumed to further weaken the nerves to a degree which could be transmitted by heredity to later generations, where there would be even more exhaustion, depravity and, ultimately, neurosis and psy-chosis.[2]

The two most prominent degenerative neuroses were hysteria and neurasthenia. Hysteria denoted a disease marked by a host of symp-toms, such as lethargy and fainting, localized losses of sensation and paralysis, narrowing of the visual field (tunnel vision), loss of speech, difficulties in walking and standing, epileptoid seizures and convul-sions, uncontrollable shouting and weeping, as well as reveries, deliria and hallucinations. As its name indicates, hysteria had originally been considered a female malady, originating in the womb (*hysteria* in Greek). Hence, for centuries its symptoms had been explained by uterine wanderings or vaporous substances exuded from the uterus. The modern, systematic study of hysteria began with Paul Briquet's *Traité de l'Hystérie* in 1859, which surveyed more than 400 hysterics, and defined hysteria as 'a neurosis of the brain, the manifestation of it consisting chiefly in a perturbation of those vital acts which are con-cerned with the expression of emotion and passion'.[3] Already Briquet no longer related hysteria to the womb, and in the course of the second half of the nineteenth century hysteria came to be acknowledged as a disorder of males as well as females.[4]

The term neurasthenia was applied to manifestations of nervous exhaustion, such as migraines, indigestion, insomnia, depression, impotence and a host of other symptoms.[5] Its theory was articulated primarily by the New York physician George Miller Beard in 1869, who considered it an American illness caused by overwork and the intensity, tension and stress caused by life in the big cities. In Europe neurasthenia soon came to be seen as typical for urbanized, hardworking Jews. In contrast to Beard's approach, European medicine regarded it also as a degenerative illness and related it to sexual excesses, masturbation and, especially, to the ambiguous idea of 'inbreeding' (*Inzucht*), which hinted both at intra-racial heredity and incest.[6]

Morel's theory of morbid heredity not only dominated the thinking of European physicians and psychologists at the time, it also became common currency in the general cultural discourse. Although there were a number of different nuances and emphases, the various theories had more or less the same message: debauchery and decadence could gain a biological momentum and produce people devoid of moral sense, who inevitably became drunkards, obsessive masturbators, madmen, criminals and prostitutes. Thus, degeneration came to be seen both as the root of vice and its punishment in modern society.

A well-known though rather eccentric and controversial popularizer of the danger of degeneration was Max Nordau. A German-speaking, Austro-Hungarian Jewish psychiatrist as well as a dramatist, novelist and journalist, he became famous as co-founder of the World Zionist Organization and as one of the leading figures of modern Zionism. In 1893, among other publications critical of European culture, Nordau published a resounding condemnation of *fin-de-siècle* aesthetics and manners, entitled *Degeneration* (*Entartung*), which appeared rapidly in several editions and translations both in Europe and in the United States. It was equally rapidly pulled to pieces by celebrities such as William James and George Bernard Shaw, who attacked the book's arrogant and dismissive moralism, and the application of concepts of criminal degeneration to artists like Wagner, Tolstoy, Nietzsche and Ibsen.[7] Yet the categories of degeneracy used by Nordau were generally agreed upon. Summing-up the established scientific opinion, Nordau claimed that 'that which nearly all degenerates lack is a sense of morality and of right and wrong. For them there exists no law, no decency, no modesty. In order to satisfy any momentary impulse, or inclination, or caprice, they commit crimes and trespass with the greatest calmness and self-complacency, and do not comprehend that other persons take offence thereat'.[8] Nordau traced degeneracy to mental and physical exhaustion caused by rising tobacco and alcohol consumption, rapid urbanization and railways. His conclusions were dire: 'to speak without metaphor, statistics indicate in what measure the sum of work of civilized humanity has increased during the half-century. It has not quite grown to this increased effort. It grew fatigued and exhausted, and this fatigue and exhaustion showed themselves in the first generation, under the form of acquired hysteria; in the second, as hereditary hysteria.'[9]

Nordau dedicated his book to Cesare Lombroso, Professor for Forensic Psychiatry at the University of Turin, and Europe's foremost authority on degeneration.[10] In his own book on the relation of artistic genius to insanity, Lombroso told the tale of the hereditary damage which alcoholism caused for a long line of generations. He mentioned one Max Jucke, whose inordinate taste for alcohol was said to have determined the fate of future generations of his family. According to Lombroso, in a period of 75 years, 200 of Jucke's direct and indirect descendants became thieves and murderers, 280 were afflicted with blindness and other terrible diseases, 90 turned into prostitutes and some 300 died an early death – in sum total, added Lombroso, this cost the state about one million dollars.[11]

This comment was typical of the way in which degeneracy was treated. If one is to believe Lombroso, with several hundred descendants in three-quarters of a century, the hereditary baggage which Max Jucke's debauchery left behind was not only degenerative, but also extremely potent. Indeed, since vice seemed to proliferate at a rapid pace through heredity, it was common for European doctors to mix concern for the nervous health of individual patients with worry for the well-being of the state, and to be troubled about the negative impact which degeneration had on their nations. This can be seen clearly from the comments which Richard von Krafft-Ebing made on the topic. Krafft-Ebing was Professor of Psychiatry at the University of Vienna and his *Psychopathia Sexualis* – first published in 1886 – became a scientific bestseller of which Freud had four copies in his personal library. According to Krafft-Ebing:

The episodes of moral decay always coincide with the progression of effeminacy [*Verweichlichung*], lewdness and luxuriance of the nations. . . . Exaggerated tension of the nervous system stimulates sensuality, leads the individual as well as the masses to excesses, and undermines the very foundations of society, and the morality and purity of family life. The material and moral ruin of the community is brought about by debauchery, adultery and luxury. Greece, the Roman Empire, and France under Louis XIV and XV, are striking examples of this assertion. In such periods of civic and moral decline [*Zerfall des Staatslebens*] the most monstrous excesses of sexual life may be observed, which, however, can always be traced to psychopathological or neuropathological conditions of the nations involved.[12]

However, it was also suggested that respectability and commitment to national values could combat nervousness. Thus, the dynamics of degeneracy were not taken to be as deterministic and inevitable as their biological rhetoric might suggest. Instead, the regeneration and social integration of the nation demanded moderation, self-restraint and even docility from individuals, who had to keep themselves virile, strong and healthy in order to remain transportable by railways, productive in industry, and fighting at the front. It was assumed that in order to alleviate or even stop degenerative processes, one had to live virtuously; that is, adopt a life-style based on principles of moral rigour, beauty, self-discipline and masculine strength. Indeed, in order to stem the tide of degeneracy which seemed to sweep over Europe in the second half of the nineteenth century, members of the European middle class – from the high to the petty bourgeoisie – united in the endeavour to maintain or recover the respectability of their nations, as well as to overcome their deep anxiety in the face of rapid modernization. They formed leagues against prostitution, social and scientific movements for moral and racial purity, temperance societies, circles promulgating eugenic policies and hygiene societies. They also founded clubs for physical education, which included both *Turnvater* Friedrich Jahn's anti-Semitic associations and Max Nordau's liberal-Zionist *Maccabi*, which was supposed to produce healthy 'muscle Jews'.[13]

Those who could not be made virtuous and healthy had to be restrained or excluded, so that they would not endanger the consolidation of modern European nation states. Conversely, by declaring certain social groups to be 'degenerate', governments could deny them political rights and access to power, and legitimize policies of exclusion. Medical and social historians have shown how the concept of degeneracy was used in the paternalist limitation of franchise in post-unification Italy, in the control of criminal rebels and sexual deviants, and finally, in the dissemination of segregationist and discriminatory eugenic practices and their related educational policies all over Europe.[14]

This juncture of politics and medicine allowed medical practitioners who concerned themselves with nervous diseases to play a prominent role as custodians of national health. This role, which carried promises of state funding and professional self-assertion, demanded not only that doctors be willing and able to appropriate nervous diseases for the medical domain, but also that they organize them in a politically useful scientific order. Hence medical attitudes and categorizations often had political implications and motives, which carried more weight than research and clinical experience.

For example, medical historian Jan Goldstein links the prominence of hysteria as a distinct medical category in the late 1870s and 1880s to the French state's attempts to use science against the Catholic Church. Obviously, symptoms of hysteria such as attacks of delusion and hallucination, sudden loss of voice or vision and paralysis, were hardly a novelty at this time. Yet Goldstein raises the question why scientific research into these phenomena flourished in this period in France. She explains that phenomena which originally were construed as religious – that is, as demonic possessions which were cured by saints, or mystical reveries and ecstasies exhibited by saints – were reinterpreted as hysterical in this era. This transformation of the supernatural into natural categories served the secularizing policies of the early Third Republic and appealed to the popular spirit of the time, which turned from religion to science. In Goldstein's words:

> The accumulation of scientific knowledge about hysteria is . . . linked to . . . the power of a profession, in collaboration with a like-minded political regime, to further its interests at the expense of the clergy; and conversely, the power of that political regime, ideologically aided and enhanced by science, to secularize French society, to remove from the nation-state the rival authority of the Church. . . . psychiatry was used first and largely for purposes of destroying remaining clerical strongholds. . . . If, at the *fin-de-siècle*, more Frenchwomen than ever before fell sick with a condition called hysteria, their illness was in part a political construction.[15]

After Léon Michel Gambetta became Prime Minister in 1881, he created a special chair in the diseases of the nervous system at the Faculty of Medicine in Paris, to which he appointed the neurologist Jean-Martin Charcot, who was head of the Salpêtrière hospital.[16] Following his appointment, Charcot (and Paul Richer) produced a volume which clearly served the anti-clerical policies of the government, in which he aimed to demonstrate that demonic possessions depicted in religious paintings and engravings were really representations of hysterics. According to Goldstein, the debunking of the demonic as hysteric was one of the constant preoccupations of Charcot's school and formed an integral part of its public image.[17]

Medical discourse on hysteria was political also in that it formed an integral part of the discourse on the nature of ethnic groups. Historian Hannah Decker explains: 'German doctors believed that even if men did have hysteria, there were fewer such men in Germany than in France. Hysterical disease was basically un-Germanic.'[18] In 1900, in a dissertation at the university of Jena, an author claimed that 'among the French – natural born and not naturalized – there are just more hereditarily tainted individuals than among the German races . . . As concerns other races, there is more hysteria among the Jews and the Slavs, especially Poles.'[19]

More than any other scholar in the field, Sander Gilman has drawn attention to the crucial role which stereotypes of race and gender played in the medical and biological discourse of the late nineteenth century. His inquiry into this discourse demonstrates that, as he puts it, '[t]here was a seamlessness to all aspects of the biology of Freud's day that made the biology of "race" a vital part of the arguments of biological and medical science'.[20] Thus the normal–pathological distinction dominant in the medical discourse of this period established a number of interrelated hierarchical distinctions, which safely separated the respectable bourgeoisie from depraved alcoholics, perverts, criminals and madmen. Similarly, this discourse drew a strict dividing line between physicians and patients, and between Germans and 'degenerate' races such as the Jews.

In France it was again Charcot who took the lead in defining Semitic illnesses, arguing that the Israelites – as he politely called the Jews – had a particular hereditary propensity for certain types of neurological disorders. Moreover, he supervised a doctoral thesis on Jewish '*vagabondage*', an allegedly hereditary pathology characterized by a morbid and insatiable need 'to wander from one homeland to another'.[21] According to Charcot, in such illnesses environmental and acquired factors were but *agents provocateurs* of secondary importance. Instead, he conceived of what he called a '*famille névropathique*' to which neurotics of the same hereditary disposition were said to belong.[22]

Like so many of his contemporaries – Jews and gentiles alike – Charcot regarded the Jews as a distinct race. Because of their tendency not to intermarry with other ethnic groups, they represented an obvious object for comparative racial studies. On the one hand, hospitalization figures indicated that Jews had a lower infant mortality and less somatic illnesses, and seemed to achieve greater longevity than non-Jews. On the other hand, the data also indicated that Jews had an especially high ratio of 'degenerative psychoses', such as imbecility, idiocy, paranoia, dementia praecox (today's schizophrenia), mania-depression and the 'degenerative neuroses', that is, hysteria and neurasthenia.[23]

The medical data indicating a higher frequency of nervous diseases among Jews made Jewish physicians uncomfortable, since they worried about potential political implications.[24] Cesare Lombroso, for instance, was not only a dominant figure in the debate on degeneracy; as a Jewish physician deeply worried about anti-Semitism, he explained that if – relatively speaking – more Jews were hospitalized with nervous diseases, this was because they belonged to an especially creative and innovative race which had to pay with madness for its genius, but which contributed to European culture more than other ethnic groups.[25]

A second, less apologetic approach shifted the explanatory weight from biology to sociology. The German-Jewish physician Max Sichel, for instance, put moral blame on the gentiles, who had turned the Jews into degenerates by forcing them into unbearable social conditions, such as life in ghettos, pogroms and persecutions, which had put a constant strain on the nervous system of the Jews. Sichel claimed that the proportionally higher ratio of hospitalized Jews by no means indicated that more Jews were actually ill. Rather, he invoked sociological factors, such as the concentration of Jews in urban areas and their greater wealth and better education, which made them more aware of the incidence of nervous diseases and allowed them to pay for hospitalization.[26] Summing up the debate on the racial origins of nervous disorders, Sichel concluded that race and heredity did play a role as etiological factors, but he emphasized that the race-biological point of view often simply expressed the inability to explain phenomena otherwise.[27] Nevertheless he still described himself as arguing from a 'race-biological point of view [*rassenbiologischen Gesichtspunkt*]'.[28]

Another variant of the shift to sociology related the high frequency of nervous diseases among the Jews to the emancipation of the Jews and to their compulsion to overexert themselves mentally in the competition for education and possessions, so as to both make up for social disadvantages and gain entrance into European society. This approach directed the moralizing fervour back at the Jews themselves, condemned their 'dance around the golden calf', as well as their 'haste and ambition', and recommended physical education to steel the body.[29] The quiet, healthy life of agriculture would provide the solution – '*Hinaus aufs Land* [Out into the countryside]' was the motto.[30]

Finally, one might also mention political publications of Zionist physicians, such as Max Nordau and Leo Pinsker, as part of this discourse. Turning medical categories back unto the anti-Semites, they characterized the latter as suffering of 'hereditary psychosis',[31] 'German hysteria', and a 'dangerous form of persecution-mania'.[32] Even though these latter formulations remained insignificant in terms of both medical and political argument, they demonstrate well that at the turn of the century even the most radical political opposition to anti-Semitism led to inversions of the hereditary paradigm, but not to a wholesale rejection of its biologistic terminology, which dominated the medico-political discourse of the period.[33]

It was not until the end of the First World War that Raphael Becker, a Swiss-Jewish psychiatrist, finally wrote dismissively of the 'dated and not very significant concept degeneration', though he still announced his treatise on 'Jewish Nervousness [*jüdische Nervosität*]', as 'a contribution to race psychiatry [*ein Beitrag zur Rassenpsychiatrie*]'.[34] His argument was openly directed against the previously undoubted and established opinion in the field. He denied all hereditary claims and substituted for them an exclusively sociological thesis, which left no room for a particular Jewish heredity. Becker argued that their legal and social situation, the introjection of anti-Semitic prejudices and the decline of religion, but not degeneration, provided decisive reasons for the high rate of nerve maladies diagnosed among the Jews.

2 Suspicious Respectability

The young Sigmund Freud must have heard Charcot's views on hysteria and heredity – and, possibly, also on demonic possession and Jews – between October 1885 and March 1886. During that period Freud spent a few months at the Salpêtrière as a neurologist on a travel grant, and audited Charcot's famous *Leçons du Mardi*. Earlier, during his medical studies in Vienna, Freud had been supervised by Ernst Brücke, a strict medical materialist from Berlin who was part of the positivist School of Helmholtz. For six formative years, from 1876 to 1882, Freud had trained in cerebral anatomy in the laboratory of Brücke's Institute of Physiology. When he finally took his medical degree, he joined Theodor Meynert's psychiatric clinic, which also was run according to staunch somaticist principles of brain anatomy. Freud had intended to continue neurological work in Paris, and to study children's brains. Confronted with disappointing Parisian laboratory conditions and the overpowering presence of Charcot – who was nicknamed both 'Napoleon of the Neuroses' and 'Caesar of the Salpêtrière' – he changed his plans after a few weeks, and devoted his time to gaining clinical experience in the study of hysteria and the use of hypnosis.

For a few years, in which Charcot remained his role model, Freud, too, adopted the degeneracy paradigm – though without its racial undertones. In 1888 he wrote, for instance, that '[t]he aetiology of the *status hystericus* is to be looked for entirely in heredity: hysterics are always hereditarily disposed to disturbances of nervous activity. . . . Direct hereditary transmission of hysteria, too is observed . . . Compared with the factor of heredity all other factors take second place and play the part of incidental causes, the importance of which is as a rule overstated in practice.'[1]

However, in 1894 Freud translated Charcot's *Leçons du Mardi* into German. In footnotes, which he added to Charcot's lectures, he expressed for the first time a substantial disagreement with his Parisian teacher's hereditary approach, stating that 'the conception of the *famille névropatique . . .* could scarcely stand up to serious criticism'.[2] To a passage declaring that heredity was the true cause of a patient's hysterical attacks, Freud added: 'I venture upon a contradiction here. The more frequent cause of agoraphobia as well as of most other phobias lies not in heredity but in abnormalities of sexual life. . . . Such disorders can be *acquired* in any degree of intensity; naturally they occur more intensely, with the same aetiology, in individuals with a hereditary disposition.'[3]

In 1894 Freud also worked on his case studies of hysteria with his Viennese mentor Josef Breuer. In the discussion of Frau Emmy von N., one of Freud's early women patients, whose symptoms and treatment he reported in *Studies on Hysteria*, he explicitly opposed his and Breuer's evaluation of their patient to those of other doctors, who stigmatized hysterical women as degenerates. According to Freud, he and Breuer used to smile when they compared their patient's character

> with the picture of the hysterical psyche which can be traced from early times through the writings and the opinions of medical men. We had learnt from our observations on Frau Cäcilie M. that hysteria of the severest type can exist in conjunction with gifts of the richest and most original kind – a conclusion which is, in any case, made plain beyond a doubt in the biographies of women eminent in history and literature. In the same way Frau Emmy von N. gave us an example of how hysteria is compatible with an unblemished character and a well-governed mode of life. The woman we came to know was an admirable one. The moral seriousness with which she viewed her duties, her intelligence and energy, which were no less than a man's, and her high degree of education and love of truth impressed both of us greatly; while her benevolent care for the welfare of her dependents, her humility of mind and the refinement of her manners revealed her true qualities as a lady. To describe such a woman as a 'degenerate' would be to distort the meaning of that word out of all recognition.[4]

Finally, in the book's concluding chapter, Freud explained that in the psychotherapy of hysterics 'we must of course keep free from the theoretical prejudice that we are dealing with the abnormal brains of *"dégénérés"* and *"déséquilibrés"* '.[5]

At the same time, however, Freud also admitted that 'Frau Emmy von N. was undoubtedly a personality with a severe neuropathic heredity. It seems likely that there can be no hysteria apart from a disposition of this kind'.[6] In his discussion of the case of Miss Lucy R., Freud put his position somewhat differently. He declared that there existed no hysteria without any pre-existing disposition, that is, without a general 'proclivity' (*Eignung*) to acquire hysteria. But he also distinguished this 'proclivity' – which in his view could be found in 'a person of sound heredity' – from a 'neuropathic disposition'.[7]

Thus, although Freud never completely denied that heredity or constitution could play a role in the etiology of hysteria, around 1894–5 he clearly departed from the degeneracy paradigm. First, as he explained in 'Heredity and the Aetiology of the Neuroses', in his view heredity fulfilled at most the role of a 'precondition' in the development of neuroses, which could bring about the onset of illness by itself and did not determine the specific form which the various nervous disorders could take.[8] Second, he stressed that even where it could be assumed to exist, a hereditary predisposition towards neuroses did not entail the disintegration of the personality or a weakness of mind, which the degeneracy paradigm implied.[9] Third, in contrast to his contemporaries Freud did not impute to hysterics a lack of ethics and respectability, or a tendency towards feeble-mindedness, corruption and crime.

Already in the 'Preliminary Communication' he stated together with Breuer that 'among hysterics may be found people of the clearest intellect, strongest will, greatest character and highest critical power'.[10] Instead, he blamed their illness on a moral rigidity which did not even allow them to become aware of sexual wishes which were incompatible with their high-minded self-image. In Freud's assessment it was the exaggerated submissiveness of middle-class women to what he called 'the demands of civilization' – which he explained as the result of an excessively strict education – that gave rise to a conflict between desire and duty, and led his patients to seek 'refuge in an illness'.[11] Freud concluded that 'a greater amount of moral courage would have been of advantage to the person concerned'.[12]

Indeed, Freud assumed that the passivity of his patients was so great that it prevented them even from responding to attacks or humiliations and thus lead to illness. As he pointed out: 'An insult that has been repaid, even if only in words, is recollected quite differently from one that has had to be accepted; and linguistic usage characteristically describes an insult that has been suffered in silence as a "mortification"

(*Kränkung*).'[13] What, then, could have brought Freud's patients to remain passive and silent in the face of abuse and humiliation? It seems that Freud regarded hysterics as caught in a constricting web of internalized social and moral principles, which burdened them with a categorical commitment to social duties of which they could not free themselves. Thus, not only their 'forbidden' sexuality, but all their emotions could turn into a threat to their overly strict and moralistic self-image. Afraid of their feelings, they were incapable of responding to aggression and abuse, and withdrew into silence. However, when hysterics tried to 'forget' traumas and avoid 'dangerous' affects, their memories and the related affects became 'strangulated' (*eingeklemmt*) in their mind. Ultimately, these unbearable affects reemerged in hysterical attacks as an unconquerable 'counter-will', in which, as Freud put it, 'distressing antithetic ideas (inhibited or rejected by normal consciousness) . . . press forward . . . and find their way to the somatic innervation'.[14]

Freud explained a patient's anorexia, for instance, by her silent acceptance of the fact that '[i]n her childhood she had been forced, under threat of punishment, to eat the cold meal that disgusted her, and in her later years she had been prevented out of consideration for her brothers from expressing the effects to which she was exposed during their meals together'.[15] Another patient whose case is told in *Studies on Hysteria* underwent training as a singer, but choked whenever she reached a certain tone level. According to Freud, her problems had started when, after her mother's death, she protected her younger siblings from their sexually offensive and oppressive father. 'Every time she had to keep back a reply, or forced herself to remain quiet in the face of some outrageous accusation, she felt a scratching in her throat, a sense of constriction, a loss of her voice – all the sensations localized in her larynx and pharynx which now interfered with her singing.'[16]

Most clearly, however, Elisabeth von R. exemplified the suffering of Freud's hysterics. As usual, he described the features of her character as incompatible with assumptions of degeneracy and her family as free of any hereditary taint. In his eyes, Elisabeth von R. was 'good-looking and unusually intelligent', though the 'independence of her nature' went further than what he took to be 'the feminine ideal'. In his words, she showed 'a considerable amount of obstinacy, pugnacity and reserve'.[17] Elisabeth von R. disliked being a woman; she wanted to study or to be trained musically rather than to get married; but she abandoned these plans and denied herself for the sake of the family, took care of her father when he was ill, and slept in his room for 18 months. While her two sisters married after his death, she continued to live with her mother, caring for her and closing herself off from the world around her. Without success, she made several attempts 'to establish a new life . . . she was never tired of repeating that what was painful about them had been her feeling of powerlessness, the feeling that she "could not take a single step forward" '.[18] This, then was the unconscious meaning of her illness. The 'proud girl with her longing for love', as Freud called Elisabeth von R., started to have difficulties with walking and developed strong pains in her legs when she could no longer avoid confronting her lack of power.[19] Without any conceivable organic causes she almost turned into an invalid. 'Till then she had thought of herself strong enough to be able to do without the help of a man; but she was now overcome by a sense of her weakness as a woman and by a longing for love in which, to quote her own words, her frozen nature began to melt.'[20] Freud explained Elisabeth von R.'s pains and walking difficulties as 'a somatic expression for her lack of an independent position and her inability to make any alteration in her circumstances'.[21] As he asked rhetorically: 'what *is it* that turns into physical pain here? A cautious reply would be: something that might have become, and should have become, *mental [seelische]* pain'.[22]

It appears that what paralyzed Elisabeth von R.'s legs in the most literal sense of the word, was the rage and resentment arising from a social situation which mortified her because she felt obliged to accept it passively and silently, and alone. In repressing their mental pain, needs, desires and anger, hysterics like Elisabeth von R. avoided above all unbearable feelings of powerlessness and humiliation. Hence the pathological 'forgetting' involved in hysteria can also be seen as a doomed strategy in which women attempted to restore a sense of power over their inner life by shrouding it in silence.

Such a reading of *Studies on Hysteria*, which focuses on social roles and hidden feelings of powerlessness of women, significantly diverges from the conclusion which Freud reached in the last chapter of the book, which he devoted to a general discussion of 'The Psychotherapy of Hysteria'. Here he claimed unequivocally that the symptoms of his patients had to be traced to sexual factors.[23] However, this conclusion contrasts significantly with the picture which he painted in the four detailed case studies, which he presented in earlier chapters and in which he referred only marginally to his patients' sexuality. In my view, Freud's case studies can easily be taken as pointing towards a political undercurrent which can be found in the symptoms of his patients.

Following a line of thought suggested by a number of Freud's feminist critics, one may interpret the symptoms of his patients as unconsciously created caricatures of modes of behaviour which were considered to be typically female in the late nineteenth century. Hysterics took female clichés one step too far, as it were. They became incoherent, irrational, unpredictable, theatrical, fragile, weak and dependent to an extent which prevented them from fulfilling the social roles allocated to them, and made them troublesome and annoying to their social environment. By stretching their socially imposed powerlessness into such hyperbolic dimensions, they resisted social conventions and recovered some power over themselves.[24]

However, it seems to me that one also has to stress another aspect of this type of social protest. When examining hysteria from a political angle, one cannot ignore that it expressed not only a protest against female powerlessness in patriarchal society, but also that it ended up reinforcing this powerlessness. By repressing their own expectations, needs and desires – instead of openly criticizing or resisting dominant social norms – Freud's patients made themselves ill. By becoming hysterics, they incapacitated themselves mentally and physically, and marginalized themselves socially.

In my view it is important to emphasize the self-defeating or pathological nature of the protest embedded in hysteria and to distinguish it from other forms of resistance, which may be termed 'normal'. Even if this distinction cannot be drawn as an unambiguous sharp line, it still is significant, both in psychological and political terms. Roughly, I would say that normal political protest arises out of a conflict in which the individual experiences his or her values, beliefs and principles as opposed to those of the surrounding society, its institutions and norms. Pathological protest, however, is the result of a conflict in which the individual is not capable of consciously opposing his or her needs, rights, demands and expectations to the opportunities and standards offered by society. Instead, it is characteristic of individuals who experience the roles which society imposes on them as severely frustrating, even though these individuals have thoroughly internalized the values and conventions of their society. Thus, they are incapable of confronting social norms and demands openly, or of admitting dissatisfaction with their social roles to themselves and to others. In the words of Michel Foucault: 'where the normal individual experiences contradiction, the ill person undergoes a contradictory experience; the experience of the first opens onto contradiction, that of the second closes itself against it. In other words: normal conflict, or ambiguity of the situation, pathological conflict, or ambiguity of experience.'[25]

Undoubtedly, it is this internal conflict, which turned Freud's patients into hysterics, that stood at the centre of his concerns in *Studies on Hysteria*. For this reason I have argued that one may 'politicize' Freud's early case studies by reading them as meditations on the etiology and therapy of a pathological form of social protest – even though this is not how their author defined them.

In any case, what made hysterics ill according to Freud, was not a degenerative hereditary process and their immorality. On the contrary, as Freud wrote in 1908, 'all who wish to be more noble-minded than their constitution allows fall victims to neurosis; they would have been more healthy if it could have been possible for them to be less good. . . . in many families the men are healthy, but from a social point of view immoral to an undesirable degree, while the women are high-minded and over-refined, but severely neurotic'.[26]

Freud attributed to hysterics not only an unreasonable moralism, but also 'an excess of efficiency' in intellectual matters – corresponding to their inordinate endeavour to be respectable, civilized and productive.[27] Here his views differed once more from the established opinion: not the exhausted and corrupt fell ill; rather, the reduction of mental capacity in hysterics had to be understood as a result of the splitting of the mind. Exaggerated parental demands, strong social pressures, strict moral conventions and harsh standards of respectability could put a strain even on people with the healthiest constitution, if they trapped their minds in irresolvable internal conflicts. If the city made one ill, it was not through its vice and corruption, as his colleagues believed, but through 'the intensification of sexual restrictions'.[28] In a radical inversion of the relation between respectability and health, Freud claimed that rather than safeguarding the health of the species by protecting it against degeneration, the often exaggerated morality of the urbanized bourgeoisie was the very reason for illnesses which his contemporaries regarded as related to degeneracy.

Freud even speculated that 'the physician finds food for thought in observing that those who succumb to nervous illness are precisely the offspring of fathers who, having been born of rough but vigorous families, living in simple, healthy country conditions, had successfully established themselves in the metropolis and in a short space of time had brought their children to a high level of culture.'[29] In other words, neurotics were often born healthy, but could be educated into illness by parents who tried too hard to make their families conform to the exaggerated standards of respectability which were typical of the urban bourgeoisie.

According to Freud, however, therapeutic progress had been hindered by a mistaken emphasis on heredity and, as he complained, 'there has been too little research into these specific and determining causes of nervous disorders, for the attention of physicians remains dazzled by the grandiose prospect of the etiological precondition of heredity'.[30] After the completion of *Studies on Hysteria*, declarations against the emphasis placed on heredity and its understanding as degenerative became a regular feature in the opening pages of Freud's papers and sometimes appear to have been their main purpose.[31]

In 1898 he advised fellow doctors that in the case of neurasthenics 'they are dealing, not with victims of civilization or heredity, but . . . with people who are crippled in sexuality'.[32] Repeating in the opening pages of his *Three Essays on the Theory of Sexuality* what by that time had become his *ceterum censeo*, he remarked that 'it may well be asked whether an attribution of "degeneracy" is of any value or adds anything to our knowledge'.[33] Finally, at a scientific meeting of the Vienna Psychoanalytic Society in May 1907, he emphasized that the concept of degeneracy 'has to be completely discarded in respect to the historic meaning which it contains: that there once actually existed a perfect generation whose descendants have gradually degenerated. Such men never existed and we are no more degenerate than our ancestors of a hundred years ago or of a thousand years ago.'[34]

Michel Foucault seems to have been the only one to note the importance of Freud's break with what he calls 'the perversion–heredity–degenerescence system'.[35] Otherwise the literature has by and large neglected to refer to the significance of Freud's rejection of the degeneracy paradigm. However, it is important to see that by arguing against the degeneracy hypothesis, Freud contradicted not only the factual, but also the moral claims of his age concerning sexuality. For him, perverse tendencies were not a symptom of the decay of an originally and naturally well-defined heterosexual sexuality. Rather, in his view, human beings were born with an originally polymorphous or diffuse sexuality. Hence, Freud claimed: 'perversions are neither bestial nor degenerate in the emotional sense of the word. They are the development of germs [*Keimen*], all of which are contained in the undifferentiated sexual disposition of the child'.[36] He pointed out that sexuality had 'uncertain boundaries' and that homosexuality had not only been tolerated by the civilized Greeks, but even 'entrusted by them with important social functions'. Moreover, Freud expressed his disrespect for what was commonly considered to be the 'civilized' (*kulturelle*) sexual morality in his time, by putting the word in quotation marks throughout an article which he wrote on the topic in 1908.

In this article he argued that a more permissive sexual morality, or the courage to feel and recognize – if not enact – seemingly illegitimate sexual desires, may keep women from falling ill. He even mentioned extra-marital affairs for women as an unlikely but potentially efficient safeguard against neurosis, and raised the question 'whether our "civilized" sexual morality is worth the sacrifice which it imposes on us'.[37]

This critical question, whose very articulation ran against the established medical morals of his age – where sexual respectability was proclaimed as the key to the future – was to remain the animating force of much of Freud's later work, such as *The Future of an Illusion* and *Civilization and Its Discontents*. However, as has been shown here, Freud formulated his basic position already in the first decade of his psychoanalytic work.

Adding insult to injury, Freud suggested in 1908 also that what his society declared to be a vice and the cause of degeneration could be quite healthy, and that some of the most valued traits of 'civilized' morality nursed on hidden perverse sexual desires. He portrayed the epitome of bourgeois respectability, the 'orderly, parsimonious and obstinate' personality, as a character which evolved in a defence against anal eroticism. He stated that 'cleanliness, orderliness and trustworthiness give exactly the impression of a reaction-formation against an interest in what is unclean and disturbing and should not be part of the body'.[38] Years later, in his *Introductory Lectures*, he summed up his position as follows: 'We cannot help observing with a critical eye and we have found it impossible to side with conventional sexual morality or to form a very high opinion of the manner in which society attempts the practical regulation of the problems of sexual life. We can present society with a blunt calculation that what is described as its morality calls for a bigger sacrifice than it is worth and that its proceedings are not based on honesty and do not display wisdom.'[39]

I agree with Erich Fromm that after Freud bourgeois respectability, decent behaviour and good intentions are no longer good enough. For now the question 'Who are you behind yourself?' can be addressed to everyone.[40] Of course, the spirit of suspicion guiding Freud's approach has accompanied thinkers throughout the ages, and in modern times there have been many who claimed, in the wake of La Rochefoucauld, that our virtues are but vices in disguise. But through Freud this spirit of suspicion found entrance into the science of mind in a three-pronged argument which traced mental illness to an exaggerated attempt to be respectable, declared immoral sexuality to be a sign of mental health, and unmasked traits of respectability as concealing 'perverse' sexual desire.

3 Portrait of the Scientist as a Young Jew

As we have seen, Freud accepted the dominant hereditary frame of reference until the middle of the 1890s. What, then, were the reasons which brought him to oppose it around 1894–5? Because Freud's break with the degeneracy model eliminated all significant differences between Jews and gentiles, commentators have been tempted to depict it as part of his Jewish self-assertion in the face of rising anti-Semitism. For instance, Larry Stewart has argued that Freud rejected claims of degeneracy for political reasons because Charcot's approach 'was used to enhance the racist ideologies of the French Right'. In 1886 the French racist Édouard Drumont referred in *La France Juive* to what he called Charcot's 'curious revelations' on Russian Jews, which he invoked as scientific evidence to support anti-Semitic claims.[1] Stewart claims that 'given Freud's immense sensitivity to anti-Semitic racism, it is clear that his appreciation of the role of heredity in character formation could not have remained unaffected by these interpretations'.[2]

Stewart creates a symmetry between Freud and his interlocutors and presents Freud's medical agenda also as overshadowed by considerations of ethnic politics. However, there simply is nothing in Freud's writings that relates his scientific claims to his opposition to anti-Semitism or to the political uses of hereditary medicine. Moreover, as I have shown above, Freud broke with the degeneracy approach in Vienna around 1895 and not in Paris ten years earlier. Stewart's hypothesis cannot explain Freud's acceptance of Charcot's views on degeneracy after the publication of Drumont's *La France Juive* and his continued use of its categories during the following years. But despite its bad timing and lack of textual evidence, Stewart's claim has been approvingly adopted in authoritative histories of psychoanalysis.[3] In fact, his argument is but one example from a large and still expanding body of literature which creates the impression that a hidden Jewish agenda underlaid Freud's work. It explains the origins of psycho-analysis as significantly influenced by Freud's ethnic identity and his reaction to anti-Semitism. In my view this literature constitutes the most sustained effort at a political or sociological explanation of the origins of psychoanalysis. It has been popular since the 1920s and still enjoys wide currency.

At first, such readings of Freud were part of an attempt to discredit psychoanalysis as a 'Jewish science', but in later years they were superseded by more detached inquiries into the status and role of Jews in late-nineteenth-century Europe. More recently they also ex-press an endeavour of Jewish scholars – especially in the United States – to reclaim psychoanalysis as part of Jewish heritage.

David Bakan is among the more eccentric but also more popular commentators of this kind. Astonishingly enough, he considers psy-choanalysis to be part of the history of Jewish mysticism; but accord-ing to Bakan, Freud hid his true colours because he feared anti-Semitic persecution. By pointing to parallels between Jewish medieval texts and Freud's approach to Moses, sexuality, dream interpretation and the curing of the sick, Bakan tries to back up his claim that Freud secretly 'conceived of himself as a Messiah in the spirit of Jewish mysticism'.[4] John Cuddihy has argued that Freud's dream theory hides the basic principles of the debate on civil emancipation and assimila-tion of the Jews which had reached Vienna from Eastern Europe. As he puts it: 'The importunate "Yid" released from the ghetto and *shtetl* is the model, I contend, for Freud's coarse, importunate "id". Both are saddled with the problem of "passing" from a latent existence "be-yond the pale" of Western respectability into an open and manifest relation to Gentile society . . . from a state of unconsciousness to a state of consciousness.' According to Cuddihy, psychoanalysis trans-posed the problems of Eastern Jews in Western Europe into a different sphere, but preserved the basic structure of their conflict. In his words, the 'social unease' of a marginalized ethnic group became 'mental dis-ease'. Western decorum turned into the superego, and sexual in-tercourse took the place of the social intercourse of Jews and gentiles. At the same time the analytic setting allowed Jews who had difficul-ties coping with the cultural code of Western society – whom Cuddihy calls '*goyim manquées*' – to 'regress back to their pre-civil id-"Yid" '. Since for Freud gentiles have the same id as the Jews, Cuddihy regards him as a great moral equalizer and psychoanalysis as 'one more ideology for the Enlightenment process'.[5]

Marthe Robert also claims that Freud's work represents a distinctly Jewish response to modernity and nationalism, and that its theoretical innovations originated in Freud's deep ambivalence about his Jewish origins and his social position as an outsider. Robert's widely-read study emphasizes Freud's boyhood experiences in Vienna, his relationship with his father and his fascination and identification with famous Semitic heroes such as Moses and Hannibal as relevant to an understanding of the origins of psychoanalytic theory.[6] Pursuing a similar line of thought, David Blatt has attempted to demonstrate that 'Freud's identification with the Patriarch Jacob exerted an important influence upon Freud's motivation to conduct psychological research'.[7] In recent years Emanuel Rice has provided detailed evidence on the genesis of Freud's Jewish identity, his family and education, which is supposed to show that Freud was more attracted to, knowledgeable about, and observant in Jewish matters than has been assumed generally.[8] Finally, in a rhetorical flourish which concludes a captivating lecture series devoted primarily to Freud's *Moses and Monotheism*, historian Yosef Hayim Yerushalmi addresses Freud directly with the following confession: 'I think that in your innermost heart you believed that psychoanalysis is itself a further, if not final, metamorphosed extension of Judaism. . . . In short, I think you believed that just as you are a godless Jew, psychoanalysis is a godless Judaism. But I don't think you intended us to know this. Absurd? Possibly. But *tomer dokh* – perhaps, after all . . .?'[9]

Adding a feminist angle to this literature, Estelle Roith has made the suggestion that Freud's controversial theories on women derived from a traditional Jewish perception of femininity and that, therefore, they should be assessed in the light of his Jewishness.[10] Combining detailed historical research with imaginative interpretation, Sander Gilman maintains that Freud displaced racial medical stereotypes into the psychoanalytic construction of gender. 'In linking the Jew with the image of the woman,' Gilman claims, 'Freud provided a place where the Jew could be made to disappear and still find a safe haven.'[11]

Of course, many more articles and books on the role of Freud's Jewishness in the origins of his psychoanalytic theorizing could be cited.[12] This literature is not only fascinating in its daring flights of imagination, it often adds valuable insights into complexities of Freud's character and enriches the history, sociology and psychology of the psychoanalytic movement and its members with admirable historical portraits. What its authors have in common, is that they consider Freud primarily as a Jew and mostly examine him within the context of the assimilated Jewish bourgeoisie of late imperial Vienna. They compare him mainly with other famous secularized Jewish contemporaries – such as Arthur Schnitzler, Otto Bauer, Victor Adler, Karl

Kraus, Otto Weininger and Theodor Herzl. This approach is also characteristic of other interpretations of *fin-de-siècle* Vienna culture, such as Carl Schorske's classic book on the subject.[13]

Dennis Klein points out rightly that such approaches have the tendency to reduce psychoanalysis to a Jewish programme – that is, to a science overshadowed by ethnic politics. However, this is not what worries Klein. He disagrees with other writers only insofar as they imply that the founding fathers of psychoanalysis were driven by a desire to integrate themselves in their surrounding society.[14] Klein, too, holds Freud's ethnicity to be crucially relevant to the origins of psychoanalysis and perceives its movement to be built on Jewish consciousness. Jewishness, he says, endowed the movement with its creative vitality.[15] But rather than a strategy of assimilation, he discerns a desire for dissimilation in the early psychoanalytic movement. According to Klein, Freud and his early followers constituted themselves as a self-consciously Jewish elite and regarded it as their ethical responsibility to bring a universalist message of reconciliation, dignity, freedom and equality to humanity. Klein speaks of an 'interpenetration of the Jewish redemptive vision with the psychoanalytic movement's redemptive hope for the eradication of neurosis'.[16]

In opposition to all these views, Peter Gay has argued that 'Freud . . . was a Jew but not a Jewish scientist',[17] and that there was no 'elusive Jewish quality that somehow, mysteriously, informed Freud's work'.[18] But though he has written extensively and perceptively on Freud's Jewishness, Gay has done little to explain the logic underlying the division which separates 'Freud the Jew' from 'Freud the Scientist'. Hence he remains vulnerable to Klein's criticism that 'it is not clear, at least from his conclusions, why Gay disregards the importance of Freud's Jewish consciousness'.[19] In a review of some of Gay's recent books, William McGrath, too, remarks that Gay's 'reluctance to deal directly with the evidence and the arguments of opposing positions is troubling'.[20]

I agree with Gay that attempts to decode psychoanalysis in terms of an underlying ethnic-Jewish unconscious are misguided. With the exception of Sander Gilman, the scholars mentioned earlier neglect to place Freud's writings in their scientific context, depreciate their role as acts of communication addressed to fellow doctors, and fail to differentiate Freud's approach from the way in which his Jewish contemporaries correlated Jewishness and nervous diseases. Moving to some extent in the tracks of Gilman's research, but making a somewhat different use of the historical sources to which he has drawn attention, I have contextualized Freud's outlook in the course of this part, in order to present it as a perspective which was unique for its period. Since Freud's radical critique of degeneracy in no way conformed to what Jewish doctors generally wrote before the First World War, it cannot simply be explained by his Jewishness. Moreover, although ethnic politics did form the backdrop to Freud's early writings, there is no textual evidence which would support the claim that they underlaid his writings on hysteria and other psychopathologies; and the effect which Freud's theory had does not, by itself, corroborate conjectures about the motives and intentions which were guiding Freud's early work. As James Tully and Quentin Skinner have stressed, one has 'to distinguish between the political point a text serves in its political context and the author's . . . point in writing it'.[21]

In this chapter I attempt to defend Gay's argument that ethnic politics did not directly motivate or underlie the origins of psychoanalysis, although they did form their background. To support Gay's position, I closely examine Freud's references to Jews and Judaism and differentiate from one another the four textual strategies which Freud adopted in his writings to express his attitude towards his ethnic identity. By no means, however, does my reading entail a neglect of Freud's Jewish consciousness; on the contrary, it means taking Freud's particular self-conception as a modern secular Jew more seriously than some of his more speculative commentators have done.

In a first textual category, constituted by private communications, Freud defiantly asserted his parochial pride in being a Jew and possessing qualities which he identified with Jewishness, and he openly expressed his ethnic or national prejudices. In such letters Freud explained most openly what meaning Jewish identity had for him. As it seems, it meant above all to possess both the emotional strength and intellectual freedom which are bred by living as an outsider. In fact, for Freud Jewishness had both 'negative' and 'positive' implications: in the first place it meant freedom from the conformism which he felt restricted gentiles and had its roots in Catholic tradition, social conventions and superstition. The earliest reference to this distinction between Jews and gentiles can be found in a facetious remark in a letter to Martha Bernays, in which he stated: 'In the future, for the remainder of my apprenticeship in the hospital, I think I shall try to live more like the gentiles [*Gojim*] – modestly, learning and practicing the usual things and not striving after discoveries and delving too deep'.[22] In the same spirit he wrote more than three decades later: 'Because I was a Jew I found myself free of many prejudices which restrict others in the use of their intellect: as a Jew I was prepared to be in the opposition and to renounce agreement with the "compact majority".'[23] In the second place – referring to the 'positive' or empowering effect of Jewishness – Freud felt that being a Jew generated the mental energy necessary for independent thought. Hence he advised his pupil Max Graf against baptizing his son – on whom he was later to write a case study under the pseudonym of 'Little Hans' – arguing that 'if you do not let your son grow up as a Jew, you will deprive him of those sources of energy which cannot be replaced by anything else. He will have to struggle as a Jew, and you ought to develop in him all the energy he will need for that struggle. Do not deprive him of that advantage.'[24] Finally, in his letters to Karl Abraham, Freud pointed out that it was easier for Jews to accept the radically subversive and innovative nature of his universalist theory and to join his movement, since they were used to being in the minority. They possessed what he called 'our ancient Jewish toughness', and were not misled by the racial myths and mystical beliefs which blinded the others to the message of psychoanalysis.[25] He explained to Abraham that the 'Aryan comrades', as he called the Swiss Protestant contingent in the International Psychoanalytic Association, were mainly necessary to prevent the movement from falling victim to anti-Semitism.[26] Freud stated that he felt estranged from Carl Gustav Jung, had a 'racial preference' (*Rassenvorliebe*)[27] for Jews, and felt close to Abraham because 'consanguineous Jewish traits' (*verwandte jüdische Züge*)[28] and a 'racial kinship' (*Rassenverwandtschaft*) bound them to one another.[29]

In contrast, a second type of Freud's writings contains prefaces, interviews, histories of the psychoanalytic movement, autobiographical comments and essays which he published, but clearly marked as non-scientific. In these published texts Freud never allowed himself to be as parochial as he was in his private letters. Though he unequivocally affirmed his Jewishness, in these instances he also insisted on the importance of overriding and transcending the boundaries of Judaism. In his 'Preface to the Hebrew edition' of *Totem and Taboo* he called himself 'an infidel Jew' and described himself as an author 'completely estranged from the religion of my forefathers', whose book 'adopts no Jewish standpoint and makes no exception in favour of Jewry'.[30] In his public address to the *B'nai B'rith* Freud wrote of an 'irresistible' attraction to the Jews, of how he was drawn to them by 'many dark emotional powers, all the stronger, the less they could be expressed in words, as well as the clear consciousness of an inner identity, the familiarity of the same psychological structure'. He explained, however, that for him to be a Jew really meant to be a humanist. In his words, 'what tied me to Jewry was – I have to admit it – neither faith nor national pride, for I was always an unbeliever and was brought up without religion, but not without a respect for the so-called "ethical" demands of human civilization'.[31]

A third textual type encompasses general, non-clinical psycho-analytic writings, such as *Jokes and Their Relation to the Unconscious* and *Moses and Monotheism*. On the one hand, such texts clearly manifest Freud's parochial fascination with Jewish folklore and tradition, but on the other hand, his analysis systematically subverts and univer-salizes their particularistic features. In the book on jokes, for instance – in which his taste for Jewish jokes is strongly evident – he put quips about Galician Jews who do not like to take baths on a par with Lessing's and Lichtenberg's sayings.[32] He commented that there was nothing that would distinguish Jewish jokes from others – other than their cruder form and weaker disguises which make it easier to ob-serve their logic. Piercing their particularistic external layers in his analysis, he reached a deeper unconscious level where he explained their dynamics by universal principles of mental functioning. Ulti-mately, as he pointed out in connection with another Jewish joke, 'the core belongs to humanity in general'.[33]

This also is the spirit in which Freud wrote *Moses and Monotheism* towards the end of his life. Referring to the book in a letter, he warned that its claims 'are particularly suited to wound Jewish feelings, inso-far as they do not want to subordinate themselves to science'.[34] In the opening pages of the book Freud explained that he had to deprive his 'people of the man whom they take pride in as the greatest of their sons', because he valued truth more highly than 'what are supposed to be national interests'.[35] As a result of this superposition of science over Judaism, the only 'positive' messages which Freud discovered in the faith of the Israelites are secular and universally applicable – such as the 'triumph of intellectuality over sensuality'.[36] Moreover, Freud's interpretation of the Moses saga turned the founder of Judaism into an Egyptian and traced monotheism and the rite of circumcision to the Egyptian religion of Aten. According to Freud the Jews had killed the man who had brought them their new faith. Hence, in terms of their historical contribution, the Jews could at best claim to have kept monotheism alive, if only out of a feeling of guilt over their crime. As he stated: 'It is honour enough to the Jewish people that they could preserve such a tradition and produce men who gave it a voice – even though the initiative to it came from the outside, from a great foreigner.'[37]

As we see, though Freud praised *Jewishness* as a sociological factor energizing independent thought, he also demanded freedom from the confines of *Judaism*, that is, from allegiance to the faith or the national creed of the Jews. As I have mentioned above, Jewishness appears in Freud's writings as a force which removes distortions and makes room for scientific truth to be told, heard and seen – a truth whose fundamental universality allows for no respect for ethnic boundaries or nationalistic pride. As Freud wrote in a letter to Sandor Ferenczi in 1913, 'there should not be such a thing as Aryan or Jewish science. Results in science must be identical, though the presentation of them may vary. If these differences mirror themselves in the apprehension of objective relationships in science there must be something wrong.'[38]

Clinical and theoretical works on psychopathology form the fourth grouping of Freud's writings. Their content constitutes the crucial test to examine claims which refer Freud's Jewishness to the origins of psychoanalysis. However, in these writings Freud maintained a complete silence on ethnic or national matters and consistently excluded all references to his own or his patients' Jewishness. From my earlier discussion of the degeneracy theory of neuroses it is evident that Freud's silence sharply distinguished him from his colleagues, Jews and gentiles alike. Obviously, my presentation of this silence has to remain short. A silence, even a stubborn one, does not lend itself to elaborate quotation. My point is, however, that not all silences are equal. Had Freud shared this silence with his colleagues, then one might have assumed that at the end of the nineteenth century it was impossible or at least highly inappropriate for an author to make an utterance on ethnicity within a medical text. But since Freud refrained from mentioning what all others were talking about, his silence assumed a polemical quality. Thus, Freud's silence on ethnicity and Jewishness in the context of psychopathology is a telling one. It proves that Freud departed no less radically from the categories used by other Jewish physicians – whose thinking remained committed to ethnic particularism – than he did from the dominant conception of nervous diseases. In other words, Freud's silence is *relevant* because it expressed his attempt to make his own and his patients' Jewishness *irrelevant* to his new science and the understanding of neuroses. As Freud commented much later: 'My background as a Jew helped me to stand being criticized, being isolated, working alone. . . . All this was of help to me in discovering analysis. But that psychoanalysis itself is a Jewish product seems to me nonsense. As a scientific work, it is neither Jewish nor Catholic nor Gentile.'[39] Isaac Deutscher's comment on Freud also is worth quoting here: 'The man whom he analyses is not a German, or an Englishman, a Russian, or a Jew – he is the universal man in whom the subconscious and the conscious struggle, the man who is part of nature and part of society, the man whose desires and cravings, scruples and inhibitions, anxieties and predicaments are essentially the same no matter what race, religion, or nation he belongs to.'[40]

4 Meaningful Sex

If Freud never wrote on hysteria as a Jew engaged in a Jewish cause, we still have to find the reason for his radical break with the degeneracy paradigm around 1894–5. In my view, the explanation for Freud's theoretical departure lies in his clinical practice. These were the years in which he started to work with Josef Breuer, examine patients and treat them in the 'talking cure'. By looking carefully at his patients' symptoms, Freud realized that contrary to common medical wisdom, 'hysteria behaves as though anatomy did not exist or as though it had no knowledge of it'. Hysterical paralyses, he discovered, did not make sense in terms of the affected limb's anatomical or physiological structure. No organic causes could be found which would explain such paralyses. Their boundaries did not follow any known pattern, and from a neurological standpoint there was nothing wrong with these patients. The nerves, as it were, were in order, and hence one could not really speak of nervous diseases. But rather than concluding that these patients were malingerers, as so many of his colleagues did, Freud tried to find an alternative explanation for these phenomena, which seemed to be beyond the conscious control of hysterics.

He noticed that they were modelled according to his patients' often mistaken common-sense assumption about anatomy. He realized that their origin, structure and dynamics could only be explained if one took 'the organs in the ordinary, popular sense of the names they bear: the leg is the leg as far as its insertion into the hip; the arm is the upper limb as it is visible under the clothing'.[1] He postulated, therefore, that with hysterics 'the lesion in hysterical paralysis will . . . be an alteration of the conception, the idea, of an arm, for instance'.[2] But though he claimed that the mind rather than the nerves produced these symptoms, he also postulated that this production occurred beyond the realm of his patients' volitional control: it was a result of *unconscious* thought processes.

The incongruence of symptoms with anatomy and physiology proved to Freud that there was an unconscious part in the mind, where there were forces – that is, ideas and affects – with the power to produce symptoms. Thus a mentalist or idealist theme entered the hitherto self-consciously organicist and materialist, but also racial, medical discourse on hysteria; for Freud's approach placed the mind above the body. By defining hysteria as an illness whose symptoms were produced by a person's unconscious ideas, Freud started what can be called a 'Copernican Revolution' in the understanding of mental illness – which put him into opposition both to the Parisian Charcot and to the German and Austrian scientific community.

In Germany and Austria doctors treating nervous diseases had developed their materialist outlook in a negative response to an earlier period, when romanticist philosophy had ruled universities in the German-speaking realm and prevented the development of an empiricist and hence more experimental and mathematical science. Only in the 1860s and 1870s had psychiatry managed to gain an institutional foothold in the medical departments in Germany's and Austria's universities and – together with several hundred public and private asylums, clinics and laboratories – had given them a scientific lead over France and Britain. When after a prolonged struggle the somaticists – that is, those who argued that the causes and origins of illnesses were organic – had gained the upper hand over their mentalist opponents, they asserted not only 'the supremacy of the brain over any other structures', as Gregory Zilboorg puts it, but also the superiority of German science over the French, whom they had defeated on the battlefield in 1870.[3]

Encouraged by the success of experimental and observational methods, university psychiatry in Germany and Austria dealt with diseases, not with patients. It was the separation of the pathological from the normal that allowed psychiatry to claim its academic independence from philosophy, and enabled it to establish a regime of scientific truth of its own. The presupposition of such a clearly demarcated boundary had formed the cornerstone of the European paradigm of psychiatry.[4] By severing the domain of the pathological from the normal, the psychiatric community had drawn a rigid biological boundary closing off the limits of its discourse, and defining a precinct where it required firm commitment to what it considered scientific method. Obsessed with demarcation from philosophy, it remained on guard against what it perceived as contamination by speculation, which, psychiatrists feared, could throw the new science back into its prescientific stage. Hence German-speaking psychiatrists restricted their research to the perfection of laboratory techniques, clinical classification and description without developing adequate therapeutic measures.[5]

It is thus not surprising that to Freud's contemporaries, his idealist approach appeared to endanger the progress of modern German-speaking science of the nervous diseases away from archaic philosophical speculation. More than twenty years after the publication of *Studies on Hysteria*, when addressing students in his *Introductory Lectures*, Freud still pointed to the fundamental divide separating his approach from that of the psychiatric establishment: 'You have been trained to find an anatomical basis for functions of the organism and their disorders . . . For that reason psychological modes of thought have remained foreign to you. You have grown accustomed to regarding them with suspicion, to denying them the attribute of being scientific, and to handing them over to laymen, poets, natural philosophers and mystics.'[6]

In *Studies on Hysteria*, Freud attributed to the symptoms of his patients a meaning which traced them to sexual traumas in their family life, which occurred around puberty. However, soon after completing this book together with Breuer, he pointed out that some of the experiences which were supposed to lead to pathological phenomena, seemed too insignificant to cause hysteria:

> In some cases, no doubt, we are concerned with experiences, which must be regarded as severe traumas – an attempted rape, perhaps, which reveals to the immature girl at a blow all the brutality of sexual desire. . . . But in other cases the experiences are astonishingly trivial. In one of my women patients it turned out that her neurosis was based on the experience of a boy of her acquaintance stroking her hand tenderly and, at another time, pressing his knee against her dress as they sat side by side at table, while his expression let her see that he was doing something forbidden.[7]

Freud reached the conclusion that the power of such apparently unimportant events derived from their associative connection with an earlier, serious trauma, which the person had suffered in early childhood but repressed from conscious memory. This conclusion reinforced Freud's opposition to the hereditary explanation of nervous disorders. As he pointed out at the time: 'If this is so, the prospect is opened up that what has hitherto had to be laid at the door of a still unexplained hereditary predisposition may be accounted for as having been acquired at an early age.'[8]

Freud postulated that not only hysteria, but also other neuroses and even psychoses originated in early sexual assaults, which occured before the age of four and in which children were molested by adults or by elder siblings who had themselves been molested at an even earlier stage. Freud stressed that such sexual relations within the family could then create an appearance of heredity, 'where there is only a *pseudo- heredity*'.[9]

Although Freud also mentioned nurses, governesses, tutors and other adults – both relatives and strangers – as possible culprits, for him the paradigmatic case of child molestation was that of a father abusing his daughter.[10] In letters to his close friend Wilhelm Fliess he referred to this hypothesis as his 'paternal etiology'.[11] In one instance he even stated that his theory implied that 'in all cases, the father . . . had to be accused of being perverse'.[12] Throughout his discussion of his hypothesis of an early sexual trauma as the primary cause of nervous diseases, Freud opposed it to hereditary assumptions. He emphasized that since adults who molest children are themselves mentally disturbed, it may seem that their illness is transmitted by heredity, when in fact 'neurosis escalates to a psychosis in the next generation – which is called degeneracy – simply because someone of a more tender age is drawn in'.[13] Thus, Freud posited that even patterns which give the impression of being the result of hereditary transmission, have their origin in instances of incestuous child abuse which traumatize the victim and result in permanent mental damage. As Freud put it in a wry comment to Fliess, 'heredity is seduction by the father'.[14]

In this fashion, Freud's hermeneutic trajectory led him away from organic explanations to an inquiry into the early childhood of his patients and their early sexual experiences. However, at that time Freud still assumed that children are asexual creatures who cannot have been aware of the nature of their abuse at the time of their victimization. Nevertheless, he argued that an unconscious memory of having been sexually abused imprints itself indelibly on the child's soul. When reactivated through the awakening of sexuality in puberty, this memory operates 'as though it were a contemporary event. What happens is, as it were, a posthumous action by a sexual trauma.'[15] Once the significance of the event is understood by a person, its memory trace becomes incompatible with this person's self-image, ethical standards and conscious feelings towards the abusing parent. Hence the memory is repressed, that is, pushed back into the unconscious and barred from access to consciousness. As long as the repression is successful, the person appears to be healthy and can deny that the unspeakable event ever occurred. But a fateful return of what has been repressed can be triggered off by later occurrences which in the victim's mind are associatively related to the 'earliest scenes' (*Urszenen*) of molestation.[16] In other words, at this stage Freud postulated that only people who repressed memories of early sexual abuse fell ill. As he pointed out: 'The scenes must be present as *unconscious memories*; only so long as, and in so far as, they are unconscious are they able to create and maintain hysterical symptoms.'[17] In contrast, those who had the moral and mental strength to consciously acknowledge and remember that they had been victimized in early childhood, were able to stay healthy.

Freud's conception of the original trauma included not only the child's shock caused by sexual abuse, but also the incapacity to cope with the ensuing incongruities and contradictions in the power structure of a family, in which a parent plays a dual role as both authority figure and molester or seducer.[18] Thus, he pointed to

> all the singular conditions under which the ill-matched pair conduct their love-relations – on the one hand the adult, who cannot escape his share in the mutual dependence necessarily entailed by the sexual relationship, and who is yet armed with complete authority and the right to punish, and can exchange one role for the other to the uninhibited satisfaction of his moods, and on the other hand the child, who in his helplessness is at the mercy of this arbitrary will, who is prematurely aroused to every kind of sensibility and exposed to every sort of disappointment . . . all these grotesque and yet tragic incongruities reveal themselves as stamped upon the later development of the individual and of his neurosis, in countless permanent effects which deserve to be traced in the greatest detail.[19]

Indeed, Freud's conception of the trauma had as much to do with complexities of authority and dependence – that is with family politics – as with sex and violence. Hence one can say that Freud's conception of an early sexual trauma as the cause of nervous disorders replaced the biologistic framework of the hereditary etiology of neuroses not only with a hermeneutic one, which placed unconscious memories in its center, but also with a *political* one.

Freud presented this etiology – which has commonly become known as the 'seduction theory' – to the Society of Psychiatry and Neurology in Vienna in April 1896; but it was not well received by his colleagues, and was dismissed by Krafft-Ebing as a 'scientific fairy tale'.[20] Undoubtedly, Freud's hypothesis was uncomfortable. However, there also was something implausible in the contention that child molestation before the age of four constituted the *necessary* cause of all mental illness. Indeed, it did not take long for Freud himself to abandon this approach, and though he repudiated it in his published work only somewhat hesitantly in the *Three Essays on the Theory of Sexuality*, privately he rejected it already in autumn 1897.[21]

The abandonment of the seduction theory led to a redirection and restructuring of Freud's hermeneutic method and, indeed, the founding of psychoanalytic interpretation as such. This development has become the subject of two narratives. On the one hand, there is the official account, created by Freud himself and adopted, elaborated and disseminated by his loyal followers. As Frank Sulloway sums it up, this tale presents Freud as a naive hero who set out alone on a perilous journey to find the truth about human nature, but who was temporarily diverted from his quest by deceptive temptresses, whose words he believed, but who in fact could not be trusted.[22]

Looking back on the early days of his work from the vantage point of 1914, Freud attributed his seduction theory to his credulity towards his patients' conscious memories. He wrote that he had been misled because he 'was readily inclined to accept as true and aetiologically significant the statements by patients in which they ascribed their symptoms to passive sexual experiences in the first years of childhood'.[23] Two decades later, in 1933, he even claimed that 'almost all my women patients told me that they had been seduced by their father'.[24] According to Freud, this error 'might well have had fatal consequences for the whole of my work'.[25] In this spirit Anna Freud commented later that 'keeping up the seduction theory would mean to abandon the Oedipus complex, and with it the whole importance of phantasy life, conscious or unconscious phantasy. In fact, I think there would have been no psychoanalysis afterwards.'[26]

However, as this tale has it, the hero realized that women's talk is fantasy. He pulled himself together before it was too late, drew back from the abyss of error and finally left the etiological darkness which shrouded his understanding of neurosis.

But there is also another, heretical account, in which Freud is portrayed as a villain who cowardly 'suppressed' the seduction theory in order to avoid ostracism by the scientific community which rejected it. Rather than as epiphany, this narrative presents Freud's rejection of the seduction theory as motivated by the wish to 'remain on the side of the successful and the powerful, rather than of the miserable victims of family violence'.[27] Most recently and most bluntly this version of events has been disseminated by Jeffrey Masson in his controversial *Freud: The Assault on Truth*, where he claims that it was Freud's opportunism which led him to dismiss his patients' accounts of their traumas 'as the fantasies of hysterical women who invented stories and told lies'.[28]

Even though they lacked access to the historical documents which were available to Masson, Erich Fromm and Alice Miller have made similar comments a few years earlier.[29] In Fromm's words, while the seduction theory had made Freud an 'accuser against parental exploitation in the name of the integrity and freedom of the child', it was Freud's patriarchal bias, 'his faith in the existing order and its authorities' that finally led him to declare that 'the child was a little criminal and pervert'.[30]

Masson, Fromm and Miller provide a political explanation of Freud's move from his trauma-based etiology to one which puts fantasy in the center of psychoanalytic hermeneutics. They explain the abandonment of the seduction theory by extraneous motives, which have to do with the power structure of the family, the academic community and patriarchal society in general. Moreover, they represent psychoanalysis as an ideological construct, designed both to conceal and perpetuate the status of women as victims in patriarchal society. According to their view, Freud not only denied the real suffering of women at the hands of abusive men, but also increased it by disbelieving his patients and portraying their stories as part of an illness which had to be overcome.

However, to indict Freud for cowardice and opportunism, as Masson does, seems strange.[31] One may wonder, in the wake of Paul Robinson, why an opportunist would go ahead and publish a lecture which had met with universal rejection, abandon it privately not long after its publication, but then wait for another decade before renouncing its offensive argument in print, so that his peers would not actually find out about his change of mind until 1905. It seems equally unconvincing that a coward would suppress the seduction theory because of its contentiousness and then substitute it by the libido theory, which was unlikely to gain more approval, since it turned all children into perverts.[32]

It may therefore be wise to look for a different explanation of Freud's change of mind. As I have mentioned earlier, in later writings Freud attributed the seduction theory to his credulity towards his patients' stories. But his early writings, which date from the period in which he still believed in the seduction theory, paint a different picture. He admitted, for instance, that 'these patients never repeat these stories spontaneously'. He pointed out that they tell their stories only 'under the most energetic pressure of the analytic procedure, and against enormous resistance', and that memories of child abuse have to be extracted 'piece by piece'.[33] Freud also conceded that only 'the strongest compulsion of the treatment can induce [the patients] to embark on a reproduction of them'. Finally, he stated that even after such memories are laboriously (re)constructed against his patients' resistance, they 'still attempt to withhold belief from them' and claim to 'have no feeling of remembering the scenes'.[34]

Rather than as a naïve believer of seductive tales of seductions (as Freud claimed in later days) or a coward denying a truth which his patients told him (as Masson would have it), Freud appears in his own original accounts as a bully who made use of his powers of suggestion in order to force speculations and interpretations upon his patients – but without much success. In the letter to Fliess, announcing his rejection of the seduction theory, Freud explained his change of theory, primarily by his therapeutic experience; that is, by 'the continual disappointment in my efforts to bring a single analysis to a real conclusion' and 'the running away of people who for a period of time had been most gripped [by analysis]'.[35]

This statement suggests to me that like Freud's earlier departure from the degeneracy paradigm, his transition from a hermeneutics aimed at uncovering the repressed memory of an underlying trauma to one directed at unconscious fantasies, can most plausibly be explained as a result of the experience Freud gathered in his clinical practice. In a close reading of Freud's letters and articles Han Israels and Morton Schatzman have shown that he abandoned the 'seduction theory' because he was unable to bring even one single analysis to a satisfactory conclusion while treating patients on the basis of this theoretical framework.[36]

Moreover, a closer look at Freud's references to child abuse in his later writings reveals that this divide was less deep than it might appear from the dramatic emplotment in Freud's autobiographical essays and Masson's problematic attempt at debunking Freud. In 1907 Freud still advised Karl Abraham that some patients' accounts of sexual traumas were real.[37] In January 1913 he wrote to the Swiss pastor Oskar Pfister that he himself had 'analysed and cured several cases of real incest (of the most severe kind)'.[38] In 1931 he described the seduction of children as 'common enough' and as an experience leaving behind 'extensive and lasting consequences'.[39] Finally, in *An Outline of Psycho-Analysis*, written shortly before his death, he repeated this statement, albeit in a somewhat different wording.[40]

What Freud gave up with his assumption of an early sexual trauma, then, was the belief that unconscious memories of sexual abuse in early childhood constitute the necessary and exclusive cause of neuroses – but not that such assaults happen and can be part of the etiology of neuroses. Most revealing of his post-1897 position is a lengthy passage in the *Introductory Lectures* in which he discussed the interplay of reality and fantasy in accounts given by neurotics during analysis. He stated that the analyst encounters a perplexing problem in that 'the childhood experiences constructed or remembered in analysis are sometimes indisputably false and sometimes equally certainly correct, and in most cases compounded of truth and falsehood . . . It is difficult to find one's way about this'. Freud suggested that in a situation in which patients do not distinguish between fantasy and reality, the proper attitude for the analyst to take is to accept their statements as having value, without attempting to verify them. As he put it, fantasies 'possess psychical as contrasted with material reality, and we gradually learn to understand that in the world of the neuroses it is psychical reality which is the decisive kind'. But as he clarified, under no circumstances at all should the patients' stories be dismissed as fantastic. Though he pointed out that accounts of sexual abuse are 'not real as often as seemed at first to be shown by the findings of analysis', and interpreted them as designed to hide shame about masturbation, he warned his listeners: 'You must not suppose, however, that sexual abuse of a child by its nearest male relatives belongs entirely to the realm of phantasy. Most analysts will have treated cases in which such events were real and could be unimpeachably established.'[41]

Thus, in his later etiology, which became crucial to the psychoanalytic framework, Freud assumed that fantasy constitutes the common cause of neurosis, but he did not completely exclude reality from the causal chain leading to neurotic symptoms. Originally Freud had considered fantasies to be obstacles on the way to the discovery of the real traumas whose memories had to be abreacted in treatment. But after he abandoned the seduction theory, he wrote to Fliess that 'phantasies are products of later periods and are projected back from what was then present into earliest childhood',[42] and in *The Interpretation of Dreams* he explained that 'hysterical symptoms are not attached to actual memories, but to phantasies erected on the basis of memories'.[43]

However, though I hold both the official and the heretic narrative to be mistaken in their characterization of the nature of the 1897 divide and its underlying motivation, I consider both of them to be right in the way in which they explain its effects on the further course of psychoanalysis. As Anna Freud has emphasized, her father's new departure enabled him to consider his patients' inner worlds of desire and fantasy as realms with reality and truth of their own, whose internal dynamics and manifold relationships with external reality could be subjected to further clinical investigation and theoretical conceptualization. Freud's abandonment of the seduction theory allowed him to concentrate on what were to become the core issues of psychoanalysis, such as infantile sexuality, libidinal drives and sexual fantasies. As he put it in his account of the history of the psychoanalytic movement: 'from behind the phantasies, the whole range of a child's sexual life came to light'.[44]

Obviously, Masson describes this development in a less positive spirit. He points out that in directing his attention primarily at his patients' fantasies, Freud turned away from the real world and marginalized the impact which the exercise and abuse of parental power had on children.[45] On this issue Masson's argument concurs again with that of a number of other authors, such as Erich Fromm, Walter Niederland, Morton Schatzman and Leon Sheleff. They have provided ample evidence from Freud's case studies to prove that he neglected to inquire into the possibility of parental violence against children, even where such an inquiry would have been appropriate.[46] Thus, although Freud never denied that children were sexually abused and that this fact could be relevant for therapy, his interpretive quest did acquire a new focus in 1897, placing psychic reality in the center of the psychoanalytic project.

Undoubtedly, there are problematic aspects to this development, as Freud's critics have stressed. However, one also has to take into account that Freud's focus on fantasy and the sexual meaning of symptoms also allowed him to develop a framework for a universal science of the mind in which national distinctions, as well as those between the diseased and the healthy, were superseded. In *The Interpretation of Dreams* Freud declared dreams to be the prototype for the understanding of phobias, obsessions and delusions.[47] As he wrote in his autobiographical article some decades later, psychoanalysis 'when it came to dreams . . . was no longer dealing with a pathological symptom, but with a phenomenon of normal mental life which might occur in a healthy person. If dreams turned out to be constructed like symptoms, if their explanation required the same assumptions . . . then psychoanalysis was no longer an auxiliary science of psychopathology, it was rather the starting-point of a new and deeper science of the mind which would be equally indispensable for the understanding of the normal.'[48]

Though always universalist, Freud's hermeneutic perspective on dreams was in the beginning predominantly directed at the personal origins and meaning of symbols. Then, in later additions to *The Interpretation of Dreams*, Freud started to give more weight to the individual's use of the cultural heritage of humankind in the production of symbols, such as 'firmly established linguistic usage', metaphors and synecdoches.[49] But despite his turn towards a collective heritage, in which hermeneutics might easily have been linked with nationalism or ethnocentricity, one finds none of them in Freud's writings. He traced the phylogenetic origins of unconscious symbols back to a mythical primeval past, before the origin of national cultures and languages, whose symbolic repertoire 'became the inherited property which, in each fresh generation, called not for acquisition, but only for awakening. . . . the "innate" symbolism which derives from the period of development of speech . . . is familiar to all children without their being instructed, and . . . is the same among all peoples despite their different languages'.[50] As he stressed in 1929: 'The first piece of work that it fell to psychoanalysis to perform was the discovery of drives that are common to all men living today – and not only to those living today, but to those of ancient and prehistoric times. It called for no great effort, therefore, for psycho-analysis to ignore the differences that arise among the inhabitants of the earth owing to the multiplicity of races, languages, and countries.'[51]

Of course, I do not wish to claim that there is a necessary and intrinsic connection between idealism and hermeneutics on the one hand, and, on the other hand, an understanding of psychopathology which is both individualist and universalist. That Freud's hermeneutics generated a general, universalist approach is but a contingent historical fact which resulted from Freud's attempt to trace the origins of the symbols and symptoms to prehistory and universal experiences, needs and desires of the body, such as eating, defecating, birth, death and sexual intercourse. However, it meant that for Freud there was no Herderian *Volksgeist* in the unconscious; no national or racial spirit hid in the mind; no archetypes differentiated between peoples or cultures; there were no German or Jewish dreams or illnesses. In his view, the mind knew only truly universal symbols and individual, personal associations.

Moreover, since Freud's hermeneutic techniques inevitably enmeshed the interpreter with the interpreted, they closed the gap between doctor and patient. In order to understand the voices arising from the unconscious inner world of patients, Freud could no longer keep the distance which characterized the relationship of observer and observed. Involved in the attempt to decipher the language of hysterics and to recover the true meaning of their symptoms, he had to abandon the extraneous and detached standpoint from which doctors like Charcot scrutinized 'their' hysterics. Thus, hermeneutic procedures led to a dialogical therapeutic practice of interpretation and intervention, construction and retrieval.

Since the scientific community refused to accept Freud's hermeneutic approach to symptoms – to a large extent, because it relied on the disreputed talking cure – he argued for it by demonstrating its adequacy in the interpretation of phenomena which did not presuppose his therapeutic technique. He applied his hermeneutic method to *The Psychopathology of Everyday Life* in 1901, to *Jokes and Their Relation to the Unconscious* in 1905, and published his *Three Essays on the Theory of Sexuality* in the same year, arguing in this last work that 'an unbroken chain bridges the gap between the neuroses in all their manifestations and normality' and 'that the disposition to perversions is itself of no great rarity but must form a part of what passes as the normal constitution'.[52]

Like all hermeneutic approaches, Freud's interpretive argument had a transgressing, expansive tendency, aiming to recover the meaning of signs and expressions by establishing connections and placing them in an increasingly wider context. Ultimately Freud's argument rested upon an appeal to his colleagues to share his understanding of human conduct as a semantic field, analogous to a text and in need of interpretation. As we have seen, this appeal ran against the most fundamental presuppositions of the somaticist psychiatric paradigm, where what Freud considered meaningful and motivated was regarded as meaningless epiphenomena of physiological processes – hence this fundamental difference in outlook was not bridged, and could not be bridged, by analogical argumentation alone. In his endeavour to establish a universal hermeneutics for the language of the unconscious, Freud could solely appeal to its partial expressions, and yet, their interpretation depended on the understanding of their ensemble.[53] Freud's work, although increasingly covering wider areas, progressed in a circle. It was destined to remain constricted within the boundaries which characterize all hermeneutic enquiry.

Nevertheless, on a political level, the hermeneutic dimension which Freud introduced into a hitherto somatic discipline subverted the interrelated hierarchical distinctions which dominated not only medical discourse of his age, but social discourse in general, separating the healthy from the diseased, the respectable from the corrupt, doctors from their patients, and Germans from degenerate races. Instead, it postulated principles of mental mechanisms with universal validity and practical, therapeutic application to all human beings.

* * *

To conclude this first part, let me sum up its arguments: extraneous interests and rhetoric – of a class, nation, state, or ethnic group – transgressed into medical theory and practice related to nervous diseases. As I have shown, it is often only a matter of emphasis whether one takes this medical discourse to be an epiphenomenon of bourgeois and nationalist ideologies in the second half of the nineteenth century, or vice versa. While neither can be fully reduced to the other or explained by it, they formed two languages which belonged to the same medico-political universe of discourse.

By placing Freud's early writings in this medico-political context, the following picture has emerged: (a) Freud argued against the established medical paradigm of his age – which attributed a crucial role to hereditarian degeneracy in the etiology of hysteria – not only on a scientific level, as it were, but also by rejecting and undermining its implicit and explicit nationalist values; (b) his opposition to the degeneracy paradigm cannot be explained by his Jewishness, that is, by the fact that he belonged to an ethnic minority which was stigmatized by nationalist and hereditary medical theories; (c) Freud was motivated in his theoretical innovations not by ethno-political considerations, but by his clinical experience with the talking cure, which led him to doubt the somatic origin of hysteria and introduce an interpretive dimension into a somatically oriented discipline; (d) the further development of Freud's theorizing away from the so-called 'seduction theory' cannot be explained by opportunist politicking, but has to be placed within the context of Freud's therapeutic practice; (e) although this practice had many problematic sides, it also led Freud to a hermeneutics of symptoms and dreams which is both radically universalist and individualist. Freud's hermeneutic principles recognize no boundaries separating the normal from the pathological, suspect the respectable, place analysts on an equal footing with analysands and refuse to distinguish among ethnic groups.

Part II

A State of Mind: Metaphorical Politics in Freud's Metapsychology

As we have seen in part I, Freud's rejection of the medical categories which explained hysteria as an organic disease led him to develop a general psychology and thus a theory of mind, aiming to explain both normal and pathological phenomena as a result of the interplay of the psyche's invisible structures and forces. The language of psychology inevitably shapes our image of the inner world of the mind by means of a vocabulary borrowed from descriptions of an apparently more accessible outer world. It transfers definitions, commonplaces and associations from social, technological, cultural or legal discourse into the mind, where it posits structures, forces and processes which conform to these descriptions. To quote Donal Carlston: 'Social psychologists equate resistance to persuasion with medical inoculation, interpersonal relations with economic processes, human memory with laundry bins, behavioral expectation with cartoon strips, impression processes with linear regression, personal space with territoriality, and attribution processes with analysis of variance.'[1]

However, Freud argued that analogies 'decide nothing', that he used them to keep 'in contact with the popular mode of thinking',[2] and that all they could do was 'make one feel more at home'[3] by conjuring up concrete pictures which adorned the abstract logic of his theory of the mind. Declaring them to be secondary to his theorizing, he demoted analogies and metaphors to illustrative embellishments and didactic props which served to convince his patients, who, as he pointed out, were 'often very intelligent, but not always learned'.[4] Thus, in *The Interpretations of Dreams*, Freud both defended his analogical mode of thought and advised his readers not to reify his tropes. Of course, he used a metaphor to do so: 'We are justified . . . in giving free rein to our speculations so long as we retain the coolness of our judgement and do not mistake the scaffolding for the building.'[5]

Pace Freud, I contend that in theories of the mind's inner world, where neither scaffolding nor building are visible or accessible, and where all we have are conjectures and interpretations of phenomena, the scaffolding *is* the building. Thus in my view metaphors are constitutive elements of theories of mind. However, in the creation of cognitive and affective links between a known external reality on the one hand, and an unknown mental domain on the other, metaphors not only fulfil a heuristic function but also a rhetorical one. Whatever metaphorical repertoire a psychological theory draws on, it always acts as a lens or a filter, highlighting some aspects of the psyche – such as particular types or a particular scope of emotion, cognition and motivation – while obscuring others.[6] Therefore, distinctions between observational and theoretical statements on the mind are impossible. Theories of the mind cannot be empirically validated as objective descriptions of a reality. At best, they can be appraised according to the ingenuity, simplicity and economy with which they are constructed, and the breadth and depth of the insight into human conduct which they provide.[7]

Freud used the term 'metapsychology' to denote the ensemble of metaphors which served him to depict processes in the mind. As he explained: 'when we have succeeded in describing a psychical process in its dynamic, topographical and economic aspects, we should speak of it as a *metapsychological* presentation [*Darstellung*]'.[8] In dynamic formulations he sought to derive 'all mental processes (apart from the reception of external stimuli) from the interplay of forces, which assist or inhibit one another, enter into compromises with one another, etc.'[9] An economic point of view added to this conflictual view of the mind estimates of the magnitude or amount of psychic energies involved in this interplay.[10] From a topographical angle, finally, he postulated psychic systems or agencies, in which or between which mental processes are supposed to take place.[11]

Metapsychological formulations have an ambiguous status in Freud's discourse. On the one hand, they usually appear clothed in a pathos of objectivity and factuality, as if to denote observable and empirically verifiable entities and processes. On the other hand, Freud repeatedly pointed out that they refer to causal connections, forces, energies and structures which can only be conjectured to exist in a non-experimental mental world. In his *Introductory Lectures* he admitted that in metapsychology 'the phenomena that are perceived must yield to trends that are only hypothetical'.[12] In *Beyond the Pleasure Principle* he stressed that topographical, dynamic or economic descriptions of mental processes were not inferred from empirical observations. Instead, he presented them as *a priori* categories, a 'figurative language' without which one 'could not have become aware' of the mental processes.[13] In the beginning of the essay he explained that 'the indefiniteness of all our discussions on what we describe as metapsychology is of course due to the fact that we know nothing of the nature of the excitatory process that takes place in the elements of the psychical system, and that we do not feel justified in any hypothesis on the subject. We are consequently operating with a large unknown factor [*mit einem grossen x*] which we are obliged to carry over into every new formula'.[14] Similarly, in *Analysis Terminable and Interminable* he referred to metapsychology as a 'witch', declaring that '[w]ithout metapsychological speculation and theorizing – I had almost said "phantasying" – we shall not get another step forward. Unfortunately, here as elsewhere what our Witch reveals is neither very clear nor very detailed.'[15]

Of course, there is nothing extraordinary in the fact that Freud's discourse on the mind builds on metaphors; for this is a basic characteristic of *all* theories of mind. Hence I fully agree with Donald Spence that 'to test the Freudian system as if it contained a set of falsifiable propositions is to overlook its essential metaphorical nature and to seriously concretize its most important concepts'.[16] Indeed, as has been pointed out even by Freud's most sympathetic commentators, none of his metapsychological hypotheses can be subjected to verification by empirical evidence.[17]

Though Freud's recourse to self-evidently metaphorical language in general, and political metaphors in particular, has been acknowledged, usually the latter have been considered as only one repertoire among the many which appear in his writings, such as imagery borrowed from hydraulics, biology, mechanics, legal procedures, archeology and history.[18] In contrast, I wish to show here that Freud's metapsychological discourse moulds the invisible world of the psyche primarily in terms of the outer world of society. Thus, part II is devoted to a reconstruction of Freud's discourse on the mind, in order to show that both its language and logic are political.

As I demonstrate in a detailed study of Freud's metaphors, his language transposes the vocabulary of imperial court procedures and manifestly political institutions and practices – such as representation, censorship and elections – into the mind. By portraying the mind as a microcosm which is analogous to the state's macrocosm, Freud's language inevitably 'politicizes' the pysche. It pictures it as an arena of political conflict, where forces analogous to those in society oppose each other, driven by contradictory motives in pursuit of their goals and divided by defences and resistances. Moreover, I maintain that even where Freud's metapsychological discourse seems non-political – for instance, when it invokes hydraulic metaphors – it not only fails to conform to principles of mechanics, but also reveals an implicit political logic. Finally, I claim that when Freud's metapsychology is seen as providing a political vision of the mind, some of its apparent problems and contradictions can be resolved, and it is revealed as an ingenious model which allows a rich and fruitful conceptualization of the workings of the inner world.

Indeed, I hold it for impossible to dismiss metapsychology as a dated and bothersome ballast which psychoanalysis would better get rid of, as some commentators have suggested.[19] As Morris Eagle has rightly pointed out, 'the very idea of a purely clinical theory untainted by any trace of metapsychology is illusory. For example, the very notion of unconscious wishes and aims, so central to the clinical theory of psychoanalysis, inevitably entails metapsychological assumptions and considerations.'[20] Instead, I regard metapsychology to be part of what Samuel Weber has described as Freud's 'willingness to negotiate with the unknown and to acknowledge uncertainty not merely as an impediment or defect, but as an integral part of thinking and writing'.[21]

5 Who Censors Whom, Where and Why?

Freud's first published model of the mind can be found in the seventh chapter of *The Interpretation of Dreams*, where he distinguished a system of *conscious* perception from one storing *preconscious* material which does not form part of the individual's consciousness at the moment, but can make its content easily available to consciousness. These two systems are separated from a third, whose material is inaccessible to both of them and thus remains *unconscious*. As Freud explained in an italicized passage in *The Interpretations of Dreams*: 'The unconscious is the true psychic reality; in its innermost nature it is as much unknown to us as the reality of the external world, and it is as much incompletely presented by the data of consciousness as is the external world by the communications of our sense organs.'[1] He often used abbreviations – in English *Ucs.*, *Pcs.* and *Cs.* – when referring to these systems as particular psychic localities with distinctive rules, processes and contents of their own. This model, which he called 'topographical', was supposed to account for the fact that crucial determinants of one's own conduct may remain unknown to oneself because they are barred by a censorship if they appear to be objectionable or reprehensible from an ethical or social point of view.[2]

Freud conceived of the process whereby access of threatening material to consciousness is denied as a form of internal 'censorship'. This notion appeared already three years before the publication of *The Interpretation of Dreams* in a letter to Wilhelm Fliess in which he asked: 'Have you ever seen a foreign newspaper which passed Russian censorship at the frontier? Words, whole clauses and sentences are blacked out so that the rest becomes unintelligible. A Russian censorship of that kind comes about in psychoses and produces the apparently meaningless deliria.'[3] In this passage Freud described censorship as a negative force, suppressing an utterance from being published and read. But when he introduced the notion of censorship in his published work and described its role at greater length, he depicted it somewhat differently:

> I will try and seek a social parallel to this internal event in the mind. Where can we find a similar distortion of a psychical act in social life? Only where two persons are concerned, one of whom possesses a certain degree of power which the second is obliged to take into account. In such cases the second person will distort his psychical acts or, as we might put it, will dissimulate. . . . A similar difficulty confronts the political writer who has dis-agreeable truths to tell those in authority. . . . A writer must be-ware of the censorship, and on its account he must soften and distort the expression of his opinion. According to the strength and sensitiveness of the censorship he finds himself compelled either merely to refrain from certain forms of attack, or to speak in allusions in place of direct references, or he must conceal his objectionable pronouncement beneath some apparently innocent disguise . . . The stricter the censorship, the more far-reaching will be the disguise and the more ingenious too may be the means employed for putting the reader on the scent of the true meaning.
>   The fact that the phenomena of censorship and of dream-distortion correspond down to their smallest details justifies us in presuming that they are similarly determined. We may there-fore suppose that dreams are given their shape in individual human beings by the operation of two psychical forces (or we may describe them as currents or systems); and that one of these forces constructs the wish which is expressed by the dream, while the other exercises a censorship upon this dream-wish and, by the use of censorship, forcibly brings about a distortion in the expression of the wish.[4]

The last sentence of this quotation would have been accurate as a summary of the censorship's role in the letter to Fliess; but it fails to sum up the very passage in which it appears, since here the act of censoring has been displaced and its goal transformed. Rather than actively interfering with the expression of another agency, the institu-tionalized existence of a censorship allows it to remain passive. Its very presence as a threat, its potential preventive and punitive power, induce the other agency to *censor itself* and express itself in allusions, symbols and hints.

As Richard Rorty and Ernest Gellner have rightly stressed, the Freud-ian unconscious is a cunning one. As Gellner puts it, 'Cunning is not just an attribute of the Unconscious. Cunning is its very essence.'[5] And as Rorty states, it is not composed of 'dumb, sullen, lurching brutes'. Rather, it is populated by 'intellectual peers of our conscious selves, possible conversational partners for those selves'.[6] Indeed, the Freudian unconscious is creative, devious, and no less clever than the conscious part of a person's mind. Hence, its self-censorship submits only partially to the exigencies of authority. By making its expressions appear harmless, it also aims at circumventing restrictions, while safeguarding the security of the agency whose expressions are considered dangerous or offensive. As Michael Levine has pointed out, in *The Interpretation of Dreams* the act of censoring no longer aims at preventing an expression, but at enabling expression to take place despite the presence of a censorship.[7] Self-censorship is thus also an act of disguise, of tricking and overcoming the censorship's constraining power.

This task is performed in an unconscious mental activity which Freud called 'dream-work', where, he wrote, 'a psychical force [*eine psychische Macht*] is operating which on the one hand strips the elements which have a high psychical value of their intensity, and on the other hand, by means of overdetermination, creates from elements of low psychical value new values, which afterwards find their way into the dream-content'.[8]

Freud conceived of several tactics in which this transvaluation of psychical values takes place. A dreamer's unconscious may hide the true meaning of a wish by turning its emotional investment into its opposite – for instance, by representing something that is desired as loathsome, or somebody disliked as appealing. Alternatively, the unconscious may *displace* forbidden wishes along associative connections from one idea to another or *condense* the expression of a whole series of impermissible ideas by its representation through an image that in the dreamer's mind is located at the intersection of several associative chains. Finally, if no such pre-existing nodal point is found, the unconscious can construct a composite figure or word out of various features of disparate ideas – such as a figure which looks somewhat similar to one particular person, while its manner of speech refers to another one, and the location in which the dream takes place indicates yet another context.

Ultimately, what mode of representation is chosen by the unconscious is a question of the relative power of the various thought-currents involved. As Freud explained:

[A] dream is not constructed by each individual dream-thought, or group of dream-thoughts, finding (in abbreviated form)

separate representation [*Vertretung*] in the content of the dream
– in the kind of way in which an electorate [*Bevölkerung*] chooses
parliamentary representatives [*Volksvertreter*]; a dream is constructed, rather, by the whole mass of dream-thoughts being
submitted to a sort of manipulative process in which these elements which have the most numerous and strongest supports
acquire the right of entry into the dream content – in a manner
analogous to election by *scrutin de liste*.[9]

Freud's reference to electoral and parliamentary representation rather
than symbolic or pictorial representation, provides an example for the
way in which his discourse always intertwines force and meaning. For
Freud the transformation of an expression from one mode to another
was never simply a matter of translation, transcription or transfigura-
tion. It always involves antagonistic forces in conflict with one another and leads to a double-edged result. Though representation
allows prohibited thoughts to be expressed in an acceptable fashion,
it also renders them incomprehensible and – in political terms –
innocuous, since they have been divested of their destabilizing power.

Sometimes, however, if the censorship is not vigilant enough, expressions may slip through into the manifest dream in a form which
is too close to the upsetting and forbidden original dream-thought. In
such cases the censorship has a further means of power at its disposal,
which still allows it to intervene after the fact. Freud explained: 'In my
view the contemptuous critical judgement "it's only a dream", appears in a dream when the censorship, which is never quite asleep,
feels that it has been taken unawares by a dream which has already
been allowed through. It is too late to suppress it, and accordingly the
censorship uses these words to meet the anxiety or the distressing
feeling aroused by it.'[10]

Moreover, the censorship remains active even after the dreamer has
woken up. When a dream is remembered, there are often doubts
which arise concerning some of its elements. Since precisely such
seemingly indistinct components are suspect as having been in the
center of the unconscious dream-thoughts, Freud interpreted such
doubts as yet another political ploy instigated by the dream-censorship: 'The state of things is what it was after some sweeping revolution in one of the republics of antiquity or the Renaissance. The noble
and powerful families which had previously dominated the scene
were sent into exile and all the high offices were filled by newcomers.
Only the most impoverished and powerless members of the van-
quished families, or their remote dependents, were allowed to remain

in the city; and even so they did not enjoy full civic rights and were viewed with distrust. The distrust in the analogy corresponds to the doubt in the case we are considering.'[11]

As we see, Freud again explained a phenomenon related to dreaming by an analogy which reveals the logic of power and authority underlying his thinking. Finally, Freud turned to the resistance which may characterize a dreamer's response to his or her analyst's interpretations of the dream. Resistance to the analyst's suggestions as to what a dream's hidden truth may be, represented for Freud 'only a putting into effect of the dream-censorship'. It proved to him, 'that the force of the censorship is not exhausted in bringing about the distortion of dreams and thereafter extinguished, but that the censorship persists as a *permanent institution* which has as its aim the maintenance of the distortion'.[12]

As Michael Levine demonstrates, Freud continuously displaced the position of the psyche's censorship, until it becomes impossible to pinpoint one stable and clearly defined place where the censoring activity could be located. What appears at first to be the specific function of a particular psychic agency, turns out to be an activity which extends throughout the mind and at each stage is performed by different actors and often with contradictory intentions.[13] This is also, it seems, how one is to understand Freud's warning in the *Introductory Lectures* not to 'take the term [censorship] too anthropomorphically' and not to 'picture the "censor of dreams" as a severe little manikin or a spirit living in a closet in the brain and there discharging his office'.[14]

Thus, Freud used political imagery whose apparent simplicity is not only persuasive, but also deceptive. However, thereby he created a discourse which mirrors the dialectics of power in the external, social world in a precise manner. The institution of a governmental agency such as a censorship always generates an intricate interplay of co-ercion and resistance, of opposition and the overcoming of opposition. Its presence affects the entire web of interactions in a given social – or psychic – framework. Rulers often realize too late that censorship may not only serve the oppressive regime of which it is part, but also lead to innovative and creative techniques by which forbidden material is presented in innocuous disguises. In real-world politics – as in dreams – both sides involved are capable of creating and interpreting meaningful artefacts, as well as disfiguring them by an exercise of force; and both sides will use these capacities to further their conflicting purposes. Moreover, in a society where there is censorship people may not only exercise self-censorship, but also pretend not to know about dangerous truths even if they recognize them, or not to have heard about forbidden texts, even if they were told about their existence – just as a dreamer may doubt elements of dreams and resist interpretations.

Thus, from a political point of view, Freud was right to present censorship as an institution which is part of a framework whose processes are interconnected and dialectical, rather than fixed and determinate. Moreover, the dialectical nature of his conception of psychic processes involved in censorship – which allow for a continuous slippage of boundaries, forces, intentions and effects – makes it obvious that the logic underlying Freud's model of the mind is sociomorphic rather than mechanistic.

6 Politics of Representation

More of the political logic of Freud's theory of mind comes to the fore in the dramatic vision of the psyche which he presented in the *Introductory Lectures*; there he compared 'the system of the unconscious to a large entrance hall in which the mental impulses jostle one another like separate individuals. Adjoining this entrance hall is a second, narrower room – a kind of drawing-room – in which consciousness, too, resides. But on the threshold between these two rooms a watchman performs his function: he examines the different mental impulses, acts as a censor, and will not admit them into the drawing-room if they displease him.'[1]

In Freud's terms, the reason for which impulses are turned back by the watchman is that they are 'inadmissible to consciousness [*bewusstseinsunfähig*]', a notion which he adopted from Breuer in *Studies on Hysteria*, where it had been constructed parallel to '*hoffähig*', the German term for 'admissible to court'.[2] Freud conceived consciousness in analogy to a social privilege: access to the psychical drawing-room is granted by virtue of an idea's social acceptability, its fitness for good society. This reflection of imperial court procedure is also apparent in Freud's use of the term '*Instanz*' (translated as 'agency' or 'system') for the elements of the psyche – which added strong connotations of legal bureaucracy or administrative echelons.[3]

In this empire of the mind, privileges are a matter of birth. The psyche's aboriginal population of infantile impulses is banned into the depth of the unconscious, where it remains separated from the subject's consciousness by an internal police force. Impulses born in the province of the unconscious remain unworthy of the privilege of becoming conscious, even if they acquire a high degree of sophistication in the course of their development. As Freud wrote: 'Their origin is what decides their fate. We may compare them with individuals of mixed race who, taken all round, resemble white men, but who betray their coloured descent by some striking feature or other, and on that account are excluded from society and enjoy none of the privileges of white people.'[4] Comparing the psyche explicitly to the multinational Hapsburg Empire, Freud depicted its 'hierarchy of superordinated and subordinated agents' also as a country divided into '*Bezirke*' (provinces) within which and between which mental processes take place, and whose boundaries act as frontiers which mental energy can sometimes cross, where it can be held up and refused entry or forced into different shape.[5]

> I am imagining a country with a landscape of varying configura-
> tion – hill-country, plains, and chains of lakes – and with a mixed
> population: it is inhabited by Germans, Magyars and Slovaks,
> who carry on different activities. Now things may be partitioned
> in such a way that the Germans, who breed cattle, live in the
> hill-country, the Magyars, who grow cereals and wine, live in the
> plains, and the Slovaks, who catch fish and plait reeds, live by
> the lakes. If the partitioning could be neat and clear-cut like this,
> a Woodrow Wilson would be delighted by it; it would also be
> convenient for a lecture in a geography lesson. The probability
> is, however, that you will find less orderliness and more mixing,
> if you travel through the region.[6]

With time Freud became dissatisfied with this model, because it portrayed the mind too much as a closed system. He developed a second, structural model, in order to account for the influence of external factors on the workings of the psychic polity. From 1923 onwards he divided the mind into three functional centers of activity – which he called '*Reiche, Gebiete, Provinzen*' (realms, regions, provinces).[7] He situated each of them in a distinct relationship *vis-à-vis* the other two and towards the outside world. Choosing simple pronouns, he called these centers 'I' (*Ich*) and 'It' (*Es*), and created the visually powerful notion of an 'Over-I' (*Überich*). He explicitly rejected scient-ific neologisms based on what he mocked as 'orotund Greek names'.[8] Nevertheless, Freud's English translator substituted for them the Latin terms 'ego', 'id' and 'superego' which, though not Greek, clearly run against Freud's intention to give non-technical names to the psyche's agencies.

Compared with the first model, the major innovation of the second blueprint of the mind was the introduction of a special agency which involves the subject in an inner dialogue with mental representatives of people whose approval was important in childhood – above all with one or both parents. As Freud put it: 'The authority of the father or the parents is introjected into the ego, and there it forms the nucleus of the superego, which takes over the severity of the father.'[9] Again, boundaries are sliding. Authority figures are not only outside oneself; surreptitiously they slip inside the mind.

To explain this crossing of boundaries which separate individuals from one another, I dwell for a moment on the notion of representation to which Freud so frequently had recourse, and which I hold to mirror the way in which representation functions in the governmental domain. In this political type of representation one person may act as a delegate for a number of other people. This relationship entails both the actual absence of the mandator – an electorate, for instance – and the presence of someone else at the seat of power – say, a parliament – who can legitimately claim that his or her actions realize not only his or her individual will, but also that of the absent mandator. The logic of political representation paradoxically entails both the representative's dependence on the mandator – that is, the duty to remain faithful to the mandator's intentions and wishes – and the representative's independence from the mandator. Even though they are supposed to represent others, delegates are also entitled and obliged to make decisions on their own and devise a course of action for new and often unexpected circumstances without having to demand specific directives.[10] Law makers are not the only people who claim to represent the will of the citizens. Law enforcement agencies, too – such as the police and the military – are supposed to represent the citizens' collective will, even when they prevent individuals or groups of citizens from realizing their personal wishes, or punish them for doing so if the law has been violated.

Freud applied this mandator–delegate logic to the mind, when he turned the superego into the mind's law-making, law-enforcing and adjudicating agency. In these functions the superego represents only partially the subject's 'I', over whom it presides. It also represents others – especially parental figures – and promotes goals which are foreign to the person in whom it enacts and enforces its laws. Its role, therefore, is rather like that of a 'garrison' set up in a 'conquered city'. As Freud pointed out, what the superego declares to be bad or evil 'is often not at all what is injurious or dangerous to the ego'.[11] Nevertheless, at the same time the superego also represents the individual's ethical standards: 'It acts as the "critical agency", performing functions of self-assessment and self-punishment, as well as providing moral ideals and judgements.'[12]

In representing and enforcing moral standards which originated outside the subject, but which have become part of its moral self-conception, the superego may act with 'cruelty'[13] and 'harshness'.[14] Indeed, Freud's eloquent description of the mental dynamics underlying depression – in which the superego crushes the ego with guilt – portrays it as a judge in a Kafkaesque trial. The superego, he writes, 'becomes over-severe, abuses . . . humiliates . . . threatens . . . as though it had spent the whole interval in collecting accusations and had only been waiting for its present access to strength in order to bring them up and make a condemnatory judgement on their basis'.[15]

At the other end of the mental apparatus, as it were, Freud placed the id, the agency expressing 'the true purposes of the individual organism's life'.[16] Full of irrational passions and desires for immediate satisfaction and pleasure, it is exclusively devoted to the satisfaction of – mostly sexual – impulses. It corresponds to a large extent to the system *Ucs.* in Freud's first topography. Without organization or collective will, 'its different urges pursue their own purposes independently and regardless of one another'. It is too chaotic and blind to give guidance to human action. According to Freud, a person could not escape death if he or she followed the id's 'blind efforts for the satisfaction of its drives' and disregarded the external world.[17] Like the superego, the id is also a dual creature: it represents interests which are foreign to the subject's self-conception, but at the same time it also constitutes the core of mental life, from which all other mental agencies originate.

Finally, the ego, described as 'the representative [*Repräsentant*] of the external world, of reality', is fully attached to the present.[18] It stands for reason and good sense and is 'governed by considerations of safety'.[19] As Freud explained: 'In each individual there is a coherent organization of mental processes; and we call this his *ego*. It is to this ego that consciousness is attached; the ego controls the approaches to motility . . . it is the mental agency which supervises all its own constituent processes . . . it exercises the censorship on dreams.'[20] In other words, the ego represents both the subject's own conscious interests and reason, and contemporary, external constraints on action. It aims at the person's safety and self-preservation and introduces criteria of the possible and useful into the mind.

In terms of its dynamics of power, Freud's model makes it impossible for any mental processes to occur without the ego's participation: 'If all the driving force that sets the vehicle in motion is derived from the id, the ego, as it were, undertakes the steering, without which no goal can be reached.'[21] If the ego is strong, it can act as a power broker. As Freud put it: 'all will be well if the ego is in possession of its whole organization and efficiency, if it has access to all parts of the id and can exercise its influence on them'.[22] But if the ego is weak, it may have to act like 'a constitutional monarch, without whose sanction no law can be passed but who hesitates long before imposing his veto on any measure put forward by Parliament'.[23] Freud dramatized this conflict:

> As a frontier-creature, the ego tries to mediate between the world and the id, to make the id pliable to the world and, by means of its muscular activity, to make the world fall in with the wishes of the id . . . It is not only a helper to the id; it is also a submissive slave who courts his master's love. Whenever possible it tries to remain on good terms with the id . . . it pretends that the id is showing obedience to the admonitions of reality, even when in fact it is remaining obstinate and unyielding; it disguises the id's conflicts with reality and, if possible, its conflicts with the super-ego too. In its position midway between the id and reality, it only too often yields to the temptation to become sycophantic, opportunist and lying, like a politician who sees the truth but wants to keep his place in popular favour.[24]

As a rule Freud described the ego as a moderate, prudent agency, which, 'driven by the id, confined by the superego, repulsed by reality, struggles to master its economic task of bringing about harmony among the forces'.[25] Often the ego feels weak compared to these other forces, and lacks the insight necessary to achieve its task. As Freud pointed out, 'if the other two become too strong, they succeed in loosening and altering the ego's organization so that its proper relation to reality is disturbed or even brought to an end'[26] – and when the ego 'has lost its unity' the person falls ill.[27] 'For our mind, that precious instrument by whose means we maintain ourselves in life, is no peacefully self-contained unity. It is rather to be compared with a *modern State*, in which a mob, eager for enjoyment and destruction, has to be held down forcibly by a prudent superior class.'[28] In 'A Difficulty in the Path of Psycho-Analysis' Freud even addressed the ego directly and reproved it for its bad politics: 'You behave like an absolute ruler who is content with the information supplied to him by his highest officials and never goes among the people to hear their voice. Turn your eyes inward, look into your own depths, learn first to know yourself!'[29]

As we see, the structural model partitions and decentres the psyche into agencies which are themselves characterized by mental and emotional attributes. Like in the example of psychical censorship, what appears at first as a simple division of the mind into functional centres, reveals itself as containing complex contradictions and dualities. All psychic agencies represent at the same time interests and forces which are intrinsic and extrinsic to the subject's self-conception. Behaving like human beings, they think, desire, remember, can be spoken to, and even speak to themselves in the political language which Freud has developed for the psyche. For instance, Freud portrayed the ego's reaction to the appearance of unconscious thoughts in neurotic disorders in the following fashion: 'Impulses appear which seem like those of a stranger, so that the ego disowns them; yet it has to fear them and take precautions against them. The ego says to itself: "This is an illness, a foreign invasion." It increases its vigilance, but cannot understand why it feels so strangely paralysed.'[30]

By referring to id, ego and superego as *dramatis personae* to whom contradictory interests and intentions are ascribed, the psychoanalytic lingua franca draws on what might possibly be the oldest metaphor for the mind – going back to Plato – where the internal world of human beings is portrayed as if it were a polis. Adopting the metaphor and turning it into the foundation of his theory of mind, Freud depicted the psyche as a political arena in which conflicting forces fight one another in order to determine the actions of the individual as a whole. He extolled the virtues of control and warned of the dangers of balance and equality, which he associated with a weakness or even a breakdown of the mind's government, while he depicted health as based on an enlightened but elitist rule.

Finally, by conceiving of agencies in the mind as internal representatives of influences and interests outside the subject, Freud undermined conceptions of the subject as a self-enclosed entity with strict, impermeable boundaries. In Freud's vision, society lives as much in the subject as the subject lives in society, while neither can be fully reduced to the other or explained by the other.

7 Mechanical Failures

So far I have discussed the politics which can be found on the 'surface' of Freud's metapsychological discourse, as it were; that is, its explicit political terminology. However, I wish to show that politics can also be found in its 'depth', concealed under an apparently mechanistic facade of language which Freud borrowed from physics.

In the second half of the nineteenth century physics was widely acknowledged as the most advanced science, and its concepts served as a source of inspiration for most other domains of exact knowledge. Moreover, Hermann von Helmholtz's famous lecture on 'The Conservation of Energy [*Die Erhaltung der Kraft*]', which he delivered in 1847 to the Physical Society of Berlin, turned energy (*Kraft*) into 'an ontological concept basic to all matter and integral to the explanation of all mechanical causes'.[1] For Helmholtz, who did not distinguish between animal, human and mechanical labour power, energy became a transcendental force, 'the groundwork of all our thoughts and acts', which was said to underlie all labour.[2]

Adopting this Helmholtzian conception, Freud transposed this energy-centred vision into the mind, to which he applied the laws of energy flow, conservation, entropy and conversion which were popular at the time. In 1894 he postulated that 'a quota of affect or a sum of excitation ... is spread over the memory-traces of ideas somewhat as an electric charge is spread over the surface of a body' and explicitly compared his theory of 'abreaction' to 'the hypothesis of a flow of electric fluid'.[3] In an unpublished manuscript addressed to his colleague neurologists – which James Strachey titled 'Project for a Scientific Psychology' – Freud attempted 'to represent psychical processes as quantitatively determinate states of material particles' in a reflex arc.[4] Five years later in *The Interpretation of Dreams* he reiterated: 'Reflex processes remain the model of every psychical function', even though he no longer attempted to reduce mental processes to neurophysiology.[5] Nevertheless, his discourse remains permeated by references to the 'flow' of a hypothetical psychical energy from a 'reservoir', through 'intercommunicating vessels' or 'channels', to its 'damming-up' or 'discharge' by 'safety- valves'.[6]

Prima facie it might seem that the political reading of Freud's metapsychology reaches an *aporia* when it is confronted with such energetic formulations. However, Freud described the psyche's energy processes in ways which fail to conform to the fundamentals of physics. For instance, when Freud wrote of the 'remoteness' of an acceptable idea from an offensive one, and of energy shifts between these ideas, it might seem as if energy travelled across some kind of psychic space.[7] Needless to say, however, the realm of the mind is beyond matter and space, and one can hardly refer to the 'distance' between ideas as anything more than a metaphor. Indeed, Freud's spatial and hydraulic terminology has to be taken as a metaphorical articulation of his intuition about the closeness and remoteness of ideas – which achieves a semblance of objectivity by being depicted in quasi-scientific imagery.

In recent years the literal understanding of Freud's notion of psychic energy has been subjected to detailed and harsh criticisms by philosophers of science and psychoanalysts alike. A survey of Freud's energy concepts ends with the statement that they 'are either impossible, useless, or mistaken',[8] and panel discussions at psychoanalytic congresses reveal that a considerable section of the community has either become doubtful about the usefulness of the energy concept or rejects it.[9] But simply to condemn Freud's references to psychic energy will not do. Once one acknowledges that Freud's energy concept is vague and inconsistent – that, as Yehuda Elkana puts it, 'physically it is total nonsense'[10] – one can still go on to examine its logic more closely. Elkana, for one, has made the point that Freud used the notion of psychic energy not so much in a scientific manner than as a loose metaphor, as an intuitively accessible image which is part of our culture and which we invoke 'colloquially in talking about our limited mental energies or about conserving our psychic forces'.[11]

Through the cracks of the mechanistic veneer of metapsychology there appears an underlying common-sensical economic logic which guided Freud's use of energy imagery.[12] Rather than to a physicalist frame of thought, Freud's references to energy are related to what he called 'the economic principle of saving expenditure'.[13] As he warned in *Civilization and its Discontents*: 'Since a man does not have unlimited quantities of psychical energies at his disposal, he has to accomplish his tasks by making an efficient distribution of his libido.'[14] Such economic ways of thinking were never far from Freud's theorizing. In

The Interpretation of Dreams he wrote: 'A daytime thought may well play the part of *entrepreneur* for a dream, but the *entrepreneur*, who, as people say, has the idea and the initiative to carry it out, can do nothing without capital; he needs a *capitalist* who can afford the outlay, and the capitalist who provides the psychical outlay for the dream is invariably and indisputably, whatever may be the thoughts of the previous day, *a wish from the unconscious*.'[15]

Moreover, as Freud's drive theory reveals, not only the economy of psychic energy was central to his thinking, but also its politics. He introduced his concept of the 'drive [*Trieb*]' in 1905, in the *Three Essays on the Theory of Sexuality*, to place his energetic notions in a differentiated frame of reference by distinguishing sexual energies from others. Unfortunately, however, by translating the German term *Trieb* into 'instinct', Strachey has brought a concept into Freud's discourse which badly blurs the distinction between organic forces determining animal behaviour on the one hand, and psychological impulses in human beings on the other. In order to restore some of the original nuances of Freud's use, I have replaced the term 'instinct' by 'drive' in all quotations from the *Standard Edition*. The latter notion is closer to the German original, which derives from '*treiben*' and evokes the indistinct driving, pressing, pushing or propelling character which sexual desire exercises on the mind.[16]

That Freud's drive concept has little to do with animal instincts becomes evident when one examines its origins and function in his discourse. Freud referred to it as '[a] basic conventional concept' which allowed him both to posit and transcend the boundary between body and psyche, while avoiding the confusing ontological issues of the psycho-physical question.[17] His search for such a conceptual bridge was the result of his repeated attempts to conceive of the structure of mind–body relations, without being capable of developing a theoretical framework which he found satisfactory. In his early essay on aphasia he related psyche and body to one another as two realms in which independent processes take place parallel to each other. Then, adopting a reductionist perspective in the 'Project' of 1895, he postulated that they were identical. With *The Interpretation of Dreams* he abandoned this position, too, warning that one should 'avoid the temptation to determine psychical locality in any anatomical fashion'.[18] Finally, in 1905, Freud's drive concept established for the first time a connection between body and mind which he maintained as adequate for more than a few years.

Originally Freud only formulated the relationship between the bodily sources of sexual desires and their effects on the mind in terms of drives. However, unlike ethologists who explain feelings of sexual arousal in terms of hormonal processes which are at least in principle measurable, Freud did not point to any conceivable endocrinological substrate of sexual drives. Their substance remains hypothetical, invisible and by definition unmeasurable. In fact, Freud's references to drives often lack clarity and are evasive – their purpose was, after all, to transcend boundaries. He situated them within the domain of psychological discourse – for him they were the 'ultimate things which psychological research can learn about' – but placed them neither in the mind's conscious or unconscious systems.[19]

As frontier creature between body and mind, Freud described the drive both as representative and mandator, depending from which angle he approached it.[20] When Freud considered 'mental life from a *biological* point of view' – that is, from a bodily perspective – he called the drive 'the psychical representative [*Repräsentant*] of the stimuli originating from within the organism and reaching the mind'.[21] In contrast, when he approached the drive from the side of the psyche and examined it 'so far as *mental* life is concerned', he described it as a mandator who remains indiscernible, unless it attaches itself to yet another representative.[22]

Let me recapitulate this complex model of a two-tiered representational framework which I extract from Freud's text: first the drive carries the body's demands to the mind, and then attaches itself in the *Ucs.* to what Freud called an 'ideational representative [*Vorstellungsrepräsentanz*]', that is, to the idea of an object promising satisfaction. It is only from the existence of such second-order representatives in the mind that the presence of drives can be inferred. As Freud explained: 'I am in fact of the opinion that the antithesis of conscious and unconscious is not applicable to drives. A drive can never become an object of consciousness – only the idea that represents [*repräsentiert*] the drive can. Even in the unconscious, moreover, a drive cannot be represented [*repräsentiert*] otherwise than by an idea. If the drive did not attach itself to an idea or manifest itself as an affective state, we could know nothing about it.'[23]

Freud's use of the political metaphor of representation to depict the function of both psychic agencies and drives, allowed him not only to portray the person as a cluster of roles and the product of social relations, but also to assign an important position to the needs and interests of the body, which put limits on the scope of socialization. Although human beings are social animals according to Freud, he also emphasized that they are bodily creatures which can never be entirely socialized. This, indeed, is one of the important implications of

Freud's model of the mind and its relation to the body. It challenges some fundamental presuppositions of much modern social thought and points to the problematic nature of social existence. Situated between body and society, the Freudian subject is never entirely free to act, but also never completely determined in his or her actions.

In 1910 Freud started to characterize activities aiming at self-preservation, too, as originating in drives. He stated: 'As the poet has said, all the organic drives that operate in our mind may be classified as "hunger" or "love".'[24] At this stage he defined drives more generally as forces which press for action with the aim to satisfy the body's demands, such as eating in the case of hunger: 'The characteristic of exercising pressure is common to all drives; it is in fact their very essence. Every drive is a piece of activity.'[25] Demands which hunger imposes on the person differ sharply from those of love. Their satisfaction requires rather well-defined objects within a more or less rigid time frame. Sexual drives, on the other hand, are malleable to a very large degree. In Freud's framework they are said to have their sources in various bodily zones; and since the objects of the drives are contingent, they can be divided into a number of component drives, as well as deflected, inhibited or ignored without endangering the person's physical existence.

This mixture of comprehensiveness and openness achieved by Freud's theory of sexual drives has again a dual – or dialectical – effect. On the one hand, it extends the realm of drive activity to a wide field of human action; on the other hand this extension of the scope and nature of forces, which are conceived as originating in the body and reaching into the mind, undermines their explanatory power as blind biological forces. Drives always leave room for a variety of strategies and tactics – which Freud called destinies (*Schicksale*) or, as the *Standard Edition* puts it, 'vicissitudes'[26] – by means of which a person may arrive at satisfaction. Therefore Freud could never fully explain human conduct in a *causal* mode, by simply invoking the pressure of drives. Rather, it is of the very nature of his explanatory construct to remain open-ended and to demand additional, *purposive* forms of explanation.[27] As he put it, even though 'the ultimate aim of each drive remains unchangeable, there may yet be different paths leading to the same ultimate aim'.[28]

Moreover, the language and logic of Freud's libido theory also intertwine the causal and the purposive by means of a repertoire of political metaphors which turn drives into energies with a history and social relations. Freud described the earliest stage in sexual development – polymorphous sexuality – as an 'anarchy' in which each of the component drives attached to the different erotogenic zones pursues its pleasures independently from the others. In his words, only with the 'subordination of all the component sexual drives under the primacy of the genitals', sexuality changes from its infantile form into maturity.[29] Freud illustrated the logic of his tolerant attitude towards what he called 'perverse' sexuality – a term he did not mean to be deprecatory – by an even more explicitly political imagery. As he put it, in both 'normal' and 'perverse' sexuality 'a well-organized tyranny has been established, but in each of the two a different family has seized the reins of power'.[30] In the political language of his discourse, this situation contrasts with infantile sexuality, where 'component drives have equal rights', that is, where they lack the authoritarian organization that structures mature sexuality and directs it towards partners in the outside world.[31] However, Freud warned that the course of sexual development is full of obstacles which may lead to an early attachment or 'fixation' of the libido to some particular bodily zone and bring the sexual development to a premature halt.[32] Even after a developmental stage has been surpassed, a return to it – that is, a 'regression' – remains always a possibility from Freud's perspective. In difficult circumstances it might be tempting to take an easy escape route into a more satisfactory past, rather than confronting the unsatisfactory present.[33] Freud illustrated his warning about the dangers looming at every juncture of human development with a military analogy: 'Consider that, if a people which is in movement has left strong detachments behind at the stopping-places of its migration, it is likely that the more advanced parties will be inclined to retreat to these stopping places if they have been defeated or have come up against a superior enemy.'[34]

As I have tried to show, Freud's discourse presents libido in military or political terms and correlates its dynamics with processes and constellations known from the social world. In this way it produces an argument which makes freedom in the external world dependent on an internal hierarchical integration of its parts. Equal rights belong to the infantile stages in sexual development and are characterized by anarchy and the lack of restraint and self-control. The purposeful pursuit of satisfaction in the external world, the finding of an object and the alteration of reality for the purpose of pleasure, are only possible in conditions of a well-established internal tyranny – either perverse or normal.

8 Occupying Forces

Hitherto I have focused on Freud's conception of mental processes, structures and agencies. Now I wish to turn to some aspects of his theory of the origins and development of psychic activity.

Freud argued that in the very beginning of life the mind is capable only of 'primary-process thought' which is driven by the quest for pleasure. According to Freud, reducing mental tension is a pleasurable experience, and he described actions pursuing this aim as governed by the 'pleasure principle'.[1] In his view an infant simply hallucinates objects which it experienced in the past as providing pleasure, such as the mother's breast. Hallucinations are possible at this stage because energy units are still 'free', 'mobile', and 'uninhibited', and thus can move in massive formations to occupy pleasurable memories.[2]

I have mentioned in my comments on dream-work that the prominence which ideas or memories achieve in the mind is determined by the quantity of drive energy with which they are occupied. In the original German, Freud likened the amount of drive energy which attaches itself to ideas to a military conquest by calling it *Besetzung* (occupation). In one instance, substituting a synonym for *Besetzung*, he also referred to such energy charges as *Positionen* (military posts).[3] Unfortunately, the metaphorical character of Freud's language has again disappeared in the *Standard Edition*'s (mis)translation of *Besetzung* as cathexis – a quasi-scientific neologism Freud was quite unhappy with.[4] To regain the original flavour of Freud's language in this instance as well, I have again modified the translation and substituted 'occupation' for 'cathexis' in the passages quoted from the *Standard Edition*.

Because they are occupied by large quantities of mental energy, hallucinations acquire great vividness and intensity, 'without the external object having still to be there' – and hence without being able to provide real satisfaction.[5] With time this mental activity leads to increasing frustration, that is, to unpleasure, and makes it obvious that a thorough reorganization of the mental processes is necessary to achieve real satisfaction.

The infantile mind abandons its restricted orientation towards pleasure, and adopts a new policy of occupation, which leads it to distribute energy to all perceptions and memories, even if they happen to be unpleasurable. Thereby the human being becomes conscious of its surroundings and learns to tolerate a certain measure of unpleasure in the hope of ultimately obtaining real satisfaction. In Freud's terms, the 'reality principle' emerges. Instead of being swept by wasteful and massive energy shifts, 'secondary-process thought' develops, in which the mind uses only minute amounts in order not to 'diminish the quantity available for altering the external world'.[6] The ability to save energy by using only small quantities of energy to test reality and thereby to anticipate possible consequences of action, endows humans with the capacity to consider the useful and not only the pleasurable. In other words, in Freud's metaphor it is economic efficiency which enables people to think according to the laws of logic and to use language.

Only impulses in the system *Ucs.* retain their original blindness and freedom. In this mental province waste and chaos continue to reign. Unruly creatures as they are, unconscious impulses press towards wish-fulfilment and continue to 'endeavour to force their way by means of the preconscious system, into consciousness and to obtain control of the power of movement'.[7] But as we have seen earlier, at the threshold to the system *Pcs.* they encounter an enemy force which inhibits their original freedom: the censorship. Where, however, does the censorship recruit the forces it needs to restrain and contain such large mobile quantities of energy reaching it from the unconscious? Freud explained the power of the system *Pcs.* to counteract pressure from the unconscious by the presence of words: 'The system *Ucs.* contains the thing-occupations ['*Sachbesetzungen*'] of the objects . . . the system *Pcs.* comes about by this thing-presentation being over-occupied [*überbesetzt*] through being linked with the word-presentations corresponding to it. It is these over-occupations [*Überbesetzungen*] . . . that bring about a higher psychical organization and make it possible for the primary process to be succeeded by the secondary process which is dominant in the *Pcs.*'[8]

As Freud pointed out, word-presentations institute a regulatory process in the mind which distinguishes human beings from animals. Their power overturns the quantitative foundations of Freud's energy model. Even though he characterized the system *Ucs.* as 'the larger sphere',[9] he claimed that the organizational superiority of the systems *Pcs.* and *Cs.* – that is, their capacity for linguistic representation – endows them with greater power. As usual, Freud illustrated the logic of his argument with an example from parliamentary politics: 'Let us imagine a country in which a certain small faction objects to a proposed measure the passage of which would have the support of the masses. This minority obtains command of the press and by its help manipulates the supreme arbiter "public opinion", and so succeeds in preventing the measure from being passed.'[10]

The words present in the systems *Pcs.* and *Cs.* endow them not only with a superior organization which allows them to tame the energy charges invading the mind from the body. Ultimately, Freud even attributed to the presence of words the power to manage and redirect such energy charges, and to force them into complete compliance with the person's conscious goals. This last step is achieved in the system *Cs.*, where mental energy is not only 'bound' to words, but made mobile again as an instrument of a 'more discriminating regulation' based on the person's purposes.[11] Thereby energy becomes usable in conscious thought, which for Freud is but 'an experimental action carried out with small amounts of energy, in the same way as a general shifts small figures about on a map before setting his large bodies of troops in motion'.[12]

As we see, Freud's metapsychological discourse refers to words not only as vehicles of signification, but also as elements which exercise power within the mind, which have the capacity to restrain and direct energies. According to Freud, they play an active part in the political struggle which takes place in the mind. As a whole, his topography of the mind interrelates energy and words in a triple-decker control system. Energy is 'free' and mobile on the first, unconscious level, but denied access to motility. It is inhibited in its movement on the second, preconscious level, where it is 'bound' to words. Finally, its quantities are regulated and coerced into actions which often run counter to their own aims on the level of consciousness. If a crucial boundary can at all be determined in Freud's model of the psyche, it has to be drawn at the entrance to the system *Pcs.*, where words are added to the pictorial mode of thought which characterizes the system *Ucs.* At this point secondary-process thought under the rule of the reality principle replaces the wasteful primary mechanisms of the pleasure principle. Since this transition is brought about by the power of words, it is no surprise that Freud admitted failure when he attempted to account for it in terms of energy processes. As he put it: 'I find it hard to give a mechanical (automatic) explanation'.[13]

The difficulties Freud encountered in these instances come hardly as a surprise. They were a result of his attempt to provide purely mechanistic and causal formulations within a theoretical framework whose political logic constantly and inevitably intertwines mechanics and meaning, and therefore can never be reduced to only one of its two dimensions. Freud's attempts at mechanical explanations were bound to reach an impasse, because the actual logic of his thinking was dialectical. The dialectical nature of Freud's theorizing manifests itself throughout his metapsychological discourse, but it is most clearly evident in the way in which he construed the dynamics between the pleasure principle and the reality principle.

In Freud's theory of mind, progress from the pleasure principle to the reality principle is achieved in an advance in which the former is overcome but not annihilated. Although it is surpassed, its goal is preserved at a higher level, leading to a unity of itself and its opposite, which Hegel has described by the term '*Aufhebung*'. Hegel used this term, since the German word '*aufheben*' can mean both 'to annul' and 'to preserve'. Thus, '*Aufhebung*' denotes a transition where a lower stage is both abolished and maintained, where an affirmative moment is preserved and contained in its negation.

Following such dialectical logic, Freud presented the pleasure principle as abandoned and superseded in mental development, not because the quest for pleasure is given up, but because it fails to reach its goal. And though the reality principle constitutes the antagonist of the pleasure principle and negates the latter in its original form, it also preserves the pleasure principle's goals by lifting them to a higher plane. In Freud's words: 'the substitution of the reality principle for the pleasure principle implies no deposing of the pleasure principle, but only a safeguarding of it'.[14] As long as we live, the pleasure principle cannot be dethroned or nullified. We all remain in its grip and, seen in this light, verbal thinking is 'nothing but a substitute for a hallucinatory wish', that is, another way of seeking satisfaction.[15] A person achieves self-mastery through the ability to handle inner and outer demands and to resist temptation to immediate and full satisfaction, which, Freud wrote, 'would often lead to perilous conflicts with the external world and to extinction'.[16] Though in the course of this passage the claim to pleasure becomes more modest as the pleasure principle gives way to the reality principle, the latter also allows purposeful action, adaptation to and control over real objects, and thus succeeds in providing real pleasure.

However, this dialectical process does not lead to an ultimate synthesis; for in Freud's framework there is no end to the dialectics of pleasure and reality. When the reality principle emerges, its forces – rational, verbal secondary process thinking – encounter opposition: 'a resistance stirs within us against the relentlessness and monotony of the laws of thought . . . Reason becomes an enemy which withholds from us so many possibilities of pleasure'.[17] Part of the mind refuses to be subjugated by language and logic and withdraws into a world of wishful pictures. As long as wishful imagination is kept within its bounds, it is not dangerous. To illustrate this point, Freud claimed that while the mind's 'front' requires strict organization because of the enemy's proximity, things can be more relaxed in its hinterland.[18] Imaginary satisfactions can even have a beneficial, compensatory effect in which a frustrating reality, although known, is temporarily bracketed, as is done in art or play, for instance. This is possible only as long as the subject can separate imagination from reality; too great a freedom from the monotonous laws of thought and from considerations of what is useful bears dangers. By liberating human beings not only from restrictions but also from pursuit of their real interests and concern with self-preservation, the pleasure principle is capable of bringing pain and death to those who fail to confine it to the nature reserve and let the sloppiness of the hinterland spread to the front.

Freud stressed the potentially destructive aspects of the blind quest for pleasure in 1920, when he concluded in *Beyond the Pleasure Principle* that 'the pleasure principle seems actually to serve the death drives'.[19] At this stage Freud decided that since in one way or another both sexual and self-preservative drives act for the preservation of the species, he could put them together under one heading, which he called Eros. The purpose of Eros, as he defined it, is 'to preserve living substance and to join it into ever larger units',[20] while he depicted the death drive as a fundamental tendency to undo connections, lead to disintegration and, as its name indicates, death. In this context Freud saw death as a complete rest, corresponding to the state of organic matter before it becomes alive. For him, life is nothing but a prolonged disturbance of matter, which is shaken out of its peaceful slumber and wants to return to it by dying. As he declared: 'everything living dies for *internal* reasons . . . *"the aim of all life is death"* '.[21] Freud chose the notion of 'Nirvana principle', as title for the death drive's tendency 'to reduce, to keep constant or to remove internal tension due to stimuli', and he explained that this tendency 'finds expression in the pleasure principle'.[22]

Strangely enough, Freud seemed to ally the pleasure principle with the death drive, while he united sexuality with the latter's antagonist, Eros. Indeed, Freud never quite managed to reconcile his theory of

Eros and death drives with his earlier drive theory, or to come clear about the relation between the death drive and aggression. For instance, in *Civilization and Its Discontents* Freud argued both that aggression originates from the death drive, whose destructive tendencies have been turned outwards and transformed into the destruction of others,[23] and that 'the inclination to aggression is an original, self-subsisting drive disposition in man'.[24]

In fact, Eros and the death drive never really became part of Freud's model of the psyche; they remained 'mythical entities, magnificent in their indefiniteness', as he called them in his *New Introductory Lectures*,[25] which he invoked primarily in writings on culture and the history of civilization. Thus, I shall neither go into a protracted discussion of the complex interrelation of Freud's notions of death, aggression and destructiveness, nor into their highly problematic relationship with pleasure and sexuality.[26] Instead, let me just state that Freud's somewhat perplexing concept of the death drive seems to me mainly a symbolic restatement of his claim that complete satisfaction is impossible in life, and that total pleasure is somehow associated with annihilation. Under the impression of the melancholy turn which his vision of human nature took in those years, Freud wrote to the Swiss vicar Oskar Pfister that 'to me my pessimism seems a conclusion, while the optimism of my opponents seems an *a priori* assumption. I might also say that I have concluded a marriage of reason with my gloomy theories while others live with theirs in a love-match. I hope they gain greater happiness from this than I.'[27]

9 Strategies of Conflict

As we have seen, independently of what drive model Freud postulated, he always regarded mental energy as a scarce commodity to be used efficiently if a person is to become capable of changing the real world into a more pleasurable one. He inevitably claimed that primary processes must be forced to accept the consequences of their blindness: after withdrawing from reality they cannot be allowed to control actions taking place in that reality. Banned into the unconscious depth of the mind, divorced from reality and consciousness, primary processes retain the core of infantile impulses which characterize individuals at the beginning of their life. Unlike the historical past, Freud maintained, the mental past cannot be destroyed; earlier stages in development are merely overlaid and continue to exist alongside what has developed from them. The nucleus of the psyche remains 'a chaos, a cauldron full of seething excitations'.[1]

The unconscious persistence of the pleasure principle turns the mind's internal state of nature into a looming threat, an ever-present potentiality of chaos akin to Hobbes' 'State of Nature'. In my view it assumes a strategic position in Freud's argument, justifying a tyranny in the mind as necessary to prevent disastrous and pathological potentialities from turning into overwhelming actuality.

Hobbes' State of Nature – a realm of never-ending war of all against all, without law, outside history and yet perpetually present – is an apt analogy for what Freud contended we all hide in our mind. The system *Ucs.* and, later in Freud's writings, the id, never achieve a unified will. They are full of contradictory demands and have no understanding of incompatibility, negation or doubt. Like Hobbes, Freud posited a fictitious State of Nature outside the domain of history and civilization in order to legitimize the existence of the Leviathan. Even though Freud elaborated extensively on primary-process mechanisms and wrote about them as if they were observable, he admitted that 'no psychical apparatus exists which possesses a primary process only and . . . such an apparatus is to that extent a theoretical fiction'.[2] Similar to Hobbes' model, which pictured not so much imaginary natural human beings as his own contemporaries in a lawless state, Freud's concept of the primary process is not truly an image of the workings of the early infantile mind, but a statement about what he thought adults would do, were they freed from the teachings of reality.[3] One could almost describe the mature and rational individual in Freud's theory in the words used by Hobbes for the *Leviathan* in the 'Preface to the Latin Edition' of his work, and call him 'an artificial man made for the protection and salvation of the natural man, to whom he is superior in grandeur and power'.[4] And, again comparable to the *Leviathan*, what a rational organization has to offer is not happiness, but the removal of at least some of the obstacles to satisfaction, promising, in Hobbes's words, 'continual success in obtaining those things which a man from time to time desireth'.[5]

What are the means necessary and available to maintain this rational organization against the continuous onslaught of unconscious forces? What political avenues are open to the mind's *Leviathan* and which of them promise success? Freud's comments on this topic are organized around the concept of repression, which he described as 'the cornerstone on which the whole structure of psycho-analysis rests'.[6] In *The Interpretation of Dreams* Freud stated that the expression ' "to repress [*verdrängen*]" . . . derived from a set of ideas relating to a struggle for a piece of ground'. His language indeed leaves little doubt that he visualized repression, too, in analogy to a military or political process, even though he warned that this should not be done 'in the most literal and crudest sense'.[7]

Repression denotes the attempt to escape from unacceptable wishes and ideas by keeping them at a distance, that is, by banning them into the unconscious and 'forgetting' them. Freud compared this strategy to an ostrich policy. The attempt to get rid of threatening feelings and ideas by their simple 'avoidance [*Abwendung*]' allows them to withdraw into what Freud called 'internal foreign territory [*Ausland*]',[8] where they form 'a State within a State, an inaccessible party [*Partei*] with which cooperation is impossible'.[9]

Though the tactics of repression are manifold, they are always absolutist, rigid, divisive, inefficient and ineffective. They lead to symptoms, paralyze the person and cannot provide any real pleasure. They are wasteful and reduce the capacity for enjoyment; in other words, they characterize neurotics.[10] Thus repression plays the role of the arch-adversary of psychoanalytic practice, and although no complete victory will ever be possible, it is by the gradual abolition and overcoming of repression that therapeutic success is defined.

In explaining why the strategy of repression is doomed, Freud again referred to words and energy as the two relevant resources of mental politics. Repression starts when the ego denies an idea the right of entrance into consciousness in order to prevent the quota of sexual energy which occupies this idea from entering with it. A kind of internal dam is constructed in the psyche, but fails in its task, because instead of having recourse to language as the major asset in the struggle against unconscious forces, the ego exclusively – and erroneously – uses energetic means. As Freud wrote, it tries to work by 'counter-occupation [*Gegenbesetzung*]' alone, but since in terms of energy quantity the ego's resources are inferior to the id's, it is bound to become increasingly incapable of mastering the repressed energy.[11]

Moreover, in Freud's framework, once a quantity of energy is repressed into the unconscious, it is able to move freely again and cannot be prevented 'from organizing itself further, putting out derivatives [*Abkömmlinge*] and establishing connections'.[12] It can occupy other, associated but more innocuous ideas, which will serve it as shelters and carriers, and ultimately allow it to return into consciousness in the form of symptoms, that is, as pathological *Aufhebungen* of what has been repressed. As always, Freud described this process in terms of a power struggle. He called it 'a rebellion on the part of the id against the external world', and defined neuroses as 'a more or less partial overpowering of the ego by sexuality after the ego's attempts at suppressing sexuality have failed'.[13]

Eagerness for pleasure has produced an unpleasurable and wasteful situation. Neurotic symptoms obviously do not bring the pleasure they were aiming at initially. Instead, the ego's imprudent strategy of repression has forced it into an endless struggle against an inaccessible and invincible enemy. Since the ego is unable to recover its legitimate sovereign position in the psyche, it will have to appeal to outside intervention in the hope of redressing the mind's internal balance of power in its favour. Freud explained: 'The position is like that in a civil war which has to be decided by the assistance of an ally from outside. The analytic physician and the patient's weakened ego, basing themselves on the real external world, have to band themselves together into a party against the enemies.'[14]

To provide a person's ego with support by acting as its ally against the forces of the id – as well as those of the superego – is the fundamental task of Freud's therapy. He asserted: 'We try to restore the ego, to free it from its restrictions and to give it back the command over the id which it has lost owing to its early repressions. It is for this one purpose that we carry out analysis, our whole technique is directed to this aim.'[15] In his *New Introductory Lectures* Freud formulated the goal of psychoanalysis succinctly by saying: 'Where id was, there shall ego be [*Wo Es war soll Ich werden*].'[16]

Nevertheless, he was modest about the goals of psychoanalysis and stressed that its practice cannot aim at a complete abolition of all repressions. At best it can hope to help an individual to find new means of control for some of them. Freud warned in *The Interpretation of Dreams* that the 'subjugation' of the unconscious by the conscious part of the mind can never be complete,[17] and in his *Introductory Lectures* he stated cautiously that after treatment a person 'has rather less that is unconscious and rather more that is conscious in him than he had before'.[18]

To reiterate this point: just as Freud's authoritarian stance is not to be confounded with an absolutist one, so his critique of the absolutism of repression is not to be confounded with an advocacy of radical liberation. He opposed both those who claim too much for liberty and those who claim too much for oppressive authority. Thus, he adopted the position of the ego whose hegemony he advocated so fiercely. As Freud pointed out at a meeting of the Vienna Psychoanalytic Society, repressed sexuality is liberated 'not in order that man may from now on be dominated by sexuality but in order to make its suppression possible'.[19] What Freud objected to in the doomed strategy of repression is its inefficiency and ineffectiveness, but not its basic aim of creating a condition where sexuality 'no longer seeks to go its independent way to satisfaction'.[20]

In Freud's framework the lifting of repressions is depicted as having many advantages. It places at the disposal of the ego energies which hitherto were either inaccessible or wasted in its efforts to maintain internal barriers. Since it becomes 'enlarged', the ego can now behave in a more conciliatory way towards the claims of sexuality.[21] It is able to allow that a certain portion of repressed desires – which can be gratified under the given circumstances without provoking danger to the individual – be given access to direct satisfaction. In exchange, the ego has now the power to tighten its control over other, more problematic sexual impulses, such as the pregenital 'perverse' ones, so that they can be employed for legitimate and socially valued cultural activities.[22]

This form of internal control is achieved by 'sublimation', a process in which a compromise-formation is forced upon the drives by the ego, combining the socially and rationally useful with the pleasurable.

Instead of blocking forbidden sexual desires which cannot be gratified under present social conditions, it desexualizes them by lifting them to a culturally higher plane, and thus provides 'a way out, a way by which . . . demands can be met without involving repression'.[23] Leading to such an alternative *Aufhebung* of forbidden sexuality, sublimation allows the individual to derive pleasure from refined intellectual work rather than from the direct satisfaction of prohibited desires. But this, Freud added, is a route 'accessible to only a few people. It presupposes the possession of special dispositions and gifts which are far from being common to any practical degree.'[24]

There is, however, also a third strategy in this conflict between desire and social necessity which, despite its importance, receives no extensive treatment in Freud's texts. In many ways, it is the inverse of repression. It divests unacceptable sexual wishes of their energy and allows their ideational representatives entrance into consciousness after they have been disarmed. As Freud explained, one of the aims of psychoanalytic treatment is to enable the patient to apply this procedure, which Freud called 'condemnation [*Verurteilung*]'. As Freud detailed in his case study of Little Hans, 'analysis does not undo the *effects* of repression. The drives which were formerly suppressed remain suppressed; but the same effect is produced in a different way. Analysis replaces the process of repression, which is an automatic and excessive one by a temperate and purposeful control of the part of the *highest* agencies of the mind. In a word, *analysis replaces repression by condemnation.*'[25]

As the term 'condemnation' suggests, bringing repressed material into consciousness does not free the patient from the need to make often difficult and painful decisions between conflicting impulses. Rather, psychoanalysis aims to turn a pathological war, in which decisions are impossible, into a normal confrontation, where decisions can be made.[26] According to Freud's well-known statement in his conclusion to the *Studies on Hysteria*: 'much will be gained if we succeed in transforming your hysterical misery into common unhappiness'.[27]

The mental agency which is supposed to do the condemning is, of course, the ego. According to Freud: 'The business of the analysis is to secure the best possible psychological conditions for the functions of the ego; with that it has discharged its task.'[28] The ego's expansion opens up a whole range of new choices for the individual – and some old ones, whose nature has changed. Freud mentioned, for instance, that successful treatment should give patients even the choice of reproducing neurotic symptoms, if they consider them appropriate –

that is, if they are no longer coerced into symptomatic behaviour by their unconscious, but choose it on their own. As he put it, 'analysis does not set out to make pathological reactions impossible, but to give the patient's ego freedom to decide one way or the other'.[29] In the *Introductory Lectures* he affirmed that as long as patients decide 'on their own judgement in favour of some midway position between leading a full life and absolute asceticism, we feel our conscience clear whatever their choice'.[30] He neither sought to prescribe one universally valid course to the good life, nor to make better human beings out of his patients. As he stated in a letter to his American follower James Jackson Putnam: 'The unworthiness of human beings, even of analysts, has always made a deep impression on me, but why should analyzed people be altogether better than others? Analysis makes for *unity*, but not necessarily for *goodness*.'[31]

Let me sum up: I have attempted to provide a reconstruction of Freud's metapsychology in order to demonstrate that its guiding principles are those of political dialectics rather than mechanics. I have found politics on the 'surface' of Freud's discourse on the mind, where the dynamics of our elusive inner world are portrayed in analogy to the outer social world, with warring forces opposing one another, driven by contradictory motives in pursuit of their goals, divided by 'defences', 'resistances' and 'censorships'. Thus, as I have shown, Freud pictured the mind as a social hierarchy whose classes are engaged in a civil war for the power to determine the actions of the individual as a whole.

I am aware, however, that historically Freud's early model of the psyche originated in the mechanistic tradition of neurophysiology, and that Freud used mechanistic metaphors throughout his writings, as if they denoted observable entities. Therefore a political reading could seem counter-intuitive and historically inaccurate. But as we have seen, Freud was alert to the inadequacy of his mechanistic formulations, which failed in crucial instances to explain the mind's complex processes. The reasons for these 'mechanical failures' have to be sought in the dialectical nature of Freud's discourse, which continuously and inextricably intertwines cause and meaning, and continuously undermines fixed and determined boundaries within and between subjects. Thus, as I have shown, even where Freud used mechanistic terminology, the logic embedded in his models of the mind is a political one.

10   Free to Choose

By constructing the mind as a polity involved in a continuous internal struggle in which the ego's rule is constantly endangered and never complete, Freud decentred the subject. In fact, Freud saw psychoanalysis as part of the great subversive movement of modern science, which was designed to destroy the illusion that humanity forms the centre of the universe. According to Freud, this decentring endeavour has three heroes. It started with Copernicus, who taught people that the earth was not the centre of the universe, continued with Darwin, who displaced humans from the centre of creation and turned them into descendants of animals. 'But', added Freud 'human megalomania will have suffered its third and most wounding blow from the psychological research of the present time which seeks to prove to the ego that it is not even master in its own house, but must content itself with scanty information of what is going on unconsciously in its mind'.[1]

In decentring the subject and postulating that individual freedom is contingent upon internal domination, Freud elaborated on a metaphor of the mind which Isaiah Berlin has vigorously condemned for providing a dangerous political momentum. Berlin claims that this metaphor leads those who are guided by it down the slippery slope to authoritarianism and coercion, and – despite good intentions – transforms the idea of freedom into a notion that sanctions oppression and violence.[2]

Berlin assumes here, as Lakoff and Johnson do in *Metaphors We Live By*, that much of our behaviour is guided by the metaphorical vantage point from which we try to make sense of social and psychic reality. As they put it: 'In most cases, what is at issue is not the truth or falsity of a metaphor but the perceptions and inferences that follow from it and the actions that are sanctioned by it. In all aspects of life ... we define our reality in terms of metaphors and then proceed to act on the basis of metaphors. We draw inferences, set goals, make commitments, and execute plans, all on the basis of how we in part structure our experience, consciously and unconsciously, by means of metaphor.'[3]

According to Berlin there are two basic metaphors – he calls them concepts – of freedom which guide political behaviour. The 'positive' concept sees the individual as internally divided and hierarchically structured. From this perspective, freedom has above all to do with intrasubjective politics, that is, with questions such as: 'By whom am I ruled?' or 'Who is master?'.[4] Answers which respond to the questions 'Who is free?' or 'When is one free?' in the terms of positive freedom, typically point to an agency internal to the person – such as reason – and claim that only this particular agency's rule will enable the individual to do what is 'truly' and 'really' his or her own will; that is, provide him or her with what Berlin calls 'freedom to'. Berlin acknowledges that the positive notion of freedom started as an ideal of self-direction which implied the rule of a 'higher' self over a 'lower' self. But he claims that – historically and psychologically – this metaphor pushed its advocates towards despotism, totalitarianism and violence.

Berlin's real foes are rationalist monists like Rousseau and Marx, with whom he identifies all thinkers adopting the positive metaphor of self-mastery. As he says, they postulate

> first, that all men have one true purpose, and one only, that of rational self-direction; second, that the ends of all rational beings must of necessity fit into a single universal, harmonious pattern, which some men may be able to discern more clearly than others; third, that all conflict, and consequently all tragedy, is due solely to the clash of reason with the irrational and the insufficiently rational – the immature and underdeveloped elements in life – whether individual or communal, and that such clashes are, in principle, avoidable, and for wholly rational beings impossible; finally, that when all men have been made rational, they will obey the rational laws of their own natures, which are one and the same in them all, and so be at once law-abiding and wholly free.[5]

According to Berlin, a person's 'higher' self comes to be conceived of as transcending the individual and is identified with the race, nation or class to which he or she belongs. In a travesty of what originally was intended as a doctrine of freedom, the positive metaphor presents the individual's coercion into a wider social framework – which might be given by the race, class or nation – as part of a process in which a 'higher' freedom is reached, thus justifying tyranny and oppression.[6]

Berlin opposes a liberal, 'negative' concept of 'freedom from' to the positive one. In this metaphor the individual figures as an internally more or less unified agent; its frame of reference is spatial and the questions it poses are 'how wide is the area over which I am, or should be, master?' or 'over what area am I master?' Hence the negative concept leads to definitions of freedom in terms of an 'area bounded by frontiers' where free movement is guaranteed and in which there are no obstructions.[7] In Berlin's view, thinking and speaking of freedom negatively – that is, in terms of an absence of coercion and interference, a negation of externally imposed obstacles and impediments – is safer, since this metaphor does not lend itself to becoming a cloak for oppression.

As we have seen, Freud conceived of a hierarchical integration in the mind, in which he posited that a person cannot be autonomous and free unless the ego achieves internal command. This approach places him in the tradition of thought which defines freedom in 'positive' terms as self-mastery. This should be more than enough to provide him with a place on Berlin's list of villains. However, Peter Gay has argued that since Freud always stressed the plurality and incompatibility of human goals and left free choice in the hands of the individual, Freud in fact conceived of freedom in a liberal sense.[8] But Gay does not explain what, precisely, distinguishes Freud's metaphor of self-mastery from the positive one which Berlin denounces, and, too keen to show affinities between Freud and Berlin, he makes nothing of the 'positive' aspects of Freud's discourse on freedom and autonomy.

In opposition to both Berlin and Gay, my view is that Freud's concept of freedom is neither liberal nor in danger of becoming part of an ideology of oppression. Rather, Freud combined the metaphor of self-mastery with a concept of individual autonomy which does not allow for its relegation to either side of Berlin's dichotomy of 'positive' and 'negative' freedom. Most simply, one might say, perhaps, that Freud differed from the people attacked by Berlin in dividing the mind into three rather than two elements. This tripartite structure allowed Freud to present outside restrictions as mediated by an agency of their own, the superego, and to oppose them with the individual's autonomous interests as represented by the ego.

On the one hand, he did not wish for the rule of the superego – the representative of a morality based on general principles and values, which is to be victorious in the rationalist doctrines attacked by Berlin. Richard Rorty has commented on this point:

> Whereas everybody from Plato to Kant had identified our central self, our conscience, the standard-setting authoritative part of us, with universal truths, general principles, and a common human nature, Freud made our conscience just one more, not particularly central, part of a larger homogeneous machine. He identified the sense of duty with the internalization of a host of idiosyncratic, accidental episodes. . . . He saw the voice of conscience not as the voice of the part of the soul that deals with generalities as opposed to the part that deals with particulars, but rather as the (usually distorted) memory of certain very particular events.[9]

On the other hand, Freud did not side with the id's wild and untamed passions, whose liberation has been advocated by those who turn Freud's approach into a revolutionary creed, such as Wilhelm Reich and Herbert Marcuse. Hence Freud's concept of positive freedom as contingent on the ego's benevolent tyranny, reinforces the vision of the individual as living in conflict with social norms and emphasizes autonomous choices.

As we have seen, in Freud's discourse self-mastery can never be complete. Though one may live with less repression, according to Freud no one will ever be completely without it. Though one can become more conscious of hidden intentions and impulses, no one will ever become fully self-transparent and self-controlled. Though one's thoughts and actions can become more rational, no one will ever be without any irrational desires and fears. According to Freud, insight into the self must also bring into awareness limitations of reason and take note of the fact that self-knowledge will always remain incomplete. To be sure, such limitations cannot free the subject from responsibility. While parts of the self will always remain beyond conscious control and knowledge, Freud was adamant that one has to take responsibility for all thoughts and feelings, whether they are conscious or not. As he pointed out, for instance, one is responsible for evil impulses in one's dream, even though their motivations and expressions cannot be controlled. In Freud's words: 'If I seek to classify the impulses that are present in me according to social standards into good and bad, I must assume responsibility for both sorts.'[10]

In contrast to philosophical arguments for the rule of reason, Freud's support for the ego's hegemony was not based on an ethical essentialism, that is, on the assumption that men ought to be rational because reason is what essentially differentiates them from other animals. Rather, Freud's argument is both hedonistic – promising a reduction in suffering and an increase in pleasure – and economic – promising less waste and more efficiency. Out of the four postulates which Berlin holds to be characteristic for thinkers of the 'positive freedom' tradition, Freud might at most be said to have endorsed the first one, which states that the purpose of human beings is rational self-direction.

Even here a few provisos are in place, not the least of which would be that Freud recognized pleasure as a rational goal. Freud did not aim at freedom from desire; in opposition to Kant and Descartes he argued that reason can never become self-sufficient and that tolerance towards human passions is of reason's essence. In Freud's words: 'The nature of reason is a guarantee that . . . it will not fail to give man's emotional impulses and what is determined by them the position they deserve.'[11] There is no doubt that the other claims of rational monists – which refer to the possibility of complete social harmony, the irrationality of all conflict, and the unanimity of all rational human beings – are as alien to the psychoanalytic *Weltanschauung* as they are to Berlin's outlook. For instance, the aims of therapeutic intervention in the psyche's civil war are presented in a fashion which clearly distinguishes Freud from the rationalist monists and their ideals of harmonious liberation. Suffice to say that Freud did not seek the abolition of antagonisms, but only their transformation from pathology to normality.

Moreover, Freud made mental health not only dependent on internal conditions of self-mastery and self-knowledge – to the extent to which he believed them to be possible. He also demanded a space where a subject is allowed to grow and mature, and gain sexual satisfaction without unnecessary restrictions, such as are imposed by social and cultural conventions. As we have seen in earlier discussions on Freud's opposition to the sexual norms of his period, he definitely demanded 'freedom from' outside interference for the individual. However, as I have pointed out earlier, he did not advocate a completely unrestricted sexual life; instead he claimed only that '[c]ertain impulses of the drives, with whose suppression society has gone too far, should be permitted a greater amount of satisfaction'.[12]

Discrepancies between Freud and Berlin run deep; they are a consequence of the differences in their very conception of human nature. Berlin regards human beings as essentially self-transparent, unified, autonomous and capable of free and rational choice. Their freedom is a good that has to be defended against unfavourable circumstances, while unfreedom is explained in terms of external interference and constraints which may inhibit individual choices, but which are extrinsic and removable. The absence of external impediments – conceived of in analogy to constraining physical obstacles such as chains, walls or locked doors – constitutes Berlin's necessary and sufficient condition of freedom. Thus, the negative metaphor of freedom derives from a mechanical picture of social causation, which portrays it as a contingent relation between two autonomous agents, one pushing and the other being pushed, one inhibiting movement and the other being inhibited.[13]

Freud, of course, rejected such visions of the subject and society. By conceiving the mind in terms of a political system of representation, whose dialectical processes allow for the *Aufhebung* of the outer world of society in the subject's inner world, Freud depicted the boundaries between self and others as permeable. For Freud society was not only a place where subjects are situated and constituted; it became itself part of the subject. As Russel Jacoby puts it: 'If Freud was "conservative" in his immediate disregard of society, his concepts are radical in their pursuit of society where it allegedly does not exist: in the privacy of the individual. Freud undid the primal bourgeois distinction between private and public, the individual and society; he unearthed the objective roots of the private subject – its social content. Freud exposed the lie that the subject was inviolate; he showed that at every point it was violated.'[14]

Freud's whole libido theory points to constraining and creative forces instilled within a person by others through means of love, fear and power, by education, training, socialization, custom, religion and morality. It confronts the various ways in which an individual's freedom can be impeded or supported by parents, teachers, priests and leaders without the erection or abolition of prison walls. Especially the notion of the superego shows how for Freud one person can become an essential and defining aspect of another, whose very identity may be dependent on the continued internalized presence of the former. In contrast to Berlin, Freud understood freedom as a good to be acquired by an initially unfree, fragmented and irrational individual.

Favourable circumstances alone, albeit necessary, are not sufficient for a free choice. Without denying the importance of negative freedom, Freud thought that those who achieve self-mastery enjoy a freedom which others do not possess under the same circumstances. Hence an individual needs to gain, tame and redirect the psychic resources necessary to ensure the internal command of the ego. In other words: Freud was concerned with the individual's *acquisition* of freedom, while Berlin's type of liberalism is concerned with its *defence*. As Mortimer Adler also put it, liberal freedom is wholly circumstantial, while Freud's concept is both circumstantial and acquired.[15]

Berlin, too, acknowledges that it might be impossible to exercise freedom if internal or material resources for its exercise are lacking; but he argues that freedom exists in all cases in which external restraints are absent. With Berlin, freedom is an *option*, not a *practice*. In my view, Berlin's identification of the metaphor of self-mastery with rationalist monism and his attempt to withdraw behind strong philosophical ramparts in order to guard himself against the dangers of the latter, has led him to limit himself to a simplistic and reductionist approach, and to blind himself to the dialectical nature of social relations.

Yet, Freud's discourse is marked by an unresolvable tension: on the one hand, he called for self-mastery and self-knowledge, and asserted the subject's total responsibility for itself. On the other hand, he pointed to an uncontrollable and unknowable core – and thus to the *limits* of self-mastery and self-knowledge – and to ways in which the self is continuously invaded by forces from within and without. The Freudian subject is condemned to live in a continuous struggle within itself and with others, which comes to an end only in death.

This is a tragic vision of the human condition. Freud's image as a gloomy thinker is reinforced when we consider the *end* for which self-mastery is to be achieved. As he put it: 'To tolerate life remains, after all, the first duty of all living beings.'[16] Indeed, rather than bringing a gratifying feeling of moral purity, happiness, superior power or complete freedom, all that self-mastery can achieve, according to Freud, is the strength necessary to endure life in unhappiness without having to escape either into individual neuroses or collective ones, such as religion. In some instances Freud blamed the necessities of life in common – which impose excessive sacrifices on us – for the inevitability of our discontent. In others he claimed that 'our possibilities of happiness are already restricted by our constitution'.[17] In any case, for Freud the aim of self-mastery and self-knowledge is to be able to accept the inevitability of unhappiness.[18] Barry Richards is right to call Freud's philosophy of human nature a 'philosophy of endurance'. As he puts it, according to Freud 'to live successfully is to endure the disappointment, guilt and fear which are ineradicably within us'.[19]

However, here Richards also points to another tragic element in Freud's understanding of self-mastery and self-knowledge: the *content* of the knowledge which humans gain in the attempt to know themselves is also a sad one. For what human beings hide from themselves are their murderous hatreds, incestuous desires, early disappointments and losses, infantile jealousy and possessiveness, haunting guilt, fears and anxieties. It is only by making conscious such aspects of the subject, which hitherto have been barred into the unconscious, that a freer, more expedient and pleasurable way to live can be found. Such a transformation also allows for a more frank and genuine way of living, which, according to Freud, *eo ipso* is a more ethical one. As Freud declared in his *Introductory Lectures*: 'We tell ourselves that anyone who has succeeded in educating himself to truth about himself is permanently defended against the danger of immorality, even though his standards of morality may differ in some respects from that which is customary in society.'[20]

As Philip Rieff has pointed out, if one can at all say that a moral end is entailed in Freud's ideal of self-mastery and self-knowledge, this end is personal honesty.[21] In this emphasis on an inner truth, Freud's approach again differs from liberal theorists. Their primary concern is with human conduct in terms of external goals, such as those which become manifest in property transactions, voting patterns, political associations and speech. They see language above all as a cognitive vehicle whose veracity can be defined in terms of its correspondence to events in the outside world. Obviously, these aspects of human conduct and expression were secondary to Freud's concerns. Inward-bound, he took the route into the individual's inner world and examined the veracity or liberty of speech and action in terms of how truly and freely they express hidden intentions, wishes and fears. Thus, notions of truth, emancipation and power acquire a new meaning with Freud, which I continue to examine in part III, where I discuss the clinical practice of psychoanalysis.

Part III

Between Two Consenting Adults: Face-to-Face Politics in the Clinical Practice of Psychoanalysis

Peter Laslett has contrasted the concept of the territorial society – that is, the state – with what he has called the 'face-to-face society'. Because of its small size, territory usually is of no importance in the face-to-face society. Its members are involved in a direct and total intercourse, and respond to one another on the basis of an intuitive psychology 'with their whole personality, conscious and unconscious, covert and overt, in all situations'. Thus, in the face-to-face society experiences are shared to a far greater degree than in the large-scale territorial society which is the subject of modern political theory. Hence, as Laslett points out, crises in the face-to-face society often are resolved by personal responses which are expressed in forms less common in interactions in the state, such as 'exclamations, apostrophes, laughter and silences'.[1] Laslett goes on to argue that political theory has failed to draw the necessary distinctions between psychological processes which characterize the face-to-face society and those which are typical of the territorial society. According to Laslett, this neglect has led to misunderstandings in the analysis of both.

Evidently, the clinical setting of psychoanalysis constitutes a dyadic face-to-face society. Encompassing conscious and unconscious dimensions, verbal and nonverbal interactions, it involves both analyst and analysand with their whole personality. I wish to show that like all face-to-face societies, the psychoanalytic situation is also politically structured. On the one hand, its mechanisms and procedures regulate the distribution and exercise of power, and on the other hand, it is situated in a territorial society with wider frames of reference which affect its power structure.[2] Two persons never encounter each other only as analyst and analysand, but always also as members of their profession, nationality, social class and gender. Thus, their interaction is always a dual one, where they act both as agents whose actions are subject to the universal rules and structures governing the internal dynamics of the therapeutic setting, and as representatives of their gender, class and nation.

In the first chapter of part III I provide a comprehensive discussion of the role which such extraneous factors played in the constitution of the psychoanalytic setting; that is, I elaborate on the effect which the male, bourgeois identity of doctors had on their encounter with hysterical women. My claim is that while such therapy-extraneous factors led many doctors to use violence against their women patients, Freud consistently eschewed coercive means of therapy, even though he, too, sought to establish an authoritarian form of treatment. Then, in a detailed historical study, I compare the conduct of analytically trained or inspired doctors during the First World War with that of non-analytical physicians. Here I demonstrate the influence of nationalist commitment on therapeutic practices in which male doctors confronted male patients. This study proves that the therapeutic approach developed by Freud led not only him but also his followers to refrain from using violence against male patients (as well as women, as will be shown below), even when social conditions allowed the use of brutal means.

Finally, in the latter two chapters of this part I turn to a detailed examination of Freud's discourse on the internal dynamics of the face-to-face politics in the psychoanalytic consulting room. Focusing on the way in which Freud conceptualized the sources of the analyst's authority over patients, its scope, limits and uses, I present psychoanalytic therapy as a social practice which aims to deploy authority for the sake of patients' emancipation.

11   A Touch of Class

As has been mentioned in part I, in Freud's time doctors were not listening to hysterics; Charcot, for instance, is said to have remarked: 'You see how hysterics shout, much ado about nothing'.[1] His motto was *'j'inscris ce que je vois* [I write down what I *see*]' and since he regarded hysterical attacks as physiologically determined *tableaux* or spectacles, he had them elaborately displayed in front of public audiences and carefully photographed.[2] While Charcot ignored utterances of hysterics, some doctors tried to eliminate their supposedly diseased organs by surgery. Others, who regarded hysterical women as malingerers, used violent means to coerce them into silent submission if they resisted their doctors' methods. Mostly, physicians conceived of their task as a combat against malingering women who had to be forced into their social roles as wives and mothers, serving their family, nation or race.

Hannah Decker reports that some late nineteenth-century gynecologists recommended to cure hysterical women by 'inserting tubes into their rectums after each hysterical episode', threatening 'hysterical girls with the application of hot irons to their spines', or cauterizing their clitorises if the disease proved 'intractable'.[3] Caroll Smith-Rosenberg comments that 'many doctors felt themselves to be locked in a power struggle with their hysterical patients' and 'felt that they must dominate the hysteric's will; only in this way . . . could they bring about her permanent cure'. In their fight with female patients, 'doctors frequently recommended suffocating hysterical women until their fits stopped, beating them across the face and body with wet towels, ridiculing and exposing them in front of family and friends, showering them with icy water'.[4]

Paul Flechsig, Professor of Psychiatry at the University of Leipzig, reported in 1884 ten cases in which hysteria was treated by the removal of ovaries, commenting that he 'did not observe a single indication of any adverse effect whatsoever on the patients' psyches'.[5] Since there was widespread opposition to ovariotomies, Alfred Hegar, a leading German gynecologist, had warned already in 1880 that the reluctance of German physicians to perform the operation 'retarded the entire development of German gynecology. If those who criticized the operation had instead performed it themselves, and then improved upon it, it would have been of immeasurable value for the entire development of the specialty in Germany. Let us not once again allow something to be taken out of our hands by foreigners!'[6]

That issues of gender and national pride were prominent in medical debates on how hysteria was to be treated, also becomes apparent when one considers the most popular form of treatment at the time: Silas Weir Mitchell's rest cure. As head of the prestigious Hospital for Orthopedic and Nervous Diseases in Philadelphia, he was as eminent in the American medical community as Charcot was in France.[7] His fame was based mainly on a method of treatment, which isolated hysterical women in silent passivity for several weeks and subjected them to a strictly regulated discipline of massages and electrical treatment, while over-feeding them on a milk diet. The rest cure was used mainly with wealthy patients, who could afford the money for such a prolonged private treatment and seemed to have had some success. Though Mitchell's therapy was not explicitly conceived as punitive – above all it was supposed to counter the patients' exhaustion and anemia – he did expand in great detail on the power struggle involved in treating hysterics. Mentioning the 'moral uses of rest and isolation', he argued that when dealing with hysterics, the doctor 'must morally alter as well as physically amend, and nothing less will answer'.[8] Therefore patients had to be removed 'from contact with those who have become the willing slaves of their caprices'.[9] He approvingly quoted a colleague who claimed that 'an hysterical girl is . . . a vampire who sucks the blood of the healthy people about her'[10] and he claimed that hysterics 'indulge themselves in rest on the least pretense'.[11] They had to be taught self-control, ordered out of bed and 'made to persist until exertion ceases to give rise to the mimicry of fatigue'.[12] In other cases, however, he agreed that patients really did need rest, though they were not allowed to get it in the way in which they wanted it:

> To lie abed half the day, and sew a little and read a little, and be interesting as invalids and excite sympathy, is all very well, but when they are bidden to stay in bed a month, and neither to read, write, nor sew, and to have one nurse – who is not a relative – then repose becomes for some women a rather bitter medicine,

and they are glad enough to accept the order to rise and go about when the doctor issues a mandate which has become pleasantly welcome and eagerly looked for. I do not think it is easy to make a mistake in this matter unless the woman takes with morbid delight the system of enforced rest, and unless the doctor is a person of feeble will.[13]

As this discourse on therapeutic measures reveals, late nineteenth-century doctors saw themselves to a large extent as representatives of their nations and the patriarchal ideology which was part of their *Weltanschauung*. Their encounter with hysterical women was a dual one: on the one hand, they were doctors seeking to help patients, on the other hand, they were men who defended the patriarchal framework of their society and aimed to break the resistance of rebellious women – and all too often the latter aspect dominated the former.

When in 1887 Freud favourably reviewed the German translation of Weir Mitchell's book, the rest cure was a widely used approach to treat middle-class and upper middle-class hysterics. A year later Freud repeated that the 'high reputation' of this method was well deserved, and throughout the late 1880s and early 1890s, when treating hysterics, he regularly employed some of its elements, such as baths, massages, electrical treatment and feeding-up.

There is even a reference to the use of 'high tension electric currents' in one of Freud's early cases, but none of the violent or coercive spirit characteristic of his contemporaries can be found in his writings. Instead, he stated that his patient, Emmy von N., 'seemed to take quite a liking to the painful shocks produced by the high tension apparatus', since she suffered from pain in her legs and the electrical shocks 'seemed to push her own pains into the background'.[14]

On the whole, however, it seems that Freud did not put his trust in any particular technique. He commented that Mitchell's rest cure, too, 'is not to be regarded . . . as something systematically complete in itself'. In Freud's view, the patient's isolation from other neurotic members of the family and 'the physician's influence remain the principal agents'.[15]

For Freud, too, treatment was above all based on the doctor's ability to impose his authority on patients – without, however, resorting to violence. In the search for an efficient means to achieve this aim, he started experimenting with hypnotic suggestion. In 1890 he stated that '[h]ypnotism endows the physician with an authority such as was probably never possessed by the priest or the miracle man, since it concentrates the subject's whole interest [*alles seelische Interesse*] upon the figure of the physician'.[16] When the topic of hypnosis came up, Freud explicitly argued against those who defended the patient's liberty. For instance, his former teacher Theodor Meynert had declared that in hypnosis 'a human being is reduced to a creature without will or reason, and his nervous and mental degeneration is hastened by it'.[17] Freud, however, asserted that 'a physician – even a non-hypnotist – is never better satisfied than when he has repressed a symptom from a patient's attention by the power of his personality and the influence of his words – and his authority'.[18]

In this period hypnotism received professional attention primarily in France, where Charcot had made it respectable. Conscious of the nationalist fervour involved in medical debates, Freud was careful to quote in his early papers not only French, but also German authorities, such as Krafft-Ebing, who had expressed their support for hypnotism. At the same time, however, he was critical of nationalist prejudices limiting the scope of science, and added in an acerbic aside: 'It will be seen that these names can satisfy, too, those who are so lacking judgement that their confidence requires of a scientific authority that it shall fulfil certain conditions as to nationality, race and geographical latitude, and whose faith comes to a stop at the frontier-posts of their fatherland.'[19]

Originally Freud had witnessed the use of hypnotic suggestion in Charcot's performances at the Salpêtrière. Fascinated by new avenues opened by such techniques, he later attended the First International Congress on Hypnotism in Paris together with – among others – Auguste Forel, Valentin Magnan, William James, Cesare Lombroso and, above all, Hyppolite Bernheim and Ambroise Liébeault from Nancy, who by then were acknowledged to be the two foremost authorities on hypnotic suggestion in Europe.[20] Bernheim had been appointed Professor for Internal Medicine at Nancy in 1879, but in 1882 he was so impressed by a provincial pastor's methods of hypnotic suggestion that he decided to adopt them. This doctor-priest, Ambroise Liébeault, treated people for free, taking only such fees as were voluntarily offered to him – and therefore, as Henri Ellenberger recounts, was thought to be not only a quack, but also a fool.[21] Hypnotizing mainly poor and uneducated patients from rural areas in a large shed in a village outside Nancy, Liébeault saw between 25 and 40 patients before noon. Together with Hippolyte Bernheim he was reputed to have sent into trance up to 20,000 of them.

Freud translated one of Bernheim's books into German and travelled in the summer of 1889 together with a woman patient to Nancy, where he spent several weeks in personal contact with the two famous hypnotists. There he 'witnessed the moving spectacle of old Liébeault working among the poor women and children of the labouring classes [*Arbeiterbevölkerung*]'.[22] Freud also observed Bernheim's hypnotic treatment of hospital patients, but when Bernheim attended to the woman Freud had brought along, he could bring no relief. As Freud wrote, she was 'a woman of good birth [*vornehme*]' and Bernheim 'frankly admitted to me that his great therapeutic successes by means of suggestion were only achieved in his hospital practice and not with his private patients'.[23]

Thus, the treatment of hysteria intertwined medicine with politics on three levels: somewhat peripherally it involved nationalist rivalry, more crucially it invoked patriarchal ideology, and in the case of hypnotic suggestion it had recourse to social practices which built on class differentials. It appears that doctors used violence more often with wealthy women in private practice, where they had a much harder time than with the poor, whom they could overwhelm by public displays of their status and authority. It seems that the magical power of hypnotic formulae depended to a large extent on the doctors' capacity to transform their social and professional superiority into verbal power over patients who had been socialized into the behaviour which the dynamics of hypnosis demanded of them: to respond with deference, acquiescence, subservience and gratitude to a doctor who helped them for free.[24]

Charcot, too, performed his public spectacles of hysteria at the Salpêtrière with poor women patients, who often were coached by his assistants, so that their performance would please the great physician and his audience.[25] Like Liébeault and Bernheim, Charcot hypnotized patients for the purpose of medical classification and public charity, with no particular concern for their thoughts, feelings and privacy. As John Forrester comments, 'the picture of the venerable country doctor, Liébeault, the university professor Bernheim's pastoral mentor, hypnotizing the poor of his parish one after the other, under each other's gazes, in a large barn at the back of his house, could not offer a more poignant contrast to the hushed, heavily carpeted private world of bourgeois front rooms and bedrooms in which Freud practiced his art'.[26] Similarly, the Salpêtrière's famous iconography of nervous diseases, for which patients were regularly photographed in the nude to record tics and sequences of movements without missing anatomical details, would have been unthinkable with the middle-class patients who became Freud's clientele.

Indeed, from a political point of view, psychoanalytic therapy can be seen as having its origins partly in Freud's lack of prejudices against a method of treatment which was generally seen as alien to German medicine. Mostly, however, it originated in his attempt to transform patient–doctor relations from a public spectacle in which members of the lower class submit to commanding talk by a middle-class doctor, into private encounters where patients are of the same class and cultural background as the doctor – and often a good deal wealthier and more powerful than the latter. Rather than illiterate, superstitious, poor peasants and factory workers, Freud's patients mostly were well-to-do women. Already in the 'Preface to the First Edition' of *Studies on Hysteria* he made explicit that his 'experience is derived from private practice in an educated and literate class [*einer gebildeten und lesenden Gesellschaftsklasse*]'.[27] But though his patients were highly articulate, self-confident, ambitious and often rebellious, he searched for a method which would allow him to treat middle-class women without having to have recourse to the violent means which some of his colleagues had made use of.

Nevertheless, it is undeniable that a strong patriarchal and authoritarian bias permeated Freud's theory in general and his perspective on the treatment of hysterical women in particular. Much has been written on these aspects of his work in the context of feminist commentary on the 'Fragment of an Analysis of a Case of Hysteria', which he published in 1905 and which tells of the treatment of the eighteen-year-old Ida Bauer, who became famous under the pseudonym of 'Dora'.[28] It is impossible here to give a detailed exposition of the way in which phallocentric ideology underlaid Freud's conduct throughout this case. Suffice to mention one example: Dora told Freud how at the age of fourteen she had been sexually attacked by a 'friend of the family', who had brought her to his office under the pretext of inviting her to see a church procession. However, in his analysis of the event Freud remained indifferent to the fact that Dora had been a minor who was tricked and trapped into this occasion against her will. When Dora reacted to Herr K.'s assault with 'a violent feeling of disgust' and a quick escape, he declared this to be but an instance of her hysteria.[29]

Feminist commentators have rightly pointed out that Dora's hysterical symptoms both sheltered and betrayed the silent rebellion of a woman who felt forced into a social role which she refused to accept, but who was incapable of open resistance. They consider Freud's psychological explanations of the young woman's symptoms as distorting the political nature of her protest. As Elaine Showalter puts it: 'Instead of asking if rebellion was mental pathology, we must ask whether mental pathology was suppressed rebellion. Was the hysterical woman a feminist heroine, fighting back against confinement in the bourgeois home?'[30] Sometimes feminist interpreters even glamourize Dora's hysteria in one way or another; Hélène Cixous, for instance, sees in her 'the core example of the protesting force of women'.[31] In contrast, Toril Moi sees in Dora's hysteria as much a sign of defeat as of protest. But she also claims that 'if the emancipatory project of psychoanalysis fails in the case of Dora, it is because Freud the liberator happens also to be, objectively, on the side of oppression. He is a male in patriarchal society, and moreover not just any male but an educated bourgeois male, incarnating *malgré lui* patriarchal values.'[32]

Undoubtedly these comments are poignant; but when one looks at Freud's therapeutic practice from a historical perspective, one also has to acknowledge that despite his patriarchal bias he oppressed hysterics less than many of his contemporaries. He rejected the moral stigmas which were attached to hysterical women, refused the use of physical violence against them, attempted to enable women to become conscious of their needs and desires even when these contradicted established conventions, and, most extraordinarily for a male physician in his period, he was ready to listen to them and learn from them.

What allowed Freud to transcend the well-established hierarchies of knowledge and gender in *fin-de-siècle* Vienna was the affinity of class, which brought doctor and patient closer to one another and made it possible for a male physician to listen to the words of female hysterics. It was his patients' *Bildung* – that is, their education and culture – as well as their wealth, which enabled them to enter into a complex and reflexive dialogue with him, which, in turn, led him to inquire into the sources of their illness.

Fanny Moser, for example, who was one of Freud's first patients and appears in *Studies on Hysteria* under the pseudonym of Emmy von N., was the widow of a Swiss-Russian industrialist and reputed to be the richest woman in Europe.[33] Freud's first and probably most important patient was Anna von Lieben, for whom he used the pseudonym Cäcilie M. As he stated in *Studies on Hysteria*, it had been the case of Cäcilie M. which led him and Breuer to publish their 'Preliminary communication' in which they outlined their theory and therapeutic practice for the first time. In his words, he got to know her 'far more thoroughly than any of the other patients mentioned in these studies'.[34] With admiration he described her as 'a highly intelligent woman, to whom I am indebted for much help in gaining an understanding of hysterical symptoms'.[35] In a comment which would have been unthinkable for Charcot, Liébeault or Bernheim to make of one of their patients, Freud even wrote to Wilhelm Fliess that if he, Fliess, knew her, he 'would not doubt for a moment that only this woman could have been my teacher [*Lehrmeisterin*]'.[36]

Peter Swales has uncovered and reconstructed biographical data on Anna von Lieben which provide a fascinating picture of the class background of this early patient of Freud's. Born in 1847 as Baroness Anna von Todesco, a banker's daughter, she grew up with nurses, governesses and tutors in a villa which served as a salon for Vienna's rich and famous. Later she moved into a Medici-style palace frequented by such celebrities as Brahms, Liszt and Johann Strauss. In 1871 she married a highly educated rich Jewish banker, Leopold von Lieben, and spent her time mostly in expensive hotels, spas and her family's palace, surrounded by chambermaids and servants. But throughout most of her life she was severely mentally disturbed, persecuted by pangs of guilt and anxiety, tortured by hysterical pains, dependent on morphine and secluded in sick rooms. Since she also suffered from insomnia, she hired a professional chess player who had to be ready all night outside her room to play the game with her whenever she wished to do so.[37]

When Freud was recommended to Anna von Lieben by his highly renowned colleague and mentor Josef Breuer in 1888, he was still a young, inexperienced and not all-too-well-reputed doctor at the beginning of his career. Hired – together with Breuer – to see this extremely rich, eccentric and ill woman in her house, his position must have been more or less on a par with that of the chess player. In a revealing sentence Freud mentioned, for instance, how one day 'the patient got me to give her hypnotic treatment'.[38] In May 1889 Freud also tried to hypnotize Fanny Moser/Emmy von N. But, having little success with the application of this method to wealthy and educated women, he quickly became dissatisfied with its uses, and later described it as hackwork, monotonous, unreliable and capable of providing short-term improvements only.[39]

Such were the complications which money, class and culture introduced into the hypnotic relationship: the doctor had to try to dominate by words a patient of a superior social status, who paid for his services, became his employer and commanded him to hypnotize her. In contrast to the brief and public encounters characteristic of Charcot, Bernheim and Liébeault, Freud was bound to his patients in an intricate and private relationship, which resulted from his employee status and a shared class background. This made hypnotizing more difficult, but allowed a confidential alliance to develop, brought mutual respect, trust, and an understanding in which hitherto unspoken disturbing sexual and familial secrets could be revealed. Thus, conventional boundaries of gender which separated male doctors from their female patients broke down.

Even when Freud attempted to hypnotize wealthy and well-educated women, he did so not in order to suppress their symptoms and command them to adopt a more acceptable type of behaviour, but to make them talk. This was a technique which he had learnt from Josef Breuer, who had become his mentor already before Freud's trip to Paris. Having experimented with hypnosis in the past, Breuer told Freud in the early 1880s of a therapeutic experience which he had gathered in the course of treating a twenty-one-year-old woman called Bertha Pappenheim, who was to become famous under the pseudonym 'Anna O.'. In his case study Breuer described Anna O./Berta Pappenheim as resistant to the type of medical authority which was brought into play in hypnotism. Breuer explained: 'She was markedly intelligent, with an astonishingly quick grasp of things and penetrating intuition. She possessed a powerful intellect . . . She had great poetic and imaginative gifts, which were under the control of a sharp and critical common sense. Owing to this latter quality she was *completely unsuggestible*; she was only influenced by arguments, never by mere assertions. Her will-power was energetic, tenacious and persistent; sometimes it reached the pitch of an obstinacy which only gave way out of kindness and regard for other people.'[40]

The strong-willed young Berta Pappenheim/Anna O., who, in Breuer's words, 'was bubbling over with intellectual vitality, led an extremely monotonous existence in her puritanically-minded family'.[41] When her father fell terminally ill, she devoted all her efforts to nursing him for several months. In the course of this period she developed a number of symptoms: a nervous cough, a squint, anxiety attacks, headaches, disturbances of vision, muscle contractures, paralyses, hallucinations, deliria, inexplicable changes and dissociations of her personality, dumbness and an inability to speak German. When her father died, she no longer even understood German, and communicated exclusively in English. Finally, repeated suicidal attempts made it necessary to transfer her from her Viennese home to the country.

There, in an innovative approach, inspired and suggested to a large extent by the patient, Breuer obliged her to talk about her hallucinations. Realizing that articulating her hallucinations in words relieved her of their force over her, calmed her down, and freed her of related symptoms, she invented the term 'talking cure' for this technique.[42]

As we see, it was a woman and a patient, who suggested to Breuer – and, indirectly, to Freud – the curative power of words. Ernest Jones even called Bertha Pappenheim 'the real discoverer of the cathartic method'.[43]

However, Breuer's success in treating his patient remains highly doubtful. Henri Ellenberger has unearthed evidence suggesting that contrary to Breuer's assertions, Bertha Pappenheim/Anna O. did at best recover temporarily and later had to be hospitalized in a Swiss clinic.[44] But whatever its results, there can be no doubt that the procedures of this patient-inspired cathartic treatment were fundamentally different from those typical of suggestion as practiced by the French hypnotists, where the doctor spoke while the patient remained silent and passive. As Freud was to explain later, the aim was to turn the patient 'into a collaborator' and to build the treatment to some extent on the patient's intellectual interest.[45]

I do not wish to give an impression of the talking cure as built on egalitarian principles. On the contrary, after abandoning hypnotic techniques, Freud sought new means to restore his authority over patients – which had been so severely undermined by the lack of class difference – and to gain the upper hand in the power struggle with his patients.

For this purpose he developed at first a somewhat theatrical 'pressure technique' in order to encourage his patients to speak. He asked them to shut their eyes and concentrate. Then he questioned them about the origins of their symptoms. Whenever answers were not forthcoming, he put his hands on their foreheads or took their heads between his hands, telling them that his pressure helped them to think of whatever they were looking for. He suggested to them that they would have a mental image at the moment at which he would relax and asked them to tell him without hesitation what occurred to them.[46] As he put it: 'It is of course of great importance for the progress of the analysis that one should always turn out to be in the right *vis-à-vis* the patient, otherwise one would always be dependent on what he chose to tell one.'[47] This posture of omnipotence and omniscience was needed to get patients to talk of things of which they clearly would have preferred to remain silent.

Only one conscious will was to govern the therapeutic dyad: that of the almighty doctor. He insisted that Elisabeth von R. had 'no right' to apply criticism to what she saw or thought: '[S]he was under an obligation to remain completely objective and say what had come into her head, whether it was appropriate or not.'[48] The patient was forbidden to exercise any conscious control over her speech: 'There is to be no criticism of it, no reticence, either for emotional reasons or because it is judged unimportant.'[49]

As these extracts from Freud's texts demonstrate, so-called 'free' associations were imposed as a duty upon women patients, rather than being granted to them as a liberty. Thereby Freud both replicated and inverted the patriarchal power structure typical of his society. On the one hand, he acted as a man who laid down rules for women and forced them to do something which they clearly refused to do out of their own free will. On the other hand, he empowered them to talk about that which a strict moral code and deep anxieties prevented them from speaking of.

This duality characterized much of Freud's attitude towards hysterical women. As has rightly been pointed out in the feminist literature, his therapy reproduced and reinforced patriarchal patterns and relied on his authoritarian relationship towards women. But as I have tried to show here and in chapter 2, his etiology of hysteria and his therapeutic practice also systematically undermined prejudices of his age concerning hysterical women, opposed violence in their treatment, aimed to wrest them out of the silence into which they had escaped, took their symptoms and speech to be meaningful and valuable for scientific understanding, and turned them into partners in his clinical practice.

Rather than forcing bourgeois women by means of violence into roles which social conventions prescribed to them, Freud attempted to make use of their exaggerated commitment to bourgeois ethics, on which he blamed their illness. As Freud explained in 1913, underlying the motivation to get well – upon which the success of psychoanalytic treatment hinges – there is an economic calculus: 'As far as the middle classes are concerned, the expense involved in psycho-analysis is excessive only in appearance. Quite apart from the fact that no comparison is possible between restored health and efficiency on the one hand and a moderate financial outlay on the other, when we add up the unceasing costs of nursing-homes and medical treatment and contrast them with the increase of efficiency and earning capacity which results from a successfully completed analysis, we are entitled to say that the patients have made a good bargain.'[50]

In other words, Freud presented psychoanalytic therapy as part of a capitalist commodity transaction, which enables patients to increase their income.[51] He both appealed to the bourgeois spirit which he shared with his patients, and tried to turn bourgeois values into the basis of a cure for the mental illnesses which they caused. He advised analysts to tell their patients openly that they had education and experience which they wanted to turn into money since they were in the market to sell their knowledge and skill. As he said, 'the psycho-analyst may put himself in the position of a surgeon, who is frank and expensive because he has at his disposal methods of treatment which can be of use'.[52] According to Freud, this frankness allowed analysts not only to help themselves economically, but also educate their pa-tients to overcome 'inconsistency, prudishness and hypocrisy' in matters of self-interest.[53]

Since Freud thought that suggestive techniques could be replaced by his patients' cooperation only if he could rely on their internalization of the bourgeois ethos and the efficiency of their economic calculus, the right of entry to the psychoanalytic setting had to be restricted to the *Bildungsbürgertum*, that is, the educated middle class. As he put it, it could be accessible only 'to the well-to-do classes, who are ac-customed to choose their own physicians'.[54] On the one hand, he claimed that those whom he characterized as 'the poor' were less likely to fall ill, since they suffered less of bourgeois values, were less inhibited in their sexual manners, and hence had imposed on themselves fewer mental renunciations and sexual deprivations than the middle class.[55] On the other hand, he argued that among those of 'the poor' who have fallen ill, the economic calculus which provided an incentive for middle-class patients to get well, constituted a powerful motive in the opposite direction: '[E]xperience shows without a doubt that when once a poor man has produced a neurosis it is only with difficulty that he lets it be taken from him. It renders him too good a service in the struggle for existence; the secondary gain from illness which it brings him is much too important. He now claims by right of neurosis the pity which the world has refused to his material distress, and he can now absolve himself from the obligation of combating his poverty by working.'[56]

To be sure, Freud did not conclude that poor neurotics ought to be unmasked as malingerers. In his view, economic considerations came into play only after a pathological condition had developed and the social and financial side effects of a disablement had been realized. For Freud, neurotics always fell ill of an internal, unconscious conflict. Only thereafter would they be tempted to stay ill for conscious, extern-al reasons if their social condition made illness seem profitable. Freud expressed regrets 'that analytic therapy is almost inaccessible to poor people'. But since he was no social reformer, he assumed that only '[l]ittle can be done to remedy this'.[57] In fact, he even portrayed psychoanalysis itself as being in the position of the poor, whom it could not help, because it was no better off then they were. As he said in his *Introductory Lectures*: 'Poor ourselves and socially powerless, and compelled to earn our livelihood from our medical activity, we are not even in a position to extend our efforts to people without means, as other doctors with other methods of treatment are after all able to do. Our therapy is too time-consuming and too laborious for that to be possible.'[58] In other words, since psychoanalysts are bourgeois professionals who need to make a living, they can do business only with members of their own class.

12 Psychiatry Goes to War

By the time of the Great War, Freud's theory had become the property of a small but active therapeutic community and determined how its members treated their patients. In my view, the way in which this group related during the war to governmental and military authority on the one hand, and to their patients on the other hand, provides significant evidence to suggest that psychoanalytic discourse played an important role in discouraging therapeutic violence. It shows that even under circumstances in which military authorities legitimized medical brutality, the therapeutic approach developed by Freud led psychoanalytically trained and inspired doctors to treat their patients in a humane manner. Thus, in contrast with non-analytic army physicians, psychoanalysts who served in the Central Powers' armies did not become ruthless when they treated 'shell-shocked' conscripts in the service of their states or nations.

As the governments of Austro-Hungary and Germany hurried to turn their citizens into soldiers in 1914, conscripts were inserted in military machineries which rearranged them on a scale and with an urgency previously unknown. In order to train soldiers for war and to increase their capacity to fight in battle, their minds and bodies were treated as objects. This imposition of military discipline on conscripts, together with the actual experience of war, caused traumatic disorders. Some conscripts became paralyzed, blind, mute or deaf, and others developed organically unexplainable trembling, twitching or cramps. Their consciousness, cognition or sensation became muddled, or they were overcome by severe anxieties, phobias and depressions. Soon such symptoms became epidemic and made a large number of soldiers unsuited for war because they were no longer able to participate in drill or battle. Such deviant behaviour brought them in conflict with the aims of their governments and armies.

Army doctors entered this conflict in an official role, in which they served their military superiors. The doctors' task was to stop the production of symptoms and return neurotics to their social role as docile fighting men for which the state had them conscripted. When treating soldiers who had developed symptoms, army psychiatrists were guided by nationalist commitment rather than concern for their patients. Whatever theoretical approach they took, they defined their therapeutic task as administrative intervention to increase the docility of soldiers to the state and its military purposes.

In the early days of the war, the psychiatric establishment in Germany and Austro-Hungary was caught in a somatic model of nervous diseases attributed above all to the work of Hermann Oppenheim in the late 1880s.[1] Hence the first soldiers who entered military hospitals with tremors, stupors or paralyses were diagnosed as suffering from an organic impairment of the nervous system – the famous 'shell shock [*Granatschock*]' – which was assumed to be caused by the explosion of shells, bombs and grenades. Since there was no medication or therapy for curing organic disorders or healing lesions of the nerves or the brain, shell-shocked soldiers were usually sent to rural areas to rest. On the other hand, as John Keegan recounts, some men whose symptoms could later be recognized as those of a mental breakdown, were shot during the first two years of the First World War, since they were suspected of malingering in order to escape from military duty.[2]

In February 1915 Max Nonne demonstrated at a medical congress in Hamburg that symptoms of war neuroses could be removed by hypnotic suggestion, a fact which clearly contradicted Oppenheim's organic etiology. At the time, Nonne's method was rejected as a return to medieval mysticism and decried as a 'disgrace [*unwürdig*]' to fighting men.[3]

However, the tides of war were soon to bring about a change in medical wisdom. Between February and June 1916 almost 300,000 German troops were sent into death at Verdun, where over 100 divisions fought a senseless battle.[4] In June, the Russian army brought the entire Austro-Hungarian front to a collapse and took a quarter of a million prisoners. As A. J. P. Taylor comments, this event 'marked the moment when the armies of Austro-Hungary lost their fighting spirit. Unity, cohesion, loyalty, vanished.'[5] Then came the battle at the Somme with a million casualties on both sides. To quote Taylor again: 'Idealism perished at the Somme ... The war ceased to have a purpose. It went on for its own sake, as a contest in endurance. ... The Somme set the picture by which future generations saw the First World War: brave helpless soldiers; blundering obstinate generals;

nothing achieved. After the Somme men decided that the war would go on for ever.'[6]

Even though there are no precise figures available, it seems that with the disenchantment in the army and the unbearable conditions of prolonged trench warfare, war neurosis seems to have become epidemic.[7] Therefore mass hospitalization seemed increasingly impractical and the medical profession reacted to the loss of hope for a quick victory by abandoning Oppenheim's organic etiological hypothesis. War neurosis was declared to be a purely mental – that is, hysterical – phenomenon, curable by psychological measures.[8] In September 1916, at the War Congress of the German Association for Psychiatry and Neurology in Munich, most of the 241 psychiatrists present switched to Nonne's psychogenic approach and thereby institutionalized a major shift in the etiology of war hysteria. Symptoms were explained as the result of a *'Willenssperrung'*, *'Willensversagung'*, or *'Willenshemmung'*, that is, a weakness or malady of the will. They were considered the consequence of an unconscious attempt to escape from duty into illness and taken as the manifestation of a 'neurosis of defense' (*Abwehrneurose*), designed to serve the individual's drive for self-preservation.[9] As Nonne stated at the end of the war: 'The term "purpose neurosis" or "neurosis of defense" is to express the fact that these neuroses serve an inner purpose and that their appearance reflects a real interest of the patient. What makes them pathological is that they do not originate in a conscious wish. A wish alone cannot create an illness. Illness is created by an unconscious drive to self-preservation mediated by strong affects with acute or chronic origins in the subconscious.'[10]

Despite such references to unconscious origins of the illness, neurotic soldiers were seen as malingerers who produced symptoms for a purpose – to receive pension payments or to avoid front line duty – and they were accused of a lack of manliness, loyalty, courage and patriotism.[11] Esther Fischer-Homberger's history of traumatic neurosis leaves no doubt that Nonne's psychogenic theory was accepted by war psychiatry to a large extent because it allowed the army 'neither to release war hysterics from duty, nor to pay them compensation'.[12] Confronted with the continuing deadlock of the war, psychiatrists not only took it upon themselves to strengthen the will of neurotic soldiers and restore them to battle fitness, but also to guard the state from the daunting financial burden of pension payments and compensations after the war.

They defined their task as preventing 'great economic damage to our fatherland', which could occur if military physicians did not cure the symptoms of what was critically diagnosed as 'greed neurosis' (*Begehrungsneurose*), or 'pension-struggle hysteria' (*Rentenkampfhysterie*).[13] If they failed, psychiatrists warned, the number of 'pension hysterics would avalanche and one would have to compensate them by payments totalling ten-digit figures'.[14] Success in their therapeutic practice, they promised, would 'increase the activity of the individual in an undreamt-of fashion and endow our people with even more nervous energy, as it has proven so far. Thus one may contend that we physicians, by conceiving of our task concerning war neuroses in this way, perform cultural work on the largest scale.'[15] Erwin Stransky of the Viennese Psychiatric Association pointed out that 'whatever therapeutic measures might seem appropriate in a particular situation, in this serious time the cardinal point of view ought not to be determined by the well-being of the individual case, but by the welfare of our so closely allied armies.'[16] The German Psychiatric Association declared officially that its members would 'never forget that we physicians have now to put all our work in the service of one mission; to serve our army and our fatherland'.[17]

Nevertheless, there was some political opposition to diagnosing German soldiers as hysterical. Some psychiatrists raised the question as to whether such an approach could not be taken as a defamation of 'courageous fighting men' who 'tired and exhausted themselves in the service of the fatherland'.[18] This issue became especially relevant for physicians who traced hysteria to heredity, since hereditary diseases were considered characteristic of deficient human beings, whose weakness of the will derived from an 'inferior nervous system' or an 'inferior or degenerate brain'.[19]

As can be seen, the medical debate was dominated by extraneous considerations of national politics. War psychiatrists were less concerned with the restoration of their patients' health and the demonstration of scientific knowledge in itself – with cure and truth, as it were – than with the military's need for fighting men at the front. Concern for the nation's power, collective health and hygiene came first. Individual soldiers were viewed as segments of an organic national body and their pathological features were evaluated in terms of the damage they were thought to inflict on the collective whole. Army doctors conceived their therapeutic task as a moral project reaching beyond their individual roles. Therefore they devised a repertoire of therapeutic techniques to deter neurotic soldiers from producing symptoms. This was done by making them understand that it would be less painful for them to fulfil their patriotic duty than to escape it by falling ill. Treatment was designed to neutralize and overcome the original psychic shock said to have triggered the neurotic escape into illness. The doctors induced another, countervailing shock to cure the soldiers of their pathological – that is, unpatriotic – intentions. In other words, by balancing the pain and fear of the front with an artificially created situation designed to be even more frightening and painful, psychiatrists tried to encourage soldiers to fight and, if necessary, die for their fatherland.

Therapeutic shocks were administered, for instance, by what Fritz Kaufmann deceptively called 'surprise method' (*Überrumpelungs-methode*). He explained that such 'a psychic shock can only be induced if one causes acute pains ... Often ... one is forced to apply strong [electrical] currents. . . . Success can only be achieved through inexorable obstinacy [*unerbittliche Hartnäckigkeit*] in the execution of the treatment.'[20] Kaufmann was one of the most prominent psychiatrists active in the German military hospitals. His 'surprise method' was widely discussed in the literature. Also called Kaufmann's 'coercive procedure' (*Zwangsverfahren*) or Kaufmann's 'method of violent suggestion' (*Gewaltsuggestionsmethode*), it was generally favorably received.[21] Even Nonne – who treated more than 1,600 soldiers by hypnotic suggestion – mentioned that whenever his patients' goodwill seemed to slacken, he reinforced it with some 'short but painful [electrical] shocks [*mit kurz dauernden aber schmerzhaften Schlägen*]'. Nonne explained: 'I had patients always undress to complete nakedness, since I found that one could thereby increase their feeling of dependence or helplessness.'[22] Others, such as Otto Binswanger, locked up their patients in isolation, declaring this to be a 'cure of psychic abstinence' (*psychische Abstinenzkur*). Kurt Goldstein claimed success by performing 'mock surgery' (*Scheinoperation*), while Weich-brod recommended 'permanent baths' (*Dauerbäder*) to 'vivaciously animate the patient's interest in his rapid recovery'.[23] After the war Nonne admitted that the choice of specific treatment methods was not so much a medical issue as a matter of the physician's personal taste. These methods all served the same aim: to create a feeling of absolute powerlessness in the soldier and to lock him in a 'duel' (*Zweikampf*) with a person who seemed to possess absolute superiority, unlimited power and uncanny perseverance.[24]

Isolation, physical pain, helplessness, a superior enemy – this is what soldiers in war fear most. As we see, in order to convince war neurotics that there was no escape, these fears were systematically reproduced behind the walls of war hospitals in the guise of 'therapies'. Wilhelm Stekel, a pacifist and an early follower of Freud who broke with the psychoanalytic movement before the war, gives a very unsettling and very personal impression of what it meant to work in the neuro-psychiatric section of a large war hospital in Vienna: 'I despised those physicians who, as slave-drivers for the war mongers, forced half-recovered soldiers to go back to the trenches. I have seen terrible examples of the work of these executioners. Convalescents, still in pain, their wounds unhealed, were marched off to their regiments. In many hospitals they were tortured with a faradic brush, so that they preferred the terrors of war to the terrors of the hospital. Every week, the chief of the hospital, a major and former dentist, came into the ward and shouted, "We must evacuate! Send fifty per cent of the patients away! A new transport is coming!" '25

By creating space for a face-to-face society in which doctors could exercise unlimited power in the name of science and state, army hierarchy and conditions of war had generated an opportunity for medical violence. War doctors were allowed to violate the bodies and minds of the soldiers in a way which about a century earlier had been declared illegal for modern criminal justice. This became possible because the military penal system was incapable of preventing soldiers from producing symptoms. Psychiatrists, in turn, were willing to inflict pain on the soldiers because they saw themselves primarily as representatives of a collective conscience, though towards the end of 1916 popular support for the war had slackened and many had become disillusioned with the pointless battles.

Nevertheless, military doctors seem to have felt that it was their mission to make soldiers realize that by pursuing selfish interests they transgressed the ethical standards of the nation and failed to fulfil their manly duty. The doctors' aim was to subordinate and harness the will of the soldiers to national purposes, to make their minds and bodies usable in the trenches. On the whole, they failed to achieve this end. Rarely were soldiers restored to battle fitness by psychiatrists. As a rule, when they were released from treatment, they were fit only for garrison service. Moreover, it appears that military authorities stopped the use of Kaufmann's surprises after a revolt took place in one of the field hospitals.26

How did Freud's conduct and that of psychoanalytically trained and inspired doctors compare with that of their colleagues? In contrast with many other doctors, Freud did not volunteer to serve in the war, even though it appears from comments in his letters during these years that he identified with the war aims of Austro-Hungary. However, he did try to separate his personal sentiments from the public medical persona as disinterested observer of universal human affairs, which he presented throughout his published work. Immediately after the declaration of war Freud wrote enthusiastically to Karl Abraham that 'for the first time for thirty years I feel myself to be an Austrian and feel like giving this not very hopeful Empire another chance'. The only thing worrying him at the time was that England was 'on the wrong side [*auf der unrechten Seite*]',[27] for otherwise, he declared: 'All my libido is given to Austro-Hungary.'[28] Since the Austro-Hungarian army had no victories of its own and disappointed Freud in its military performance, he lived like most of his countrymen 'from one German victory to the next'. With Freud, this euphoric mood 'expressed itself in increased work energy'.[29]

Publicly, however, Freud lamented the partisan attitudes of scientists who were carried away by the emotions of the war. In a short essay, written about six months after the war broke out, he commented: 'We cannot but feel that no event has ever destroyed so much that is precious in the common possessions of humanity, confused so many of the clearest intelligences, or so thoroughly debased all that is highest. Science herself has lost her passionless impartiality; her deeply embittered servants seek for weapons from her with which to contribute towards the struggle with the enemy. Anthropologists feel driven to declare him inferior and degenerate, psychiatrists issue a diagnosis of his disease of mind or spirit.'[30]

As soon as he had finished writing this article, he privately dismissed it in a letter to Abraham, calling it 'a piece of topical chit-chat [*zeitgemässes Gewäsch*] about war and death to keep the self-sacrificing publisher happy'.[31] Only in communications to close friends living in the domain of the Central Powers, such as Abraham or Sandor Ferenczi, did Freud admit his nationalist sentiments and his identification with the aims of the Austro-German side. In November 1915, he again published comments of a disenchanted, scientific observer about how the war had 'shattered our pride in the achievements of our civilization' and 'our hopes of a final triumph over the differences between nations and races'.[32] Privately, however, even though Freud's confidence diminished towards the end of 1915, it took him a rather long time – until May 1917 – to call the war a 'disaster [*Unglück*]' and to start longing for peace.[33] Finally, when defeat was imminent, Freud wrote to Ferenczi in a pessimistic mood: 'I expect frightful things in Germany . . . There will be resistance there, bloody resistance. That William is an incurable romantic fellow; he misjudges the revolution just as he did the war. . . . As for the downfall of Old Austria I can only feel deep satisfaction. Unfortunately I don't consider myself as German-Austrian or Pan-German.'[34] Freud's strict separation of his private nationalism from his public universalism stands in stark contrast to the politically committed rhetoric of mainstream war psychiatry. What is known of the therapeutic practice of his leading followers who served as medical officers in the armies of the Central Powers is even more instructive in drawing a line between the psychoanalytic movement and the psychiatric establishment.

Karl Abraham volunteered for the German Army in the beginning of the war and worked at first as a surgeon. In March 1915 he was put in charge of a medical unit in East Prussia 'that served as a clearing house for psychiatric cases on the Eastern front', and in some instances he had up to 90 patients in treatment at the same time.[35] At a psychoanalytic congress in Budapest towards the end of the war – which is discussed in detail below – he reported on the further course of his army service: 'When I founded a unit for neuroses and mental illness in 1916, I completely disregarded all violent therapies as well as hypnosis and other suggestive means. I allowed patients to abreact while they were awake and tried to explain origin and nature of their suffering by means of a kind of simplified psychoanalysis. Thus I managed to create a sense of being understood in patients and achieved comprehensive relaxation and improvement.'[36]

The Hungarian physician and analyst Sandor Ferenczi was at first stationed in a small town garrison as the chief medical officer of a squad of hussars.[37] Later he became head of the psychiatric section of a military hospital in Budapest. In a paper delivered at a scientific congress in 1916, Ferenczi explained that already after two months in the hospital he 'had about two hundred cases under observation'.[38] His paper attempted to demonstrate that all war neurotic symptoms could be described in psychoanalytic categories, because they conformed to patterns of either conversion hysteria or anxiety hysteria. Though Ferenczi made no specific reference to therapeutic technique, his systematic application of Freud's theory to war neuroses suggests that his practice also proceeded along Freudian – that is, non-coercive – lines.[39]

Victor Tausk, originally a lawyer, completed his medical degree in June 1914 and was called up in August 1915. From December 1915 he served as a psychiatric expert for the Austrian army at a military court in Lublin. Tausk used his medical authority to intervene on behalf of soldiers who were to be court-martialed as deserters. After the war – and Tausk's death – Freud praised what Paul Roazen has called Victor Tausk's 'genuine heroism in using psychiatric diagnoses for human ends'.[40] Freud commented with admiration that 'during the war [Tausk] threw himself wholeheartedly, and with complete disregard of the consequences, into exposing the numerous abuses which so many doctors tolerated in silence or for which they even shared the responsibility'.[41] Tausk dared to question publicly the support of war psychiatrists for the aims of their military superiors. In a paper on 'The psychology of the war deserter', delivered in March 1917 at the Ninth Medical Officers Seminar in Belgrade, he pointed out that 'the military view of the deserter differs from the psychologist's, who is not concerned with whether or not the consequences that follow from his investigations harmonize with the requirements of the army, or the political situation'.[42]

Ernst Simmel, a physician previously unconnected to psychoanalysis, spent the last two years of the war as senior medical officer in charge of a field hospital for war neurotics in Posen. He developed a short symptomatic therapy on the basis of his clinical experience and his reading of Freud.[43] Simmel made no use of medication or force. Instead, he combined hypnosis, analytic conversation and dream interpretation into a cathartic treatment in which soldiers enacted their aggression against a dummy and were allowed to experience the pain, fear or aggression involved in the trauma underlying their illness.

The efficiency of psychoanalytic methods in treating war neurotics drew official attention to their techniques. Ernest Jones reported on the atmosphere in the end of 1918: 'A book by Simmel early that year, together with the excellent practical work performed by Abraham, Eitingon and Ferenczi, had made an impression, if not on the general medical public, at least on the high-ranking Army medical officers, and there was talk of erecting psycho-analytical clinics at various centers for the treatment of war neuroses.'[44]

A great moment had come for psychoanalysis. Officials from Germany and Austro-Hungary contributed financial support to – and attended – the Fifth Psychoanalytic Congress, which took place in the hall of the Hungarian Academy of Sciences in Budapest at the end of September 1918. As Sandor Ferenczi remarked ironically in his address: 'You see, ladies and gentlemen: the experience with war neurotics led finally even further than just to the discovery of the soul – it led the neurologists almost to the discovery of psychoanalysis.'[45] Ferenczi's critical survey of the literature established that the war had brought an important gain in prestige for the psychoanalytic approach. Therapeutic experience had corroborated the basic tenets of psychoanalysis on a mass scale. Faced with war neuroses, mainstream psychiatrists had abandoned their somatic etiology and had come to accept psychogenic concepts of mental disorders. At last they recognized the importance of unconscious impulses.

Abraham's paper emphasized the narcissistic nature of war neuroses, while Simmel gave a detailed and comprehensive account of the psychic mechanisms involved. He made clear that psychoanalysts redefined the meaning of neurotic symptoms, which were not to be seen as a ruse serving the soldier's selfish purposes. Instead, they constituted a behaviour pattern that the soldier had not consciously initiated, over which he had no control and whose true motives remained unknown to him. Rather than symbolizing illegitimate freedom, they announced the defeat of the soldier's conscious ego under the onslaught of unconscious forces that forced the ego into a painful and pathological escape from inner tensions. Such tensions could be created in conscripts by the contradictory demands of military discipline, moral conscience, emotional needs and physical survival. As Simmel pointed out, by suffering physical injuries or witnessing the death of comrades, forced to live under conditions of affective deprivation, separated from family and often humiliated by superiors, a conscript was made to feel that 'he is worth nothing as an individual, and only constitutes a negligible part of a crowd'.[46]

Strong feelings of anxiety, rage and resentment against superior officers arose as a result of the narcissistic injuries inflicted, but since they stood in opposition to the soldier's conscious loyalty to his army unit, country and nation, they caused him guilt and anxiety. Though repressed, they unconsciously continued to exercise power. Symptoms brought this internal conflict into the open with the purpose of restoring the soldier's self-esteem. Even soldiers who seemed to simulate symptoms to gain pension payments were not primarily interested in money. Financial compensation served merely as a means to recover part of their lost self-value as autonomous individuals. Analytic treatment would restore the soldier's conscious and rational self-control, that is, enable him to stay healthy despite inner conflicts. Instead of futile attempts to press soldiers back into combat, therapy had to allow forbidden feelings to surface into consciousness, induce a catharsis and enable the patient to work off his anger, thereby confirming his value as a subject. This, Simmel argued, would enable soldiers to return to front-line duty with strengthened psychical capacity to withstand the demands of active service.[47]

The debate at the Budapest Congress was free of the nationalist rhetoric and derogatory views on war hysterics which characterized war congresses of the medical establishment and legitimized almost any method by which traumatized soldiers were coerced back into their patriotic duty. Psychoanalysts opposed the infliction of pain, recommended words as the only therapeutic measure and proposed a cooperative therapeutic approach instead of deterrence and degradation. Above all, they referred to their patients as suffering individuals, who had lost their sense of autonomy in the wake of conscription, which had turned them into the cogs of a military apparatus and exposed them to unspeakable fears in the trenches. By locating the purpose of war neuroses – to escape from military service – beyond the soldier's conscious control, their theory freed war neurotics from moral condemnation and threats of violence. Despite personal enthusiasm for German and Austro-Hungarian war aims during most of the war – illustrated by Freud's letters and the willingness of analysts to volunteer for duty – psychoanalysts never put their science as blindly into the service of the governmental apparatus as their mainstream colleagues did.

Hence it seems misleading to state, as Louise Hoffman does, that while 'many psychiatrists thought war neurotics were malingerers and treated them as such, psychoanalysts knew that they were not but treated them as malingerers anyway'.[48] Nevertheless, Hoffman is right in pointing out a fundamental ambiguity underlying the psychoanalytic position during the war. As a rule psychoanalysts simply tried to abstain from politics. Like Freud, they separated their private and public personae from each other and avoided references to collective goals and values. Political abstinence of this kind allowed them to continue to use humane methods and to define their therapeutic obligation to their patients' well-being; but such abstinence also empowered the state to take possession of psychoanalytic practices, a process in which analysts – with the exception of Tausk – were willing partners. They accepted a military criterion as the standard of the soldier's recovery: his ability to fight and die in the front line. To quote Louise Hoffman once more: 'Most of these analysts, despite their marginal professional and ethnic status, seem to have accepted patriotically the military demand that war neurotics be treated so as to enable their fastest return to the front lines.'[49]

In contrast with techniques developed by the war psychiatrists, psychoanalytic methods had been carried over from peacetime practices. Yet, even though they were neither coercive nor violent, they did serve the army by restoring and reintegrating individuals into a social role imposed on them by conscription. Obviously, state officials attended the Budapest Congress in 1918 not because psychoanalysts were humane, but because their cathartic therapies appeared to provide an efficient means of sending neurotic soldiers back into battle. For their part, psychoanalysts hoped for an even more explicit and extensive colonization of their therapeutic techniques by the state. They thereby expected to gain the scientific and social authority hitherto denied to them by the medical establishment and government.

Since government support appeared to be forthcoming for psycho-analysis, Freud no longer thought it necessary to limit its practice to the middle class. State funding could extend the reach of psychoanalysis beyond the bourgeoisie. Official recognition and government funds seemed to enable the establishment of psychoanalytic centres in which observation and treatment could be conducted on a mass scale.[50] Freud avoided comments on the treatment of war neuroses – probably because he lacked all practical experience. Instead, he painted a rosy picture of the future, in which 'the conscience of society will awake' and make psychoanalysis available to the poor: 'When this happens, institutions or out-patient clinics will be started, to which analytically-trained physicians will be appointed, so that men who would otherwise give way to drink, women who have nearly succumbed under their burden of privations, children for whom there is no choice but between running wild or neurosis, may be made capable, by analysis, of resistance and of efficient work. Such treatments will be free.'[51]

Though he indicated that therapy for the poor necessitated the reintroduction of elements from hypnotic suggestion into psychoanalysis, Freud refused to compromise on fundamental elements of his doctrine. In his view, 'whatever form this psychotherapy for the people may take, whatever the elements out of which it is compounded, its most effective and most important ingredients will assuredly remain those borrowed from strict and untendentious psycho-analysis'.[52] Presenting an internal argument on therapeutic technique, Freud reminded followers and officals that the task of the analyst consisted exclusively in 'making conscious the repressed material and uncovering resistances'.[53] In his words: 'We refuse most emphatically to turn a patient who puts himself into our hands in search of help into our private property, to decide his fate for him, to force our own ideals upon him, and with the pride of a Creator to form him in our own image and see that it is good.'[54]

Even when dealing with the masses, for whom Freud had no high regard, authoritarianism in therapy had to be strictly circumscribed. Freud prided himself on being able to help his patients 'without affecting their individuality', and emphasized that 'the patient should be educated to liberate and fulfil his own nature, not to resemble ourselves'.[55]

As we see, although Freud remained silent on the obvious political issues involved, indirectly and subtly he made a political statement after all. In a time in which the state and war psychiatry were ready to coerce neurotics into military duty by violence, he stressed the social duty of the state towards those suffering from neuroses. He presented psychotherapy as a matter of public health care, a practice that had to respect and serve the individuality and autonomy of its patients.

With the armistice agreement in November 1918 all official interest in psychoanalysis came to a halt, as the army no longer had any need for it. It remained for Karl Abraham to remark in a mood of sour grapes that 'I cannot even say that I am unhappy about this, for I did not like the idea that psycho-analysis should suddenly become fashionable because of purely practical considerations. We would rapidly have acquired a number of colleagues who would merely have paid lip service and would afterwards have called themselves psycho-analysts. Our position as outsiders will continue for the time being.'[56]

After the war, under a new government a 'Commission for Enquiry into Violation of Military Duty' was appointed by the Austrian Parliament, investigating the role of military psychiatrists. The principal target of accusations of malpractice was Julius von Wagner-Jauregg, Titular Professor of Psychiatry and Neurology at the University of Vienna and Director of the Department of Psychiatry at the Vienna General Hospital – the foremost representative of the Hapsburg Empire's psychiatric establishment.[57] Freud was invited to testify for the commission and submitted a written 'Memorandum on the Electrical Treatment of War Neurotics', thus making an official appearance in the question of war neuroses.[58] As a final illustration of the intricate interrelation of political power and psychiatric knowledge, this appearance took place in a courtroom.

Out of a feeling of patriotic duty Wagner-Jauregg had volunteered to treat neurotic soldiers during the war. As he reported in his testimony, he regarded them as insufficiently motivated, with a tendency to put their personal welfare above the future of their country. Though Wagner-Jauregg seems not to have been directly involved in excesses of electrical shock treatment, the minutes of the hearing confirm the appalling picture of the treatment of war neurotics. Wagner-Jauregg's assistant had applied painful electrical shocks to soldiers' nipples and genitals.[59] Physicians without any neurological or psychiatric background were put in charge of departments in field hospitals in which nervous illnesses were treated. Isolation cells, cold showers, straitjackets, electrical shocks, naked exposure and public humiliation were common practices. These gruesome means were commonly used in a desperate bid to stem the tide of war neurotics and often caused irrevocable harm: electrical treatment was terminal for about twenty patients in German field hospitals.[60]

In his written memorandum Freud argued that psychiatric brutality was not based on mistaken theoretical conceptions held by physicians in good faith. Rather, brutal means were adopted by them against their better scientific judgement because of their political commitment to interests of state: 'It seemed expedient to treat the neurotic as a malingerer and to disregard the psychological distinction between conscious and unconscious intentions, although he was known not to be a malingerer.'[61] In his oral testimony Freud was even more condemning of his medical colleagues; he blamed them for ignoring the fact that neurotic symptoms appeared as the result of the defeat of the soldiers' conscious will by uncontrollable unconscious affects that had gained the upper hand: 'All neurotics are malingerers; they simulate without knowing it, and this is their sickness. We have to remember that there is a big difference between conscious inability and unconscious inability.'[62] Rather than aspects of the soldier's personality, Freud singled out conscription – that is, an action of the state – as 'the immediate cause of all war neuroses'. In his words, the compulsory draft created 'an unconscious inclination of the soldier to withdraw from the demands, dangerous and outrageous to his feelings, made upon him by active service. Fear of losing his life, opposition to the command to kill other people, rebellion against the ruthless suppression of his own personality by his superiors – these were the most important affective sources on which the inclination to escape from war was nourished.'[63]

A hostile attitude to war neurotics was not only factually misguided and therapeutically ineffective; it was also unjust towards neurotic soldiers. This was especially true of soldiers who tried too hard to be loyally devoted to the state and nation and could not allow their fears and aggressive feelings to become conscious. Hence they were most likely to fall ill in the attempt to repress them. As we can see, in his testimony Freud invoked a line of reasoning which he had used two and a half decades earlier in *Studies on Hysteria*. He pointed out again that it was not the patients' immorality which had caused their neurotic disorders. Rather, it was their sincere allegiance to conventional social norms which at the same time were also severely frustrating and anxiety-provoking to them, which gave rise to unresolvable inner conflicts and finally led to symptoms. Moreover, like in his case studies on hysteria, Freud's etiology of war neurosis explained mental disorders by an underlying all-pervasive experience of powerlessness rather than by sexual determinants. Finally, there are a number of parallels between Freud's opposition to the commonly accepted concept and treatment of hysteria in the late nineteenth century and his critique of the role which the psychiatric establishment played during the First World War. He defended shell-shocked soldiers against the contempt and hostility which they received, just as he had defended hysterical women against stigmas which the dominant medico-political discourse had attached to them. And in both instances he condemned the tendency of doctors to regard patients as enemies and to use violence in order to force them into prescribed social roles. Freud denounced war psychiatrists for adopting a therapeutic procedure which, in his words,

> bore a stigma from the very first. It did not aim at the patient's recovery, or not in the first instance; it aimed above all, at restoring his fitness for service. Here Medicine was serving purposes foreign to its essence. The physician himself was under military command and had his own personal dangers to fear – loss of seniority or a charge of neglecting his duty – if he allowed himself to be led by considerations other than those prescribed for him. The insoluble conflict between the claims of humanity, which normally carry decisive weight for a physician, and the demands of a national war was bound to confuse his activity.[64]

What had made Freud abandon his earlier position of abstinence and ambiguity and brought him to reflect publicly and critically on the relations between the state and medicine, the army and psychiatry – if only as an after-thought? Austria's military defeat had resolved some of the contradictions inherent in the position adopted by Freud and other psychoanalysts during the war. It certainly had cooled Freud's patriotic enthusiasm, thus allowing for a reconciliation of his private pro-Austrian feelings and public role as a detached scientist. Finally, some of the social aspirations of psychoanalysis seemed to have been fulfilled during the war. Freud's invitation to the hearings and the official interest in the Budapest Conference indicated that Freud's new science had gained political and scientific recognition, albeit as an outsider. Psychiatry's move from somatic to psychic etiology of war neuroses made psychoanalytic therapeutic techniques appear to be based on more solid theoretical ground. They had proven to be not only impartial and humane, but also efficient and usable for collective purposes. War psychiatry, on the other hand, had acquired a bad name through its failures and violence. Thus, the Wagner-Jauregg hearings allowed Freud to demarcate psychoanalysis as an autonomous discipline as opposed to psychiatric brutality which had developed in subservience to the old regime. Freud could confidently condemn opportunism, confusion and cruelty, speaking from the vantage point of therapeutic success, scientific independence and objective truth.

Despite his critical stance, Freud played the role of a loyal opposition to mainstream psychiatry. First, he honoured the medical *ésprit de corps* and put no blame on Wagner-Jauregg, thus avoiding the issue of the accused physician's personal liability. Second, rather than placing responsibility for their actions on the shoulders of the army psychiatrists, he presented the conditions of conscription as the ultimate cause of medical brutality – despite the fact that psychoanalysts treated their patients under the same conditions without resorting to violence. Instead of assigning blame, he compared the psychiatrists' excessive enthusiasm for their duty to the nation to the soldiers' rigid and exaggerated attempt to remain moral and respectable. In his eyes, the practitioners of war psychiatry had been caught between contradictory commitments to their patients on the one hand, and to the army on the other hand. Contrary to the true aims of their profession they let their quest for respectability determine their activity. As a result, they found themselves in a situation similar to that of the neurotic soldiers whom they tried to cure. As Freud explained to the commission, the inhumanity of psychiatric practice was also a symptom of a fundamentally pathological condition:

> The physicians had to play a role which turned them into something like machine guns behind the front, of driving fugitives back. This certainly was the intention of the War Office . . . But then, this was rather an unsuitable task for the medical profession. The physician should primarily act as the patient's champion, not somebody else's. His function is impaired as soon as he starts serving someone else. At the moment at which he is ordered to make people fit for active duty as soon as possible, there necessarily arises a conflict for which one cannot possibly blame the medical profession. There is no compromise between subordination to humanitarian principles and general conscription.[65]

Undoubtedly, the conduct of psychoanalytically inclined and trained doctors in the First World War and of non-analytically inclined physicians constitutes an instructive chapter in the history and politics of medicine. It shows how the state can attempt to colonize therapeutic techniques for its purposes and illustrates the dangers inherent in a situation in which medical authority is backed up by military hierarchy. The behaviour of the large bulk of non-analytical army psychiatrists confirms once more claims concerning the readiness of doctors to subordinate medical theory and practice to political goals. Moreover, this episode shows that in the peaceful times of the late nineteenth century this hierarchy of values led doctors mainly to victimize women, but that conditions of war brought them to use brutal means against men as well. Since hysterical symptoms were explained as signs of unreliability, depravity, weakness of will and boundless selfishness, physicians inflicted physical pain on all those who fell ill and seemed to resist more moderate methods of treatment. In the guise of therapy they used methods of torture against their patients, men and women alike, if the demands of a collective – race, society, nation, state or army – legitimized them in doing so. However, this story of the treatment of war neuroses also demonstrates that even when the values of such collectives legitimized the use of violence and coercion in therapy, psychoanalytic practitioners abstained from having recourse to such means, because their theoretical and clinical framework ruled them out unequivocally.

Finally, one may examine the epidemic of war neuroses on the level of patients rather than doctors. From this perspective one notices that when men were caught in a prolonged and pervasive experience of powerlessness, but also attempted to remain loyal to frustrating and anxiety-provoking social norms, substantial numbers of them responded by producing symptoms – just as hysterical women had done in times of peace.[66] As Elaine Showalter has said: 'shell shock was the body language of masculine complaint, a protest against the concept of "mainliness" as well as against war.'[67] Thus, although in the second chapter I have explained hysteria as an unconscious and pathological protest of women against restrictive gender roles, the war neuroses demonstrate that this phenomenon and its explanation cannot be limited to women.

13 Authority for Hire

It appears that the war had given new life to questions concerning the limits of legitimate therapeutic authority and the dangers of its abuse, questions which troubled Freud throughout his therapeutic practice. In this chapter I wish to explore Freud's thinking on the problems and dynamics of the analyst's authority *vis-à-vis* patients, patients' resistance against analytic authority, as well as their submission to it. After the Wagner-Jauregg proceedings were over, the first essay which Freud published was *Group Psychology and the Analysis of the Ego*. He had completed a draft of the essay in January 1920, the month in which he was not only asked by the Wagner-Jauregg commission to submit a written statement on the treatment of war neurotics, but also met its chairperson and wrote his memorandum. Moreover, the Wagner-Jauregg hearings took place only a few months before he gave his essay its final form.

In this essay – which deals with mass psychology and is discussed in detail in chapter 17 – Freud returned to his early experience with hypnotic suggestion in Nancy. More than two decades after his trip to Liébeault and Bernheim he emphasized the principled nature of his opposition to suggestive hypnotism. Retrospectively, he could 'remember even then feeling a muffled hostility [*Gegnerschaft*] to this tyranny of suggestion. When a patient who showed himself unamenable was met with the shout: "What are you doing? *Vous vous contre-suggestionnez!* [you counter-suggest yourself]", I said to myself that this was an evident injustice and an act of violence. For the man certainly had a right to counter-suggestions if people were trying to subdue [*unterwerfen*] him with suggestions.'[1]

Later in the same paper, Freud developed a three-sided analogy, comparing three forms of the dynamics of love and power by juxtaposing the complete dependence of the hypnotized on the hypnotist with the obedience of a crowd to their leader and the 'bondage

[*Hörigkeit*]' of a person in love in the hands of the beloved. According to Freud's critical comments, in all cases '[t]here is the same humble subjection [*demütige Unterwerfung*], the same compliance, the same absence of criticism, towards the hypnotist as towards the loved object. There is the same sapping of the subject's own initiative.'[2]

As we see, Freud presented his reticence from the dynamics of absolute authority and dependence as having been motivated from the very beginning by a libertarian outlook on therapeutic politics. However, while Freud disapproved of all coercive or imperative expressions of authority in therapeutic settings, he certainly did not object to the therapeutic use of authority *per se*. On the contrary, as I have pointed out earlier, throughout the late 1880s and early 1890s he was in search of means to establish therapeutic authority over patients. In fact, in those early days of the talking cure he asserted that 'a physician – even a non-hypnotist – is never better satisfied than when he has repressed a symptom from a patient's attention by the power of his personality and the influence of his words – and his authority'.[3]

Indeed, much of Freud's discourse on therapeutic technique can be read as an extended meditation on the sources, limitations and functions of the analyst's legitimate authority in the consulting room. This discourse presents the face-to-face politics of psychoanalytic practice as embedded in a dialectical structure: it is based on a voluntary contract which deploys the analyst's authority in order to free the patient from unconscious forces leading to submission to authority.

In Freud's view psychoanalytic practice can succeed only if it is recognized by both sides as an agreement concluded by independent agents. As he put it, he tried to follow the rule 'of not taking on a patient for treatment unless he was *sui juris*, not dependent on anyone else in the essential relations of his life'.[4] In another instance he emphasized by italics that 'if the right of a patient to make a free choice of his doctor were suspended, an important precondition for influencing him mentally [*seelische Beeinflussung*] would be abolished'.[5]

In fact, Freud depicted the analytic contract as based on principles which are analogous to the ones which provide the ground of the social contract in liberal political theories. Its foundation is the analysand's free choice of, and consent to, an authority who is given the power to lay down the law under which the analysis is conducted, on condition that its regulations serve to promote the analysand's well-being and respect his or her autonomy. Freud stated that analysis both 'presupposes the consent of the person who is being analysed and a situation in which there is a superior and a subordinate'.[6] He also placed strict limitations on the analyst's exercise of power. As he pointed out, beyond the determination of basic conditions designed to make the analysis possible at all, such as the 'stringent régime' of money, time and physical posture, the analyst is not to structure the analytic process.[7] Indeed, even though Freud intended the analyst to interpret the patient's utterances, the only obligation he explicitly imposed on him was a negative one, demanding the analyst to refrain from exercising any directive control over the patient. Instead, the analyst has to become an authority without qualities: 'The doctor should be opaque to his patients and, like a mirror, should show them nothing but what is shown to him.'[8]

However, the reality of Freud's psychoanalytic practice was some-what different from its ideology; that is, from the way he portrayed it in general declarations of principle. In contrast with the latter, Freud did accept patients who did not come to his consulting room out of their own free will and who certainly did not pay for his services out of their own money. For instance, when Dora/Ida Bauer arrived at Freud's house in autumn 1900, she did not come there willingly. 'It was,' Freud wrote, 'only her father's authority [*Machtwort*] which induced her to come to me at all'.[9] This beginning of one of Freud's most famous case studies clearly contradicts the liberal principles which Freud presented as the basis of the analytic alliance. In fact, as Freud explained, Dora/Ida's father had decided to hand her over to the physician at the Berggasse, with the plea to 'bring her to reason' after his daughter had started to interfere with his extra-marital affair, fainted and left a suicide note.[10]

Moreover, as any reader of this case study notices, Freud did not limit himself to playing the role of a blank screen. Throughout his treatment of Dora one finds Freud proceeding like a master detective intent on demolishing a defendant's alibi and on extracting a confession by confronting her with overwhelming circumstantial evidence. His style is far from the elegance of a Sherlock Holmes; rather, Dora is faced with the bullish forcefulness of a Hercule Poirot, who uses her recollections 'against her', while she persists 'in denying' his contentions, until finally the young woman gives in.[11] In Freud's words, 'when the quantity of material that had come up had made it difficult for her to persist in her denial, she admitted'.[12] According to the Swiss psycho-analyst Raymond de Saussure, who was analyzed by Freud in 1920, 'Freud was not a good psychoanalytic clinician. . . . he had practised suggestion too long not to have been materially affected by it. When he was persuaded of the truth of something, he had considerable difficulty in waiting until this verity became clear to his patient. Freud wanted to convince him immediately. Because of that, he talked too much.'[13]

However, Freud's account of Dora's case not only bears witness to his active and interfering behaviour, it also provides a telling illustration of a contractual right which patients retain throughout psychoanalytic therapy, namely, the right to terminate treatment at any time they wish. Dora broke off her therapy with Freud just as his 'hopes of a successful termination of the treatment were at their highest',[14] leaving him with nothing but a 'Fragment [*Bruchstück*] of an Analysis of a Case of Hysteria' in his hands, as the title of Freud's case study acknowledges.

What, then, are the obligations which the analytic contract imposes on patients? According to Freud, it stipulates that as long as a patient is in analysis, he or she should 'relate everything that his self-observation can detect, and keep back all the logical and affective objections that seek to induce him to make a selection from among them'.[15] Freud pronounced the obligation to associate freely as the 'fundamental rule' or 'sacred rule' of the analytic setting, which the patient has to 'obey'.[16] In his words, the patient's commitment not to consciously withhold anything that might come into his or her mind, even though it might seem irrelevant, unpleasant or nonsensical, 'is henceforward to govern his behaviour towards us', making thereby 'a duty of the most complete honesty'.[17] Freud recounted how another of his famous patients, the Rat Man, at one stage interrupted a difficult session, 'got up from the sofa and begged me to spare him the recital of the details. . . . naturally I could not grant him something which was beyond my power. He might just as well ask me to give him the moon.'[18]

As these examples show, and as I have mentioned in the discussion of *Studies on Hysteria* above, the term 'free associations' which Freud used to describe this obligation is somewhat misleading, since it invokes liberal rhetoric and appears to offer the patient the right of free speech. But rather than granting a liberty to the patient within the psychoanalytic setting, 'free' associations are an obligation which the analysand has to consent to as part of the contract. Confronted with a patient attempting to resist the terms of the fundamental rule, Freud played the role of loyal guardian of the psychoanalytic constitution and acted as if he was a strict law-enforcing authority which could not tolerate any violations of its charter, even though he admitted: 'One hardly comes across a single patient who does not make an attempt at reserving some region or other so as to prevent treatment from having access to it. . . . Analytic treatment does not, of course, recognize any such right of asylum.'[19]

Freud justified the demand for the patient's submission to the fundamental rule as being a necessary requirement to enable the unconscious to insurrect against its habitual suppression by the patient's self-censorship and to take over the direction of his or her speech. However, by denying patients the right to exert rational and moral self-control over their words, the terms of the analytic contract clearly violate fundamental liberal principles of individual privacy and autonomy – even though the agreement itself is based on the patient's consent. These contractual terms turn a patient's speech and silence, activity and passivity into part of the analytic setting, legitimizing the analyst to consider everything that occurs within fixed boundaries of time and place as falling within the scope of interpretation.[20] In this way the analytic encounter takes on features of a 'total institution' which allows the analyst to interpretively appropriate all of the patient's utterances and silences. Hence Michel Foucault has suggested that Freud 'focused upon this single presence – concealed behind the patient and above him, in an absence that is also a total presence – all the powers that had been distributed in the collective existence of the asylum; he transformed this into an absolute Observation, a pure, impassive Silence, a Judge who punishes and rewards in a judgement that does not even condescend to language'.[21]

On the one hand, Foucault seems right in stressing that psychoanalytic practice proceeds in a strictly regimented space, in which the patient is deprived of any possibility to change the rules, and is asked to reveal his or her secrets in 'free' speech, while the analyst is invisible and responds with parsimonious, neutral and calculated utterances or silences.[22] On the other hand, however, there is an obvious and significant difference between Freud's consulting room and the asylum, which Foucault neglects. Rather than a warder acting in conditions of confinement, the analyst is a partner to a contractual agreement which the analysand can choose to terminate at any given moment. Although it seems inevitable that an analysand's abrupt departure will be interpreted by the analyst, the consulting room is not locked, the patient will not be stopped and does not even have to listen to the analyst if he or she chooses not to.

Thus, the analytic setting is constituted as an incongruous duality of liberal and authoritarian elements and cannot be reduced to either of them. This duality is reflected in Freud's texts, which depict analyst and analysand as two individuals meeting in one social space both as allies and antagonists. As Freud pointed out, while the analyst's interpretations are considered legitimate interventions undertaken by force of the authority delegated by the patient, he finds himself resisted against by the patient. According to Freud, in such cases the patient denies the analyst's authority and behaves 'as though he were outside the treatment and as though he had not made this agreement with the doctor'.[23]

Paradoxically, in the course of their analysis patients end up resisting the one fundamental rule to which they have given their original consent, sabotaging thereby the very purpose for which they have come to see their analyst. According to Freud, such resistances come in various shapes and forms, but they all have the same purpose: to exert a countervailing force against the analyst's attempts to obtain access to the unconscious.

'Resistance' (*Widerstand*), this most military of terms in Freud's vocabulary for the analytic process, is central to Freud's discourse on therapeutic technique. Already in *Studies on Hysteria* Freud described the work of the analyst in the language of strategy and warfare; in his words:

> We force our way into the internal strata, overcoming resistances [*Widerstand*] all the time; . . . we experiment how far we can advance with our present means . . . we are constantly making up arrears . . . By this method we at last reach a point at which we can stop working in strata and can penetrate [*vordringen*] by a main path straight to the nucleus of the pathogenic organization. With this the struggle is won. [*Damit ist der Kampf gewonnen*], though not yet ended. . . . But now the patient helps us energetically. His resistance [*Widerstand*] is for the most part broken.[24]

From early on Freud defined the task of treatment as 'combating'[25] or 'lifting'[26] resistances, and in his case study of the Rat Man he declared '[t]he overcoming of resistances' to be 'a law of the treatment'.[27] In this fashion Freud depicted the analytic process as a prolonged confrontation between analyst and patient in which '[t]he patient brings out of the armoury of the past the weapons with which he defends himself against the progress of the treatment – weapons which we must wrest from him one by one'.[28] As Freud explained, in therapeutic warfare '[t]he length of the path of development and the wealth of the material are not the decisive factors. It is more a question of whether the path is clear. An army can be held up for weeks on a stretch of country which in peace time an express train crosses in a couple of hours – if the army has to overcome the enemy's resistance there.'[29]

Thus, while Freud's discourse represents the framework of psychoanalytic practice as a liberal contract, it depicts its internal dynamics as those of a war, in which the analysand struggles against the analyst's authority. This duality is the necessary result of the fact that the same individual who consents to analysis also opposes its procedures.

How does this duality come about? As Freud saw it, patients seek therapeutic help because they are immersed in a pathological internal conflict which drains their energies, but which they are incapable of resolving. In Freud's words: '[T]he pathogenic conflict in neurotics is not to be confused with a normal struggle between mental impulses both of which are on the same psychological footing. In the former case the dissension is between two powers, one of which has made its way to the stage of what is preconscious or conscious while the other has been held back at the stage of the unconscious. For that reason the conflict cannot be brought to an issue.'[30]

Incapable of gaining the upper hand, the patient's rational, conscious 'I' seeks someone who can provide support 'in order to subdue portions of his id which are uncontrolled – that is to say to include them in the synthesis of his ego'.[31] In Freud's view the patient's conscious ego concludes the contract with the analyst in order to regain both the forces which repression has restricted to the unconscious and those which the ego has to expend in order to maintain these repressions. However, since the ego is simultaneously involved in maintaining repressions – and thus resistances – and seeking an ally against them, it is ambivalent towards the goal of analysis. On the one hand it seeks an ally and on the other hand it 'treats recovery itself as a new danger'.[32] Hence the analysand both is ready to accept the analyst's authority as part of the contract and opposes it in order to prevent what has been repressed – that is, has been deemed to be unpleasant, immoral, or shameful – from entering consciousness.

What is the aim of the analyst in this complex contractual confrontation? Freud stressed that analysts should not try to solve their patients' conflicts, establish a harmonious inner order, suggest specific forms of behaviour or lead one psychic agency to a decisive victory over another. As Freud put it most famously in the conclusion to *Studies on Hysteria*, the talking cure cannot promise happiness; at best it can transform 'hysterical misery into common unhappiness'.[33] In other words, the purpose of analysis is to transform a pathological – that is unresolvable – conflict into a normal one, in which opposing forces actually come in contact with one another. As Freud pointed out: 'A true decision can only be reached when they both meet on the same ground. To make this possible is, I think, the sole task of our therapy.'[34]

To put it differently, the goal of psychoanalytic therapy is to dialectically overcome a pathological conflict, to achieve an *Aufhebung* in which the conflict is abolished in its original, pathological form, but lifted to a higher, more conscious plane, while the discordant elements involved are preserved as such. Not the pursuit of any particular course of action, but the ability to make autonomous choices, manage and resolve conflicts, provides proof of therapeutic success or cure. The face-to-face politics in the psychoanalytic consulting room are to lead to the patient's individual self-mastery, in the sense which has been clarified in chapter 10. As Freud put it, 'if, having grown independent after the completion of their treatment, they decide on their own judgement in favour of some midway position between living a full life and absolute asceticism, we feel our conscience clear whatever their choice'.[35] True to liberal ideals of pluralism and tolerance, Freud argued against those who recommended that 'psycho-analysis should place itself in the service of a particular philosophical outlook on the world and should urge this upon the patient for the purpose of ennobling his mind. In my opinion, this is after all only to use violence, even though it is overlaid with the most honourable motives.'[36]

In order to portray the psychoanalytic setting as an arena of face-to-face politics, I have discussed until now various aspects of the historical context of the psychoanalytic setting, its contractual foundations, structure and purpose, as well as Freud's assumption that patients are incapable of keeping the contract. However, nothing has been said about the processes which are supposed to lead to the disruption of the contractual agreement and the technique which is to be used to understand and overcome patients' resistances. This is so because I have left out that which lies at the very heart of psychoanalytic practice and which Freud denoted by the term 'transference' (*Übertragung*).

In Freud's parlance it is transference which makes patients behave in an inappropriate manner, provides the material to be interpreted by the analyst, and explains patients' resistance to these interpretations, as well as their readiness to accept them. In short, transference is the motor of psychoanalysis; it is what makes it work and allows analysts and patients to reach their aim. As Freud put it, it constitutes the 'battlefield' where 'all the mutually struggling forces should meet one another'[37] and where 'victory must be won'.[38] What Freud termed 'transference' involves a *'mésalliance'* or a 'false connection'[39] in which unconscious wishes and fantasies are displaced from the past into the present, from childhood into adult life and from early love objects and authorities to later ones.

For Freud nobody ever lives fully and exclusively in the present. All human beings acquire early in life certain unconscious but prototypical patterns which mould the way in which they relate to others as objects of their love and authority figures. As Freud explained, especially for neurotics – whose emotional life is dominated by the past to a higher degree than that of 'normal' people – relationships in the present are but 'new editions or facsimiles'[40] of an infantile *cliché* which is maintained in their unconscious, and in whose mould current behaviour is each time printed afresh.

Obviously, much of Freud's discussion of transference has to do with libidinal impulses and love which are transferred to the analyst. However, as I argue in part IV, in Freud's discourse love and power are always intertwined, for in his view love provides the foundation of authority, and authority, in turn, evokes love. Here, however, I wish to show that underlying Freud's discussion of transference, too, there is a political discourse *par excellence* which is concerned with the vicissitudes of authority in the face-to-face politics of the psychoanalytic setting.

On the one hand, transference 'clothes the doctor with authority', by putting the analyst in place of the patient's father or mother.[41] However, what distinguishes psychoanalysis from other methods of treatment, is not the existence of transference *per se*, which Freud took to be an inevitable part of all social relations. Rather, since the analyst is present only as an opaque authority, which remains mostly invisible, silent and passive, disclosing little about his or her own feelings, the patient's fantasies and wishes towards authority figures can come to the fore.

The nebulous presence of the analyst in the clinical setting of psychoanalysis provides patients with an object, in reference to which their neurotic patterns reproduce themselves under controlled conditions. The artificial creation of such a 'transference neurosis' constitutes the principal ruse of psychoanalysis, for it makes manifestations of the unconscious accessible to the analyst's observation and intervention.

Hence the consulting room was for Freud the only social space where the neurotics' unconscious, infantile attitudes to love objects and authority figures can be unmasked as powerful factors which interfere with their lives. As Freud explained: 'while the patient experiences [transference] as something real and contemporary, we have to do our therapeutic work on it, which consists in a large measure in tracing it back to the past'.[42] The ability to make patients aware of transference constituted for Freud the major clinical achievement of psychoanalysis and distinguishes the latter sharply from suggestive methods, where 'we can observe transference occurring with the greatest intensity and in the most unworthy forms, extending to nothing less than mental bondage'.[43] While other physicians reinforce their patient's subservience through their treatment, the task of the analyst is 'constantly to tear the patient out of his menacing illusion and to show him again and again that what he takes to be new real life is a reflection of the past'.[44]

As long as the effects of the transference are positive and reinforce the analyst's authority over the patient, Freud saw no reason for it to be interpreted. His advice was to wait 'until the transference, which is the most delicate of all procedures, has become a resistance'.[45] However, transference needs to be analysed when it turns negative and undermines the analyst's authority, that is, when a patient 'does not *remember* anything of what he has forgotten and repressed, but *acts* it out. He reproduces it not as a memory but as an action. . . . For instance the patient does not say he remembers that he used to be defiant and critical towards his parent's authority; instead, he behaves in that way to the doctor.'[46]

Yet, even in such cases transference can be used in the analysis, since by presenting the analyst with 'a piece of real experience'[47] the patient repeats an infantile pattern of his relationship with authority figures. As Freud pointed out: 'The hostile feelings are as much an indication of an emotional tie as the affectionate ones, in the same way as defiance signifies dependence as much as obedience does, though with a "minus" instead of a "plus" sign before it.'[48]

However, rather than exploiting the transference in order to maintain and bolster his authority status, the analyst systematically aims at its abolition by revealing its unreal aspects to the patient and by making it clear to the latter that he is being given a fantasy role which he refuses. Instead of simply benefitting from the authority with which transference has endowed him, the analyst undermines it 'by pointing out to the patient that his feelings do not arise from the present situation and do not apply to the person of the doctor, but that they are repeating something that happened to him earlier'.[49] By revealing behaviour which stems from transference as being incongruous with the rational contractual analytic setting, the analyst can make unconscious elements conscious to the patient and turn the latter's attitudes towards authority – such as unconscious compulsions to fear, flatter, placate, escape, defy or resist authority figures, and to regard them as benevolent, aloof, critical or punishing – into a crucial issue of the therapy.[50]

Freud considered the ability to get patients to recognize transference for what it is, to be contingent upon the very authority which the analyst seeks to undermine: 'The intellectual content of our explanations cannot do it, for the patient, who shares all the prejudices of the world around him, need believe us as little as our scientific critics do. The neurotic sets to work because he has faith in the analyst, and he believes him because he acquires a special emotional attitude towards the figure of the analyst. Children, too, only believe people they are attached to.'[51] In other words, the analyst's authority and the patient's way of responding to it is not only the subject-matter of psychoanalytic practice, it also constitutes its medium. According to Freud, if understanding is to liberate patients from the trappings of their past, it cannot do so on its cognitive merits but has to win cunningly by exploiting the false connection which furnishes it with mistaken authority. In order to be an effective therapist, the analyst has to use the parental authority with which the patient has endowed him.

The dialectics involved here are precisely those which Thomas Wartenberg has defined as typical of the exercise of 'transformative power', which he contrasts with paternalism.[52] In a paternalistic relationship a dominant agent exercises power over a subordinate agent in the name of the latter's interests, assuming that the subordinate agent cannot recognize or realize them. Hypnotic suggestion entails a paternalistic use of power: as we have seen, it makes use of patterns of social domination, such as class differentials and habitual deference, for the benefit of the subordinate agent. As Wartenberg explains: 'In a transformative use of power, a dominant agent also exercises power over a subordinate agent for the latter's benefit. In doing so, however, the dominant agent's aim is not simply to act for the benefit of the subordinate agent; rather, the dominant agent attempts to exercise his power in a way that the subordinate agent learns certain skills that undercut the power differentials between her and the dominant agent. The transformative use of power is a use of power that seeks to bring about its own obsolence by means of the empowerment of the subordinate agent.'[53]

In opposition to the paternalistic exercise of power – which is characteristic of suggestion – the analyst's use of his authority is self-transcending. He deploys his authority strategically, in order to create a social experience which teaches patients about unconscious elements which make it impossible for them to act as reasonable partners in a contractual agreement. In this way patients can gain control over these elements and learn to act as autonomous agents. Therefore I consider the transformative dialectics of psychoanalytic practice to be political: they are structured around issues of consent, resistance and authority, and Freud invoked imagery of conflict, alliances, rights and warfare in order to portray them. Most importantly, however, Freud placed the dynamics of the psychoanalytic dyad in the service of a political goal: the abolition of dependence and the promotion of individual autonomy. As he put it:

> If the patient puts the analyst in the place of his father (or mother), he is also giving him the power which his super-ego exercises over his ego. . . . The new super-ego now has an opportunity for a sort of *after-education* of the neurotic; it can correct mistakes for which his parents were responsible. . . . But at this point a warning must be given against misusing this new influence. However much the analyst may be tempted to become a teacher, model and ideal for other people and to create men in his own image, he should not forget that this is not his task in the analytic relationship, and indeed that he will be disloyal to his task if he allows himself to be led by his inclinations. If he does, he will only be repeating a mistake of the parents who crushed their child's independence by their influence, and he will only be replacing the patient's earlier dependence by a new one. In all his attempts at improving the patient the analyst should respect his individuality.[54]

14 Mighty Words

As we have seen earlier, Freud 'politicized' the clinical setting of psychoanalysis through the use of a repertoire of metaphors and analogies which portray the therapeutic process by comparisons to large-scale public institutions of power and authority. Now I wish to show that Freud also structured the clinical setting of psychoanalysis as an arena for verbal politics, where speech acts as a weapon of attack, control, coercion, domination, defence and liberation. In fact, words are the only means of power which Freud allowed in the carefully isolated social space of the analytic consulting room. This political conception of psychoanalytic practice, I contend, corresponds more closely to the logical and linguistic structure of Freud's discourse on therapy than the two approaches currently prevalent in the literature, which refer to therapeutic practice either as a hermeneutics concerned with meanings and purposes, or as a scientific investigation of causes and mechanisms (I return to this comparison in my conclusions). As we have seen, the main work of the analyst is to interpret patients' transference and resistances; that is, to decipher speech and behaviour which diverge from the contractual agreement and to trace them to underlying latent or hidden causes. Obviously, this also obliges the analyst to speak in response to the speech of patients.

Freud stressed the role of the analyst's words as vehicles of influence in the face-to-face politics of the consulting room because it is not the patient's ignorance which is at the root of neurosis, but the forces of repression and resistance. The analyst battles with an invisible, cunning and devious opponent who will use every possible trick to conceal hidden desires and wishes, and resist the knowledge which psychoanalysis may bring.[1] As Freud explained:

> The pathological factor is not his ignorance in itself, but the root of this ignorance in his *inner resistances*: it was they that first

called this ignorance into being and they still maintain it now. The task of the treatment lies in combating these resistances. Informing the patient of what he does not know because he has repressed it is only one of the necessary preliminaries to the treatment. If knowledge about the unconscious were as important for the patient as people inexperienced in psychoanalysis imagine, listening to lectures or reading books would be enough to cure him. Such measures, however, have as much influence on the symptoms of nervous illness as a distribution of menu-cards in a time of famine has upon hunger. The analogy goes even further than its immediate application; for informing the patient of his unconscious regularly results in an intensification of the conflict in him and an exacerbation of his troubles.[2]

Victor Wolfenstein has rightly pointed out that interpretations are neither scientific hypotheses to be tested in a laboratory, nor exegetical exercises performed on narratives provided by the patient.[3] They are not statements of a disinterested observer and demand neither the patient's assent as corroboration, nor do they accept dissent as refutation. Rather, the analyst's words constitute tactical moves in face-to-face politics, which involve both partners to the analytic contract with their entire subjectivity in a complex interplay of conscious and unconscious forces.

Already in 1890 Freud wrote that 'words are the most important media by which one man seeks to bring his influence to bear on another',[4] and in 1893 he reminded his readers that 'as an English writer has wittily remarked, the man who first flung a word of abuse at his enemy instead of a spear was the founder of civilization. Thus words are substitutes for deeds, and in some circumstances (e.g. in Confession) the only substitutes.'[5] In the same spirit Freud admonished an imaginary interlocutor in *The Question of Lay Analysis* not to underestimate the power of the word: 'After all it is a powerful instrument; it is . . . our method of influencing other people. Words can do unspeakable good and cause terrible wounds. . . . originally the word was magic – a magical act; and it has retained much of its ancient power.'[6]

What magic, then, are the words of the analyst supposed to perform? Adopting a distinction made by Leonardo da Vinci, Freud compared the power of psychoanalytic interpretations to sculpting on the one hand, and, on the other hand, likened the commanding or prohibitive speech of the hypnotist to painting. While the analyst removes material, as the sculptor does, the hypnotist proceeds like a painter who covers a canvas with the strokes of his brush. Thus, the latter '*superimposes* something – a suggestion – in the expectation that it will be strong enough to *restrain* the pathogenic idea from coming to expression'. Analytic therapy, explained Freud, 'does not seek to add or to introduce anything new, but to *take away* something, to *bring out* something'.[7]

In order to illuminate the characteristics of the analyst's exercise of his verbal power, one may distinguish two concepts of power, parallel to Isaiah Berlin's two concepts of liberty, which I have discussed in chapter 10. A 'positive' notion of power can be identified, which designates actions in which one agent aims to force or manipulate another agent to think, say or do something in accordance with a particular discipline, ethic or ideal, which has been imposed on the latter by the former. On the other hand, a 'negative' concept of power describes actions by which one agent obstructs or prevents thoughts, actions or words of another agent.

By restricting the analyst's interventions to interpretation, Freud excluded both the positive and the negative exercise of power from the face-to-face politics of the psychoanalytic setting. Both in its negative and positive form, the exercise of power precedes the action of an agent who is to be forced into a certain course of behaviour or prevented from it. In contrast, it is characteristic of interpretation that it always follows the patient's speech and actions. Rather than to impel or prevent words or actions, psychoanalytic interpretations aim to undermine some of them in order to facilitate others. Though psychoanalytic interpretations are vehicles of power by means of which the analyst endeavours to bring the patient to do or say something which he or she otherwise would not do or say, the analyst's verbal power is always exercised subsequently to the patient's silence, talk or action in the consulting room, rather than before them, and ultimately aims to enable speech rather than to direct it.

There is thus an emancipatory project inherent in psychoanalytic practice, which commentators such as Jeffrey Abramson, Jürgen Habermas and Victor Wolfenstein have pointed out.[8] However, the notion of 'emancipation' is often used without clarification of what it involves. Therefore I explicate here both the general characteristics of emancipatory practice, as I see them, and the way in which they apply to the specific case of psychoanalytic practice.

Emancipatory practice, as we know it from the large-scale politics outside the consulting room, aims to unmask hidden cultural, social and economic forms of domination which force social agents – individuals and groups – into social roles which reproduce the existing

power structure and constrain full self-development. It seeks to uncover the connections which exist between parts of peoples' lives,
thereby allowing one to see these lives in the whole and enabling one
to grasp the significance of particular forms of behaviour in terms of
this whole. The result of this sort of analysis is a kind of enlightenment
in which various meanings of actions are made transparent. Thus
emancipatory practice attempts to facilitate forms of speech, behaviour and social organization which, rather than repeating established
patterns, transcend the limitations of the existing social order and its
conceptual schemes. It discloses the hidden logic of such dominant
conceptual schemes by means of which the social reality of a given
society is constituted and defined, the ways in which such schemes
frustrate the satisfaction of needs of some social actors, and the manner in which they serve the purposes of others. Inevitably, this endeavour leads to the reappraisal and subversion of the meaning
attributed to basic assumptions around which self-conceptions of
societies, groups and individuals are constructed. These consist of
notions of private and public, rights and obligations, private property
and the role of work, human needs and values, masculinity and
femininity, nature and culture.

Moreover, it is one of the aims of emancipatory practice to provide a
historical account of the origins and development of the existing
social order – its constitutive myths and cultural framework – in order
to reveal its partial and contingent nature. As long as social actors
consider that which is actual also to be rational and necessary, and are
capable of conceiving themselves and their social framework only in
terms of the meanings which are attributed to such notions in a given
social order, possibilities of alternative social organizations are pre-
cluded. Only by making social actors aware of the biased nature of
such patterns can distributions of power be renegotiated or negated
and processes of social transformation initiated. In other words,
emancipatory practice is dialectical. By placing actual social practices
in a wider context it seeks to reveal their negative character, negate the
negation immanent in them, and transcend limitations of the actual.

For instance, in order to bring about a revolutionary consciousness
of the working-class, Marxist theorists have undertaken to reconstruct
the history of the world from a materialist point of view. They have
attempted to reveal hidden forms of oppression and exploitation, and
the way in which assumptions and definitions concerning the nature
of political rights, private property, labour, and capital serve to perpetuate the class structure in capitalist societies and commodify human
relations. Similarly, feminist writers have re-written history from a

women's point of view and have aimed to disclose the way in which conventional definitions of the family, femininity, reproduction and the gendered nature of social discourse in general sustain, the patriarchal order. Questioning conventional social categories, such as those of the public–private and nature–nurture distinctions, they aim to open the road to a new self-conception of women, which allows them to break out of conventional social roles as daughters, wives and mothers which patriarchy has assigned to them.

What, then, are the characteristics which define the analyst's exercise of power as part of emancipatory practice? First, parallel to efforts to disclose constraining effects of social forces and cultural meanings, analytic interpretations expose processes in the patient's mind, of which the patient is unaware and which therefore have the power to structure the latter's behaviour in ways over which he or she has no control.

Second, analytic interpretations have a practical aim. As Freud clarified in his case study of Little Hans, 'a psychoanalysis is not an impartial scientific investigation, but a therapeutic measure. Its essence is not to prove anything, but merely to alter something.'[9] Hence, without the ensuing production of speech even the patient's explicit consent to an interpretation is without relevance, since it provides no indication that the transference has been resolved. As Freud put it: 'The [patient's] "Yes" has no value unless it is followed by indirect confirmations, unless the patient, immediately after his "Yes", produces new memories which complete and extend the construction. Only in such an event do we consider that the "Yes" has dealt completely with the subject under discussion.'[10] Freud underscored that '[o]nly the further course of the analysis enables us to decide whether our constructions are correct or unserviceable'.[11]

Third, as Freud's link between the correctness and the effectiveness of psychoanalytic interpretations shows, they form part of a politics of truth. The recollection of what is 'forgotten' or excluded from conventional discourse is said to be an accurate and complete representation of reality – in Freud's case, of the inner reality of the patient's mental world. At the same time, however, this truth is supposed to be politically efficacious. In other words, emancipatory practice is built on the assumption that it leads to truth, and that the truth of its interpretations constitutes part of their subversive power. Indeed, without the claim to truth and its liberating potential, emancipatory social movements cannot assert that they lead to freedom, rather than substituting one form of social oppression for another.

Similarly, Freud was emphatic in his rejection of claims that psychoanalysis is 'nothing more than a particularly well-disguised and particularly effective form of suggestive treatment'. He admitted that suggestion may play a role in psychoanalytic practice, and he stressed that the analyst's authority is instrumental in overcoming the patient's initial resistance to interpretation. But he consistently denied that suggestion could effect the permanent transformation in the patient's psychic world, which psychoanalysis sought to achieve. Speaking of the patient's readiness to accept the analyst's authoritative utterances, Freud explained: 'The doctor has no difficulty, of course, in making him a supporter of some particular theory and in thus making him share some possible error of his own. In this respect the patient is behaving like anyone else – like a pupil – but this only affects his intelligence, not his illness. After all, his conflicts will only be successfully solved and his resistances overcome if the anticipatory ideas he is given tally with what is real in him. Whatever in the doctor's conjectures is inaccurate drops out in the course of the analysis; it has to be withdrawn and replaced by something more correct.'[12]

Fourth, theories of emancipatory practice emphasize that truth has to be related to an actual social experience to be effective. In Marx's view, for instance, the working-class is likely to acquire a revolutionary consciousness only when social conditions are ripe for it, that is, when capitalism is at its height and workers experience the destructive and self-destructive character of its dynamics. Similarly, Freud also claimed that the analyst has 'to wait till he has come so near to the repressed material that [the patient] has only a few more steps to take under the lead of the interpretation you propose'.[13] Moreover, since the analyst's words are to stir a recollection in the patient, they have to refer to the patient's actual behaviour in the consulting room, that is, to instances in which unconscious impulses manifest themselves *in vivo* in transfer-ence and resistance. Only when they are brought into the contractual setting as 'a present-day force [*eine aktuelle Macht*]',[14] these impulses enter into the scope of the treatment, and can be interpreted and overcome. As Freud commented pointedly: 'it is impossible to destroy anyone *in absentia* or *in effigie*'.[15]

In other words, psychoanalytic interpretations seek to provide knowledge which is related to the patient's experience in the analytic relationship, in order to facilitate the initiation or resumption of a process of self-development that previously has been ruled out by a neurotic conflict.

Fifth, emancipatory practices have to overcome resistance. Obviously, the social agents which have had a part in the establishment of a *status quo*, or those which dominate it and benefit from it at present, have a vested interest in its maintenance. They tend to oppose emancipatory endeavours which might undermine their power and dismantle existing social structures. However, even those who are placed in a subordinate position by a social order often identify with its values and their social role, and are reluctant to embrace doctrines of change and liberation.

Similarly, as I have pointed out in chapter 13, the analyst has to overcome the patient's resistance. Freud depicted even the ego, which has been weakened by the waste of energy brought about by the mechanism of repression and has sought an ally who can support it in the psyche's civil war, as unwilling to lift the barriers of repression. Even though repression has led to an unresolvable pathological conflict, it has given the patient the benefit of not having to face that which has been expelled into the unconscious and is feared as being unpleasant, painful or immoral.

Sixth, analytic interpretations aim to overcome the compulsion to repeat old patterns by providing a history of that which has been repressed and 'forgotten'. Such genetic 'constructions' trace the origins of unconscious elements to pieces of the patient's early history, which, because they have been forgotten, the patient is compelled to repeat in adult life. As Freud explained: 'unconscious impulses do not want to be remembered . . . but endeavour to reproduce themselves. . . . The doctor tries to compel him to fit these emotional impulses into the nexus of the treatment and of his life-history, to submit them to intellectual consideration and to understand them in the light of their psychical value.'[16]

As Freud stated in various places, the aim of psychoanalytic practice is to replace repetition by remembering.[17] Intellectual knowledge acquired from the outside is of no therapeutic value. The aim of interpretation is, rather, to set in motion a process whereby a hidden inner knowledge is allowed to become conscious. By bringing such material into consciousness, the dimension of time – which is absent from the unconscious – can be imposed on it, and it becomes integrated into the subject's conscious self-conception. Obviously, this psychoanalytic task parallels attempts of emancipatory movements to recover 'forgotten' aspects of their history. Just as remembering is to free the patient from the need to repeat patterns of behaviour over which she or he has no control, Marxists and feminists argue that the achievement of historical self-awareness is necessary in order to create a collective self-conception among workers and women which will enable them to transcend the social roles ascribed to them in capitalism and patriarchy.

However, there are also six important aspects in which psychoanalytic therapy differs from emancipatory practices outside the consulting room. First, it is performed within a contractual agreement with a professional who is paid for his or her services. Second, it is conducted under conditions of confidentiality. Third, it aims at the emancipation of individuals only. Fourth, it seeks emancipation from oppressive inner, mental forces, rather than from dominant cultural, social, political or economic formations. Fifth, as both the feminist critique of Freud's behaviour in Dora's case, and my study of the activity of psychoanalysts during the Great War have shown, psychoanalysts return patients to their social roles even if these roles have been imposed on patients by coercion. Sixth, psychoanalytic practice severely proscribes its scope and aims. As I have pointed out before, Freud was weary of promises of total liberation. He rejected suggestions that psychoanalysts should try to push patients beyond the limits of their 'narrow personality',[18] and advised analysts to 'be tolerant to the weakness of a patient' and to 'be content if one has won back some degree of capacity for work and enjoyment for a person even of moderate worth'.[19]

Throughout this chapter the emancipatory project in psychoanalytic practice has been discussed from the point of view of the analyst, as it were. However, as has been pointed out earlier, in order to be able to act in an emancipatory fashion, the analyst has first to be accepted voluntarily as an authority by the patient. Indeed, the exercise of all forms of emancipatory or transformative power demands a relationship which is grounded in trust, in which an authority is acknowledged by a person or a group which freely adopts a subordinate position. As history has taught us, even though the initial establishment of such a hierarchical relationship is based on consent, it may lose its dynamic and self-transcending character and become stabilized into a paternalistic power structure.[20]

Ernest Gellner has argued that psychoanalytic practice is inherently self-stabilizing in precisely this fashion. In a *Huis Clos* presentation of the psychoanalytic setting, Gellner describes the patient entering into the consulting room as passing 'through a kind of "conceptual valve", permitting entry but blocking an exit'.[21] In his view, the terms of the analytical setting to which the patient consents, systematically delegitimize any criticism of the analyst, since such criticism is inevitably seen as driven by unconscious motives which can be exposed by the analyst's interpretation. As Gellner puts it: 'The patient is and must be deprived, if he is cooperating with the therapy, of retaining some stance from which he could attempt a critical evaluation of it.'[22] In addition, Gellner points to the transference as 'the real central emotional bond' which keeps the patient on the couch and in dependence on the analyst, so that the contractual framework which allows the patient the freedom to terminate the analytic relationship, becomes vacuous.[23] Thus, by raising high hopes, but without making any explicit promises of cure, the analytic setting places the patient in a powerless position from which there is no escape without the analyst's assent.

Gellner is right in pointing out that the ground rules of psychoanalytic practice do not place analysts and patients on an equal footing and make it unlikely that the latter may ever win in an argument with the former. However, it seems to me that he measures the analytic encounter too much by the yardstick of an intellectual debate. Moreover, a degree of voluntary dependence based on trust is not to be mistaken for complete powerlessness. A patient's ego which is strong enough to carry the burden of analysis, is also able to retain some independent capacity for criticism. As Dora's case exemplifies, a patient is capable of leaving treatment if she feels she is not really listened to, even if her analyst is a famous doctor and she is a young woman. Thus, even though Gellner points to a danger which is part of every emancipatory project, it appears that the protection which the psychoanalytic contract provides to those who seek its emancipatory action, is better than that which most other forms of emancipatory practice can offer. After all, licensing an analyst to interpret and thereby evade criticism is not the same as giving authority figures the power to silence their critics and though analytic consulting rooms have not turned into places of liberation for all, they have not become prison cells either.

Yet, though it does not seem to me that psychoanalytic practice inherently and inevitably turns into a paternalistic, oppressive practice, there can be no doubt that the trust placed in psychoanalytic practitioners has been betrayed in too many cases. Freud's own detailed case studies reveal that he never quite practised what he preached about therapy and that he was far from being a successful practitioner of the art which he had invented. As a number of commentators have pointed out, he adopted a more paternalistic and interfering attitude towards patients than his clinical principles allowed – sometimes with disastrous consequences.[24] However, the historical record which I have presented here also shows that the therapeutic principles initiated by Freud led him and his followers to relate to the weak and powerless – that is, to women and conscripted soldiers – in a manner that was consistently less coercive and more humane than that of other therapeutic practitioners. It seems to me that this should not be forgotten when one reads some of the recent vituperative attacks on Freud's therapeutic practice, which present it as totalitarian.[25]

Yet rather than dismissing critics of psychoanalysis in the same way in which they dismiss psychoanalysis, they should be taken as voicing a warning which is to be taken seriously by analysts and patients alike; for they point to a danger which cannot be ignored. They remind one rightly that psychoanalytic practice is set within a hierarchical framework, and that any such framework can easily deteriorate into an oppressive structure if there are no built-in safeguards which protect those who are placed in a subordinate position. It seems to me that this warning should be heeded precisely by those who wish to preserve and develop psychoanalysis as an emancipatory practice. It is to be hoped that by setting the historical record straight – as I have tried to do here – one can help encourage psychoanalytic practitioners to feel less on the defensive and become more prepared to uncover and combat abuses of power in the face-to-face politics of the consulting room, and to develop preventive measures against them – so that psychoanalysis can truly become the emancipatory practice Freud designed.

Part IV

Empires of Passion: Oedipal Politics in Freud's Writings on Social Relations

In earlier chapters I have maintained that much of Freud's thinking on therapy was concerned with the foundations and transformations of authority, its uses and abuses, and the dialectics of obedience, resistance and liberation. In the last part of this study I wish to establish that Freud's writings on the family, tribal society and crowds provide an unmistakably political and dialectical elaboration on the origins, development, dynamics and structure of these social phenomena.

As I show in the course of my discussion, Freud understood all social authority as structured according to an Oedipal pattern, where the child accedes to the father's injunctions and gives up incestuous sexual desires which are directed towards the mother. According to Freud, people who become authorities and elicit obedience from others are to be seen as father figures not only if they impose their laws in the face-to-face politics of their biological families, but also if they rule in the larger sphere of public politics. However, I suggest that while Freud traced all public forms of authority to Oedipal interactions, he also portrayed the dynamics of early sexual development in political terms. On the one hand, Freud presented politics in the public domain as shaped by an unconscious familial dynamics. On the other hand, he prefaced this depiction of public politics by the politicization of childhood sexuality.

By transposing the Oedipal dynamics from his libido theory to society at large, Freud created a social vision which is strikingly different from other perspectives on society in that it stresses the nature of human beings as bodily creatures driven by sexual desires which conflict with the demands of life in common. As we shall see, Freud's presentation of social relations elucidates that no society can completely ignore sexuality and that no individual can disregard the necessities of social life. It is because human beings are reluctant to renounce their pleasures for the sake of society that restrictions have to be imposed on them by father figures whose prohibitions they are ready to obey.

I also wish to show that Freud's social vision is dialectical; it suggests that paternal authority can never be completely obliterated. At most it can be dialectically overcome or *aufgehoben*, that is, abolished in its original form, but at the same time also lifted to a higher level where it is preserved. As I explicate in the course of this part, Freud used this dialectical conception of the Oedipal nature of authority in defence of authoritarianism. Moreover, in his writings on large-scale social processes Freud introduced a Lamarckian concept of an acquired phylogenetic inheritance into psychoanalysis, and thus reformulated basic tenets of psychoanalysis in an unfortunate manner. Finally, while I have argued that in his early writings on hysteria and in his clinical practice his attitude was more favourable towards the plight of women in the late nineteenth century than feminist critics have acknowledged, there can be no doubt that Freud's social vision exhibits a strong patriarchal bias. He presented all politics in terms of father–son relations and therefore as an activity in which only men take part, while he relegated women to the role of passive objects of male desire. Since I am critical of social theories which rely on hereditary assumptions and promote authoritarian and patriarchal values, I am less sympathetic towards Freud in this part than I have been in the first three parts.

15　Body Heat

According to Freud, the first social framework within which human beings have to cope with the conflict between sexual pleasures and social demands is the family. Referring to the child as a political creature as much as a *homo sexualis*, Freud construed the family as an arena of power struggles, which contains processes of submission, legitimation and liberation. In this way he extended the scope of politics into the nursery and the earliest days of human life, and turned love into an instrument of power. He attributed to the various stages of infantile sexual development not only erotogenic zones on the body of the child – from which desires are said to originate and where they can be satisfied – but also specific forms in which the child is said to conceive of itself in relation to its parents.

I intend to demonstrate here that each stage in the individual's sexual development gives rise to a different political style designed to cope with parental figures. To this end, this chapter is devoted to a reconstruction of the libido theory as a political rather than a sexual tale:

libidinal stage:	child's conception of relations with parents:	political style:
autoerotic	none	self-sufficiency
narcissistic	child above parents	domination
oral	child dependent on parents	compliance
anal	child opposes parents	defiance
phallic/Oedipal	child desires and fears parents	subordination
genital	child becomes free from parents	independence

Let me elaborate in detail what I regard as the politics of Freud's libidinal theory. His depiction of the first, autoerotic stage presents the infant entering life as an unorganized bundle of drives which have not yet been placed under a particular 'sexual régime', and whose activity

is under the exclusive control of the pleasure principle.[1] These component drives are not only isolated from one another, but also independent from the outside world; therefore Freud called them
'autoerotic'.[2] This autoerotism reflects the infant's original lack of
awareness of itself as a cohesive and coherent subject and of others as
potential objects of its desires.

According to Freud, after some time the infant unifies the sexual
drives and directs them towards a first object: its own body. This
unification occurs in the second, narcissistic stage, where the infant is
both subject and object of its own desires, and fantasizes that it is
omnipotent and self-sufficient, that is, capable of satisfying all its
wishes on its own. As long as the baby manages to maintain itself in
the fantasy of having absolute power over its desires, it loves itself
and no one else. Freud calls the narcissistic infant 'His Majesty the
Baby'[3] and describes it as a megalomaniac who is unaware of the
existence of others as independent beings.[4]

In fact, the baby is entirely dependent on its mother for nourishment. By failing in its practical activities – such as satisfying hunger
and thirst, sitting, standing-up or walking – it becomes conscious of
its limitations and its complete reliance on another person. In Freud's
words, the baby's ego which becomes conscious of these limitations is
'first and foremost a body-ego'.[5] Freud explained: 'In this way there is
for the first time set over against the ego an "object", in the form of
something which exists "outside" and which is only forced to appear
by a special action.'[6] This feeling of powerlessness, Freud argued,
'establishes the earliest situations of danger and creates the need to be
loved which will accompany the child through the rest of its life'.[7]

It seems that Freud presented childhood sexuality as crucially important for human development because it constitutes the first field of
power in human experience. At this primary stage of cognitive and
emotional development the infant finds itself locked into a closed
framework, where survival is dependent on parents who exercise
absolute control over its bodily needs and pleasures. Thus, for Freud
the child's love of parental figures and the latter's authority have their
common source in the control which parents exercise over their baby.
In his words, it is the baby's awareness of its real physical dependence
which brings forth its first love towards both 'the woman who feeds
him' and 'the man who protects him'.[8]

As we see, Freud postulated that domination evokes love in the
dependent party, and love in turn 'becomes an important, if not the
most fundamental source of authority'.[9] As he put it: 'Being loved by
an adult does not merely bring a child the satisfaction of a special

need; it also means that he will get what he wants in every other respect as well.'[10] Freud attributed to the baby a differentiated vision of its parents, where the mother appears primarily as a nurturing figure, while the father is seen as a protective authority. It may be true that in its complete dependence on the parents a baby cannot but regard them as persons of importance on whose recognition and care its well-being depends. The question remains open, however, why a baby should differentiate between female nurturance and male protection in the way in which Freud postulated, and why early experiences in child–parent relations could give rise to the father's protector image in the baby's mind.

Freud claimed that the baby's growing awareness of its dependence leads it to abdicate its fantasy throne and instead to crown its parents as a supreme authority. This new awareness of dependence comes to the fore especially in the third, oral stage, in which the baby's social relations still consist mainly of sucking at its mother's nipples. In contrast to the earlier autoerotic stage, however, the baby realizes now that the mother's breasts are not as completely under its control as it had imagined at first, because they belong to another person.

Confronted with this fact of life, the baby becomes ambivalent towards the breast that feeds it. Freud stated that the baby is tempted to bite it with the aim of 'abolishing the object's separate existence'.[11] According to Freud, the baby seeks to devour the breast as much as to gain nourishment from it, so that it will be 'assimilated by eating and . . . in that way annihilated as such'.[12] In Freud's view, by attempting to incorporate the mother's breast into itself, the baby aims to resolve its ambivalence towards the mother's power, that is, her ability to provide or withhold food. Freud claimed that the child's recognition of the parents' control over its needs and wishes also makes a possible loss of their love a dreaded prospect. Because children fear to lose their parents' love, the latter can grant or refuse affection at will and thus deploy it as an instrument of domination and control.[13]

In the fourth, anal stage, toilet training puts the child in a dilemma. It has to choose between, on the one hand, the parent's love and the security which it promises and, on the other hand, sexual pleasures which the child still exclusively derives from its own body. Freud assumed that retaining faeces in the bowels provides the child with pleasure. Urged by the parents to release them, the child can either give in to their pleading or assert its own will against theirs, at the cost of losing – temporarily – some of their love. In Freud's discourse faeces become the currency of the child's consent to authority: 'He either parts obediently with his faeces, "sacrifices" them to his love, or else retains them for purposes of autoerotic satisfaction and later as a means of asserting his own will.'[14] Or, as Freud put it in another instance: 'By producing them he can express his active compliance [*Gefügigkeit*] with his environment and, by withholding them, his disobedience [*Trotz*].'[15]

In the course of these struggles the father's image seems to change in the eyes of the child. Originally he appears as a protector, then his role becomes above all that of a restrictive, punishing figure. According to Freud: 'In the son's eyes his father embodies every unwillingly tolerated social restraint; his father prevents him from exercising his will, from early sexual pleasure and, where there is common property in the family, from enjoying it.'[16] The mother is at first presented as a person giving the baby food and warmth, and then as a frustrating object of infantile sexual fantasies, who fails to provide the satisfaction her child desires.

This transformation of the parents' role, as well as the conflict between the child's own will and that of the parents, comes to a head in the phallic period, in which penis and clitoris become the leading erotogenic zones in children. In this period masturbation is the characteristic form of gratification. However, because it is accompanied by Oedipal fantasies, Freud did not consider it a form of autoerotic sexuality.[17] As Freud put it, in the phallic stage there is for the first time 'a sexual object and some degree of convergence of the sexual impulses upon that object'.[18]

Freud assumed that the mother constitutes the sexual object of both sexes. According to him, only male sexual identity exists during this period, without there being a corresponding independent female identity. In Freud's words, in this phase the antithesis is 'between having a *male genital* and being *castrated*'.[19] This difference in the self-conception of boys and girls, which Freud portrayed as a result of their anatomy, leads to two ways in which the Oedipus complex is said to proceed from there on until it is superseded.

Boys desire the mother, but perceive her exclusive tie to the father. In the wake of more or less explicit threats of castration uttered by parents and nurses in response to masturbation, and the observation of sexual differences when they see a child of the other sex naked, they develop fantasies concerning the father's potentially castrating violence. Under the impact of such real and imagined threats of bodily mutilation, Freud explained, 'the child's ego turns away from the Oedipus complex'.[20] Thus, in Freud's discourse it is the exercise of parental authority which leads to the latency period in which sexual desires are largely abandoned until they reawake during puberty.[21]

While boys may never completely recover from the fear of losing their penis, girls come to accept themselves as castrated males. However, because they regard their mother as responsible for their lack of the penis, they too, turn away from her. Girls are also influenced by external threats – that is, parental authority – as well as a feeling of humiliation, to lower their sexual interests and to enter the latency period. However, Freud pointed out that in contrast to boys, 'girls remain in [the Oedipal complex] for an indeterminate length of time; they demolish it late and, even so, incompletely'.[22] In contrast to his discussion of male development, which contains concerned comments on the potentially grave effects of an unsuccessful resolution of the Oedipus complex, Freud claimed that 'it does little harm to a woman if she remains in her feminine Oedipus attitude' since this means that 'she will in that case choose her husband for his paternal characteristics and be ready to recognize his authority'.[23] According to Freud problems arise, rather, when women refuse to accept male authority; in his words, in such cases 'there comes to light the woman's hostile bitterness against the man, which never completely disappears in the relation between the sexes, and which is clearly indicated in the strivings and in the literary productions of "emancipated" women'.[24] It hardly needs to be spelled out that such an approach severely discredits the demand of women for equal rights.

Only by overcoming and resolving the Oedipal complex can the child mature into an independent adult and finally achieve what Freud called 'the liberation [*Ablösung*] of an individual as he grows up, from the authority of his parents'.[25] Otherwise neuroses develop, whose main characteristic is that they do not allow full sexual independence. In such cases 'the son remains all his life bowed beneath his father's authority and he is unable to transfer his libido to an outside sexual object'.[26] However, even when the Oedipal complex is superseded in a normal course of development there are long-term results. According to Freud, the dissolution of the Oedipus complex leads to the establishment of the superego in the child's mind: 'By means of identification he takes the unattackable authority into himself. The authority now turns into his superego and enters into possession of all the aggressiveness which a child would have liked to exert against it.'[27] Thus, as Freud explained, the Oedipal complex 'initiates all the processes that are designed to make the individual find a place in the cultural community'.[28]

In other words, the body politics of the family lead up to a stage of sexual development in which the contradiction between desire and society can be overcome in the following three ways:

First, the dissolution of the Oedipal complex brings about the abolition of paternal authority in its external form and its transformation into an agency in the child's the mind. Although the superego continues to represent the father's authority, it is located within the individual. Evidently, what the libido theory describes here is a dialectical *Aufhebung* of paternal authority in all the senses which Hegel ascribed to the term.

Second, Freud argued that when sons and daughters accept the limits which paternal authority has placed on their sexuality and ascend to the final, genital stage – in which their aim is to gain satisfaction by heterosexual intercourse – 'the sexual drive is . . . subordinated to the reproductive function; it becomes, so to say, altruistic'.[29] He called genital sexuality altruistic because in contrast to the earlier forms of infantile sexuality, it combines social demands – the need for the reproduction of the species – with the sexual satisfaction of the individual, thus superseding an original conflict by creating a synthesis in which the interests of both parties are preserved, but divested of their antagonistic quality.

Third, while genitality takes the place of the earlier manifestations of sexuality – such as anal or oral desires – in determining the end-pleasure of sexual desire, it preserves all of them as possible preparatory acts, which may encourage full heterosexual intercourse, and from which 'fore-pleasure' can be gained.[30]

As I have shown, Freud's description of libidinal development tells a political tale of human growth and maturation: from illusionary self-sufficiency, through self-loving majestic megalomania, slavish compliance, hostile defiance and rebellious urges, to autonomous self-assertion by internalization of parental law. However, even though in the last stage of sexual development the individual can be both independent in pursuit of satisfaction and serve the demands of society, the dialectical finale of the libido theory does not lead to a fixed and stable conclusion of the conflict between sexuality and society, desire and authority.

Freud pointed out that even when children grow up and leave their families in pursuit of heterosexual genital satisfaction, they are not allowed a free sexual life. Society constantly imposes new restrictions on sexuality, since, as he claimed, there is an 'inverse relation holding between civilization and the free development of sexuality'.[31] He explained that in successively narrowing the realm of legitimate sexual satisfaction 'civilization is obeying the laws of economic necessity, since a large amount of the sexual energy which it uses for its own purposes has to be withdrawn from sexuality. In this respect civilization behaves towards sexuality as a people or stratum of its population does which has subjected another one to its exploitation. Fear of a revolt by the suppressed elements drives it to stricter precautionary measures.'[32] Freud claimed that this exploitation of sexuality by society had reached 'a high-water mark' in his age, which permitted sexual relationships only 'on the basis of a solitary, indissoluble bond between one man and one woman'.[33] Thus, modern society continually forces the individual 'to live psychologically beyond his means, while the unsatisfied claims of his drives make him feel the demands of civilization as a constant pressure upon him'.[34]

However, Freud also acknowledged that in order to make communal life possible, 'a restriction upon sexual life is unavoidable'.[35] Though he advocated a freer sexual morality than was common in his age, he never preached sexual revolution. In his view, the antagonism between sexuality and society could be alleviated and contained, but there was no end to the conflict between these two forces, which accompanies all human beings from cradle to grave. As Freud put it poetically: 'Human civilization rests upon two pillars, of which one is the control of natural forces and the other the restriction of our drives. The ruler's throne rests upon fettered slaves. Among the drive components which are thus brought into service, the sexual drives, in the narrower sense of the word, are conspicuous for their strength and savagery. Woe, if they should be set loose! The throne would be overturned and the ruler trampled under foot.'[36]

16   Brothers in Arms

In 1912–13, when Freud published the four essays which he then collected in *Totem and Taboo*, he turned the Oedipal conflict between sexual desire and paternal authority into the origin and essence of all civilization. In these essays he presented a genealogy which traces the dialectical interplay of power, sexuality and obedience back beyond individual development (ontogeny) to a developmental sequence originating in a mythical childhood of humanity (phylogeny), which Freud located in the dark ages of prehistory. However, as I see it, rather than a scientific explanation of the sources, evolution and dynamics of civilization, Freud's account of all that he considered prehistoric and primal, and endowed with the German prefix *Ur* – such as the primal horde (*Urhorde*), the primal father (*Urvater*) and the primal murder (*Urmord*) – constitutes itself a political myth to be interpreted.[1] In this chapter I discuss the internal logic of this myth and the role it played in Freud's theorizing on history and society. At the same time I compare its structure and argument with those typical of other such myths, which have achieved canonical status in the history of political theory.

Freud himself was ambivalent about the scientific status of his reconstruction of primeval events in *Totem and Taboo*. He admitted that his hypotheses may seem fantastic and that the earliest state of society which he portrayed in his essay, 'has never been an object of observation'.[2] In a footnote he even conceded that '[t]he determination of the original state of things . . . invariably remains a matter of construction'.[3] Almost a decade later, in *Group Psychology and Analysis of the Ego*, he described as 'not unkind' a critic who called *Totem and Taboo* a 'Just-So Story'.[4] A few pages later Freud referred to his own depiction of the primal horde as a 'myth'.[5] Nevertheless, when he summarized the essential themes of *Totem and Taboo* in *Moses and Monotheism*, he asserted: 'There is nothing wholly fabricated in our construction, nothing which could not be supported on solid foundations.'[6]

I read Freud's story of the primal horde as part of a rhetorical strategy which is well-known from the writings of social contract theorists such as Thomas Hobbes, John Locke and Jean-Jacques Rousseau. By depicting human beings as endowed with certain attributes in a hypothetical state of nature which is claimed to precede the social contract, these thinkers aimed to emphasize the conceptual priority of these aspects of human nature and to illuminate the essence and purpose of government. Like them, Freud also presented a hypothesis about a primeval stage in social development which was supposed to have preceded the establishment of political authority and law as we know them. However, Freud's myth remains unique in the history of political thought in that it envisages this archaic state as already characterized by a political structure, that is, by an absolutist regime and mechanisms of dependence and coercion.

What, then, did Freud assume happened in primeval times? *Totem and Taboo* tells the story of a period in which males took females as permanent sexual partners in order to ensure that their sexual needs would be satisfied on a regular basis. In this archaic mating process women agreed to become sexual objects in order to ensure their own safety as well as that of their children – they seemed to have no sexual needs of their own. According to Freud, the primal family served male sexuality and was based on the superior physical power of men. Males had no interest in their offspring and their children were not bound to them by an emotional link comparable to that which tied them to their mothers. As Freud pointed out in a letter to Jung: 'A father is one who possesses [*besitzt*] a mother sexually (and the children as property [*Eigentum*]). The fact of having been engendered by a father has, after all, no psychological significance for a child.'[7]

Freud regarded male sexual desire not only as possessive, but also as exclusive and insatiable. Therefore each primal patriarch not only controlled his children by means of physical force, but also jealously kept to himself as many women as he could obtain and support. Violent brute that he was, and endowed with absolute power, he deprived his sons of all sexual satisfaction and punished opposition with death, expulsion or castration. As Freud put it in *Moses and Monotheism*: 'The strong male was lord [*Herr*] and father of the entire horde and unrestricted in his power [*Macht*], which he exercised with violence.'[8]

The father's primal authority was based not only on his physical superiority, but also on the sons' emotional dependence, which was reinforced by their sexual frustration. Though this prevented them from becoming rebellious, the sons' feelings towards their father was ambivalent: 'They hated their father, who presented such a formidable obstacle to their craving for power [*Machtbedürfnis*] and their sexual desires; but they loved and admired him too.'[9]

Like the libido theory, Freud's myth of the primal horde presents a story of body politics. Intertwining sexuality and power, it depicts a primeval society governed by the primal father's bodily strength, whose absolutist rule was driven by his sexual desire. Again, like in the case of the individual infant, Freud presented the rule of the pleasure principle as self-defeating. According to Freud, the sons managed to escape from their father's control. Organizing themselves in a community of their own, 'united to overpower their father', they created an egalitarian social order. Similar to the father's rule, Freud also grounded this original egalitarian social organization in sexual relations and bodily desire.[10] As he explained, partly at least, the sons achieved their liberation from dependence on the father through 'homosexual feelings and acts'.[11]

However, the strongest feeling which brought the sons to join each other in their first free community, was their common desire for their mother and their shared hatred for their father. Out of heterosexual, incestuous lust and hatred they proceeded to commit what Freud depicted as the first collective political act in human history: murder for sex, or, to be more precise, parricide for the sake of incest.

Freud believed that this act occurred repeatedly in primeval times. Primal sons overwhelmed and murdered their primal fathers, and, according to Freud, '[c]annibal savages as they were, it goes without saying that they devoured their victim as well as killing him'.[12] In the act of cannibalizing, the sons accomplished what – according to Freud – all later sons have aimed to achieve symbolically in the dissolution of the Oedipal complex: they introjected him, so that each of them acquired some of the father's strength.

Again, we see that Freud's tale underlays politics with bodily processes: sexual desires bring about equality and independence from authority. They lead, in the most literal sense of the word, to the physical annihilation of paternal government. But the Oedipal dialectics set in motion by the bodies of the father and his sons do not lead to the fulfilment of incestuous desire. After the primal parricide the sons realized that none of them actually could take the place of the father. As Freud explained: 'Each of them would have wished, like his father, to have all the women to himself. The new organization would have collapsed in a struggle of all against all, for none of them was of such overmastering strength as to be able to take on his father's part with success.'[13]

Through their complicity in murder, the brothers experienced the superior bodily power vested in the group and realized the weakness of each as an isolated individual. Moreover, Freud assumed that at this stage, at which the sons were still not capable of governing themselves properly, the women of the horde inherited part of the father's power and established a matriarchal interregnum, which was later replaced by a new patriarchal order.[14]

Social contract theories of canonical political philosophers are usually marked by the absence of women from their discourse. However, since Freud's myth traces the origins of political order to the body and sexuality, women are present, even though they are continually denied the status of political subjects. At best, Freud's myth allows them a short interregnum at a time at which men are incapable of organizing themselves. In general, their bodies and the sexual satisfaction which they provide constitute but the passive objects of male political action. Not even the power to withhold pleasure from males is accorded to them by Freud, even though visions of such female power have been part of male thinking at least since Aristophanes' *Lysistrata*. Moreover, by presenting males as fundamentally uninterested in their offspring, Freud's myth denies that the reproductive capacity of females might endow women with a biological power which can create insecurity in males by making the future of their possessions dependent on the actions of women.[15] In Freud's discourse the specifically female capacities of their bodies can never serve women as a resource of power *vis-à-vis* their sexual partners.

Freud's myth also differs from conventional social contract theories in that it presents not an original State of Nature without government, but a primal stage of human development in which political processes still are physical. The father's despotism over the primal horde was achieved, maintained and abolished by the direct contact and use, mutilation and destruction of bodies. Cognizance of the self-defeating nature of such a body politics – which blindly realized the program of the pleasure principle and was based on violence – led the sons to the recognition of the need for law and self-imposed legitimate institutions.

In Freud's myth, civilization started with the transition from an original state of body politics, in which obedience was imposed externally by physical coercion, to a new form of obedience, which was based on the internalization of rules. This transition was made possible by a social contract concluded by the sons. They pledged to renounce despotism, declaring that 'no one could or might ever again attain the father's supreme power [*Machtvollkommenheit*], even though that was what all of them had striven for'.[16] As Freud put it in *Moses and Monotheism*:

> A realization of the dangers and uselessness of these struggles, a recollection of the act of liberation which they had accomplished together, and the emotional ties with one another which had arisen during the period of their expulsion, led at last to an agreement among them, a sort of social contract. The first form of social organization came about with a *renunciation of drives*, a recognition of mutual *obligations*, the introduction of definite *institutions*, pronounced inviolable (holy) – that is to say, the beginnings of morality and justice. Each individual renounced his ideal of acquiring his father's position for himself and of possessing his mother and sisters. Thus the *taboo on incest* and the injunction to *exogamy* came about.[17]

The insatiable and possessive sexual desire which Freud attributed to male bodies alone, necessitated social controls in the form of taboos and the enforcement of a distinction between a daughter, sister and mother on the one hand, and a sexual partner – possibly a wife – on the other. Even though this distinction among women demanded a renunciation of male desire, it constituted the necessary condition for all viable social frameworks and cultures. In Freud's discourse the internalization of rules, agreements and authorities became necessary, because males are bodily creatures which can only continue to live and experience pleasure if they agree to live in a stable social framework, in which they have to renounce incestuous pleasures. As Freud explained in *Civilization and Its Discontents*: 'Human life in common is only made possible when a majority comes together which is stronger than any separate individual and which remains united against all separate individuals. . . . This replacement of the power of the individual by the power of a community consitutes the decisive step of civilization. The essence of it lies in the fact that the members of the community restrict themselves in their possibilities of satisfaction, whereas the individual knew no such restrictions.'[18]

It might almost seem as if Freud's social contract tells of sons who came to reason and learned to govern themselves autonomously. But this is not the whole tale. According to Freud the transition from primal individualism to a communal self was not achieved by the power of reason alone. He postulated that after the brothers had lived out their rage and hatred, killed and cannibalized their father, and thus emptied themselves of their pent-up aggression, the other side of their ambivalent relationship with their father started to reemerge and they felt remorse over the crime which they had committed. They recalled him as having been good, protective and indulgent, and therefore felt guilty for having killed him. These feelings of guilt and remorse – a paradoxical result of their uprising – ultimately led to the father's symbolic resurrection as totem animal of the brother clans. It 'embodied the unlimited power [*Machtfülle und Unbeschränktheit*] of the primal father against whom they had once fought as well as their readiness to submit to him'.[19] As Freud put it, by submitting to the totem animal the sons attempted to 'appease the father by deferred obedience [*nachträglichen Gehorsam*] to him'.[20]

In other words, as much as a result of reason leading to autonomous self-restraint, Freud depicted the social contract also as based on posthumous obedience to the father's authority, aiming at the latter's symbolic restoration. In the Freudian social contract the sons not only bound themselves to one another as members of a community; by submitting themselves to the totem animal they also concluded a 'covenant with their father' after his death.[21]

Moreover, by exaggerating the power of the dead father into imaginary dimensions, the sons extended the scope of his posthumous authority without limits: 'The dead father became stronger than the living one had been.'[22] If we are to believe Freud, the memory of the dead primal father also underlaid the monotheistic construction of a paternal deity. Freud claimed that monotheistic religion resurrected, on a cosmic scale, the dependence and submission of the sons to paternal authority. Monotheism enthroned the father in a Kingdom in Heaven, thereby symbolically nullifying the unconscious guilt over the killing of the primal father: 'Totemic religion arose from the filial sense of guilt, in an attempt to allay that feeling and appease the father by deferred obedience to him. All later religions are seen to be attempts at solving the same problem. They vary according to the stage of civilization at which they arise and according to the methods which they adopt; but all have the same end in view and are reactions of the same great event with which civilization began and which, since it occurred, has not allowed mankind a moment's rest.'[23]

In order to explain the indestructibility of the primal father's authority, Freud invoked the concept of a phylogenetic inheritance or archaic heritage he supposed to have preserved the memory of the primal murder and to have transmitted it by heredity across generations since the dawn of history. The highly problematic assumption of such a hereditary memory-trace relied on the doctrine of Jean-Baptiste Lamarck concerning the inheritance of acquired characteristics, which was discredited already when Freud adopted it. Despite the wide-spread criticism of Lamarckian ideas and attempts of Freud's followers to convince him to reject them – since they had long been given up by biologists – Freud stubbornly held on to them until the end of his life. As Jones puts it: 'Freud never gave up a jot of his belief in the inheritance of acquired characters.'[24]

For the first time, Lamarckian assumptions figured prominently in 1912–13 in *Totem and Taboo*. The recently discovered manuscript of *A Phylogenetic Fantasy*, written in 1915, shows that in the following years Freud continued to be concerned with this topic.[25] In 1915 Freud also added to the *Three Essays on the Theory of Sexuality* that over the ages the incest taboo had become part of an 'organic inheritance' of the human race.[26] In 1916 he appended a number of arguments and explanations to *The Interpretation of Dreams*, which aimed at absorbing a notion of universal symbolism – developed by Jung – into his own method of dream interpretation.[27]

Consequently, in the *Introductory Lectures* of 1916–17, Freud referred to 'symbolic connections, which the individual has never acquired by learning' and which could 'be regarded as a phylogenetic heritage'.[28] Moreover, he postulated 'primal phantasies' which originated in primeval experiences and argued: 'It seems to me quite possible that all the things that are told to us to-day in analysis as phantasy – the seduction of children, the inflaming of sexual excitement by observing parental intercourse, the threat of castration (or rather castration itself) – were once real occurrences in the primeval times of the human family, and that children in their phantasies are simply filling in the gaps in individual truth with prehistoric truth.'[29] In 1918 Freud even compared this phylogenetic heritage to the '*instinctive* knowledge of animals',[30] a comparison which he reiterated in *Moses and Monotheism*, where he also provided the most detailed discussion on the concept of an inborn archaic heritage.[31]

Thus, starting with *Totem and Taboo*, Freud attributed to the human race 'a collective mind, in which mental processes occur just as they do in the mind of an individual'.[32] According to Freud, this collective mind was universal and contained a number of primal fantasies which formed part of a 'store of unconscious phantasies of all neurotics and probably all human beings'.[33] These primal fantasies were residues 'from the prehistory of the primal family, when the jealous father actually robbed his son of his genitals if the latter became troublesome to him as a rival with a woman'.[34] Therefore Freud claimed unequivocally in *Moses and Monotheism* 'that men have always known (in this special way) that they once possessed a primal father and killed him'.[35] In this fashion Freud's discourse turns the collective memory of a murdered primal father into part of a human instinct, which leads people to seek father figures, makes them dread them, and revolt against them.

It seems that Freud was partial to Lamarckism because it allowed him to expand the realm of psychoanalysis over all human behaviour, individual and collective alike. As he explained: 'If we assume the survival of these memory-traces in the archaic heritage, we have bridged the gulf between individual and crowd psychology: we can deal with peoples as we do with an individual neurotic.'[36] However, Lamarckism also allied psychoanalysis closely with highly questionable quasi-scientific approaches, such as recapitulation theories. These postulated that ontogeny – that is, individual development – constituted a repetition of the development of the species or phylogeny. Such recapitulation theories were quite popular at the turn of the century and led to comparisons between savages, children and a phylogenetic past which they were said to replay. According to Stephen Gould these theories 'stood second to none in the arsenal of racist arguments supplied by science to justify slavery and imperialism'.[37] Though Freud's universalism may have prevented these implications of the Lamarckian approach in psychoanalytic discourse, his Lamarckism clearly fulfilled an ideological function. It provided quasi-scientific underpinnings for the authoritarian bias in Freud's presentation of social relations, allowing him to depict humanity as driven by an inborn and ineradicable thirst for obedience, and to dismiss fears of authority figures as an irrational remnant from primeval times.[38]

Freud's Lamarckism shows again that in Freud's discourse paternal authority can only be *aufgehoben*, but never annihilated. The primal father can be overcome and cannibalized, but his authority cannot be obliterated. What may appear to be autonomy and self-rule, turns out to be but another form of obedience to the father. Thus the primal parricide leads to a transformation of paternal authority into part of a collective unconscious and raises it to a higher level – into Heaven – where it is preserved and perpetuated.

There are thus two strands in Freud's presentation of the social contract: one depicts it as the product of the brothers' transformed self-conception, which, in turn, is the result of reason and insight into the destructive dynamics of a politics based on sexual desire, physical strength and violence. The other, however, traces the contract to the sons' love for the father and an irrational longing to submit to his authority. Therefore two contradictory readings of Freud's social contract theory seem possible: one would make the contract appear as an act based on self-understanding, which allows liberation from paternal absolutism and the creation of communal self-government, self-restraint and mutuality. The other would turn the social contract into a reactionary event, where possible self-rule is given up in favour of self-inflicted tutelage under a dead father's eternalized and imaginary authority.

In my view these two strands in Freud's myth cannot be separated. Freud conceived prehistoric humanity in analogy to the individual child which cannot overcome the Oedipus complex without the establishment of a superego in its mind, in which the father's authority and the paternal prohibition against incest are preserved. Similarly, according to Freud the murderous mob of brothers could not transform itself into a self-governing community without submitting to a symbolic figure – first the totem and then God – which perpetuated the primal father's authority. On the one hand the self-imposed obedience to a father symbol enabled humanity to liberate itself from the constraints of body politics and subjection to the primal father; but on the other hand it prevented growth into full maturity.

In *The Future of an Illusion* of 1927 Freud was optimistic that ultimately humanity would overcome its dependence on paternal deities and that science would usher in a new age of reason.[39] He praised 'our god Logos' who, even though 'not a very almighty one' could 'increase our power'.[40] Even in 1933, the year in which Hitler came to power in Germany, Freud still declared in his *New Introductory Lectures*: 'Our best hope for the future is that intellect – the scientific spirit, reason – may in process of time establish a dictatorship in the mental life of man. The nature of reason is a guarantee that afterwards it will not fail to give man's emotional impulses and what is determined by them the position they deserve. But the common compulsion exercised by such a dominance of reason will prove to be the strongest uniting bond among men and lead the way to further unions.'[41] Freud regarded it as a task of psychoanalysis to help ease the transition into a post-religious age, which would be based on the 'primacy of the intellect'.[42] He suggested in *The Future of an Illusion*: 'Our behaviour should . . . be modelled on that of a sensible teacher who does not oppose an impending new development but seeks to ease its path and mitigate the violence of its irruption.'[43]

In such passages, in which Freud postulated the possibility of liberating humanity from its subjection to the authority of the primal father's divine heirs, he transposed the emancipatory message of his therapeutic outlook to the human race as a whole. However, Freud's optimism was not consistent. Already in 1930 he had stated his belief that 'the great majority of mortals will never be able to rise above this [religious] view of life',[44] and in the end of the 1930s Freud finally noticed that rather than ascending to a higher universal unity based on the rule of reason, humanity was on the verge of an abyss.

In a 'Prefatory Note' to *Moses and Monotheism* he remarked with astonishment 'that progress has allied itself with barbarism'. In his eyes the Soviet Union was one example of such an alliance. Its regime attempted to improve living conditions, withdrew the 'opium' of religion from the people, and granted them a reasonable amount of sexual liberty; but at the same time the Soviet regime also 'submitted them to the most cruel coercion and robbed them of any possibility of freedom of thought'. Freud's other example of an alliance of progress and barbarism was fascist Italy, where he deplored the violent means used to instil in people such positive qualities as 'orderliness and a sense of duty'. Nazi Germany, however, was a different case for Freud. It provided proof for him that 'a relapse into almost prehistoric barbarism can occur as well without being attached to any progressive ideas'. On the whole, he admitted, 'things have so turned out that to-day the conservative democracies have become the guardians of cultural advance and that, strange to say, it is precisely the institution of the Catholic Church which puts up a powerful defence against the spread of this danger [of barbarism] to civilization – the Church which has hitherto been the relentless foe to freedom of thought and to advances towards the discovery of the truth!'[45]

17 Big Daddy

Freud's comments on the Soviet Union, fascist Italy and Nazi Germany cannot be taken as a critique of authoritarianism *per se*. Astonishingly enough, historical developments in Europe failed to alert Freud to the perils inherent in all authoritarian regimes. Freud's portrayal of modern society exhibits a striking blindness to the dangers emanating from charismatic leaders; somehow he seemed to have forgotten that – in his own terms – they are heirs to a killing and castrating patriarch. Instead, he regarded them as necessary for social cohesion and the control of 'the masses', whose lack of restraint he feared. While he was an old-style liberal, he was by no means a democrat. Moreover, Freud's outlook was not only authoritarian, it was also elitist. He never believed it possible to achieve a working social order without the submission of the majority under the command of a minority. He always drew a clear distinction between 'the masses', whom he thought to be driven by the impulses and passions of their bodies, and a minority of people, who organized their lives according to the reality principle and accepted the demands which social necessities imposed on them. Freud's elitism, the emphasis he placed on the role of leader figures and the political concerns underlying his crowd psychology, form the topic of this chapter.

Already in 1883, before the dawn of psychoanalysis, Freud mused in a letter to Martha Bernays – who was later to become his wife – on the difference which in his view separated the lower classes from the bourgeoisie:

The mob [*Gesindel*] gives vent to its appetites, and we deprive ourselves. We deprive ourselves to maintain our integrity, we economize in our health, our capacity for enjoyment, our emotions; we save ourselves for something, not knowing for what. And this habit of constant suppression of natural drives [*Triebe*] gives us the quality of refinement. . . . Thus we strive more toward avoiding pain than seeking pleasure. . . . Our whole conduct of life presupposes that we are protected from the direst poverty and that the possibility exists of being able to free ourselves increasingly from social ills. The poor people [*die Armen*], the masses [*das Volk*], could not survive without their thick skins and their easygoing ways. . . . The poor are too helpless, too exposed, to behave like us. When I see the people [*das Volk*] indulging themselves, disregarding all sense of moderation, I invariably think that it is their compensation for being a helpless target for all the taxes, epidemics, sicknesses, and evils of social institutions. I am not going to pursue this thought any further, but it would be easy to demonstrate how "the people" judge, think, hope and work in a manner utterly different from ourselves. There is a psychology of the common man which differs considerably from ours.[1]

This elitist approach also guided statements which Freud made more than four decades later in the opening pages of *The Future of an Illusion* – the essay in which he was optimistic about the capacity of humanity to emancipate itself from its self-imposed subjection to paternal deities. In fact, in this essay Freud adopted a sharper, less understanding tone. He no longer showed any consideration for the reasons underlying the lack of enthusiasm of 'the masses' for drive renunciation, which he had explained earlier by inferior social conditions and powerlessness. No longer did he write of the easy-going ways of the people. Instead he declared: 'it is just as impossible to do without control [*Beherrschung*] of the crowd [*Masse*] by a minority as it is to dispense with coercion in the work of civilization. For crowds are lazy and unintelligent; they have no love for the renunciation of drives, and they are not to be convinced by argument of its inevitability; and the individuals composing them support one another in giving free rein to their indiscipline.'[2]

It seems that according to Freud only those who exercise self-mastery are entitled to govern society. However, Freud assumed that the control of what he called 'the crowd' (*die Masse*) could not be handled by the brute force of an elite. It necessitated father figures, who presumably originated from the elite and who could inspire masses to restrict themselves, while keeping the means of power in their hands – that is, act as fathers of society. As he explained in *The Future of an Illusion*:

It is only through the influence of individuals who can set an example and whom crowds recognize as their leaders [*Führer*] that they can be induced to perform the work and undergo the renunciations on which the existence of civilization depends. All is well if these leaders are persons who possess superior insight into the necessities of life and who have risen to the height of mastering their own drive wishes. But there is a danger that in order not to lose their influence they might give way to the crowd more than it gives way to them, and it therefore seems necessary that they shall be independent of the crowd by having means to power [*Machtmittel*] at their disposal.[3]

Freud argued that throughout history breakthroughs to a higher and more rational cultural system had been initiated by outstanding individuals who devoted themselves to a higher purpose and managed to mesmerize the masses to do the same. Therefore he reserved 'a place for "great men" in the chain, or rather the network, of [historical] causes', and contrasted his approach with modern scholarship, where emphasis was placed primarily on impersonal forces, such as economics, the development of tool production, migration and climatic changes.[4]

The Biblical Moses was Freud's paradigmatic example of a leader capable of shaping history according to his will. In his eyes, Moses was 'an outstanding father-figure'[5] who acted not only as 'the political leader of the Jews settled in Egypt but was also their law-giver and educator and forced them into the service of a new religion'.[6] While Moses clearly was one of Freud's heroes, Freud subjected another person who left his mark on world history to a condemning analysis. In the early thirties Freud collaborated with his former patient William C. Bullitt in the writing of a book on Woodrow Wilson, which for a number of reasons was published only in 1967. The hostile and simplistic approach of this book makes it a notorious example of how political psycho-biographies ought not to be written.[7] Devoid of any historical and sociological analysis, the book reduces all of Wilson's politics to an unresolved Oedipal complex. Even though only the introduction was actually written by Freud, and Bullitt did the writing of the rest of it, there can be no doubt that Freud was an active collaborator and that the book's argument largely reflects his ideas, albeit in a crude manner.[8]

As Philip Rieff put it, for Freud Wilson was 'another false Messiah, a focus for popular illusions of a radically new order of social life – peace on earth'.[9] In his introduction Freud confessed his antipathy for Wilson. He regarded the American president as a person who never quite came to terms with reality. According to Freud, for Wilson '[n]othing mattered except noble intentions'. He ignored the facts and his 'insincerity, unreliability and tendency to deny the truth', his religious conviction and 'his alienation from the world of reality' led him to pursue illusory and deplorable policies.[10] Freud blamed Wilson for promising to create a just peace in Europe after the First World War, but then agreeing to the transformation of his Fourteen Points into the Treaty of Versailles, and thus bearing a large part of the responsibility for the economic collapse in Germany and Austria. Freud is said to have remarked that he detested Wilson because 'as far as a single individual can be responsible for the misery of this part of the world, he surely is'.[11]

Although there may have been a number of other reasons for Freud's dislike of Wilson, there can be no doubt that Freud saw in Wilson the antithesis of the leader figure which he described in *The Future of an Illusion*. In Freud's eyes Wilson possessed no insight into the necessities of life and failed to master his own wishes. Thus, rather than raising the human race to a higher level, he allowed the world to fall into decline.

According to Freud the fate of all enlightened fathers/leaders, who aim to elevate humanity to a more advanced stage of development, is a tragic one. His speculative account of how and why Moses was murdered by his people forms a case study, as it were, of how such leaders 'have perished in misfortune'.[12] The drive renunciation – that is, obedience – which they impose on their followers in the name of the reality principle and progress is disliked even where it finds acceptance at first. Freud thought that the unwillingness to abandon satisfactions led the Israelites to murder their 'great leader [*Führers*] and liberator [*Befreiers*]'.[13]

In Freud's discourse rebellions inevitably appear as the deed of people who refuse obedience to leaders because they cannot suffer the restrictions on satisfaction which such father figures impose on them. However, while *Totem and Taboo* represents the restrictions which the primal father imposed on his sons as exaggerated and serving his selfish pleasure-seeking aims, later father figures and their laws are said to encounter opposition because they represent the demands of reason. Nowhere in Freud's writings can one find an instance where people rebel against despots because their lives and property, rights and interests have been threatened or violated by autocratic leaders. Even Thomas Hobbes, whose writings constitute a classic defense of absolutism, was aware that the concentration of power in the hands of an autocratic sovereign could also be dangerous to those subject to the latter's government (though less dangerous than life in the State of Nature).

Freud's obtuseness to the dangers of paternal authority, when it is transposed into the public realm, appears most strikingly in his dedication of a copy of *Why War?* – his exchange of letters with Albert Einstein on the possibility of a world peace – to: 'Benito Mussolini with the respectful greetings of an old man who recognizes in the ruler the cultural hero'.[14] Although this dedication contrasts with Freud's critique of fascist Italy which he put in his preface to *Moses and Monotheism*, it is no lapse. As the passages quoted earlier demonstrate, it is complemented by a number of statements on the need for independent leaders with means of power. In addition, Freud warned of what he called the 'psychological malaise of crowds [*das psychologische Elend der Masse*]' in *Civilization and Its Discontents*. He held such a malaise to be imminent where 'the bonds of a society are chiefly constituted by the identification of its members with one another, while individuals of the leader type [*Führerindividualitäten*] do not acquire the importance that should fall to them in the formation of a crowd [*Massenbildung*]'.[15]

Such assertions were the logical outcome of the Oedipal analytical grid by means of which Freud interpreted social processes and structures. It allowed him to present submission and obedience to father figures as necessary for social bonds and development, and to discount the dangers of authoritarianism. Thus, Freud justified his authoritarian position by the universalization of the father–son relationship into a prototypical mould underlying all political formations. He inevitably depicted society as divided into masses/sons on the one hand and leaders/fathers on the other. He decoded its large-scale conflicts as expressing an underlying and unconscious intergenerational conflict, which centers on the father's request for the sons' obedience and the sons' questionable willingness to submit to their father's demand.

Above all, Freud's bias against those whom he called 'the masses' can be discerned in *Group Psychology [Massenpsychologie] and the Analysis of the Ego*. The Standard Edition misleadingly renders Freud's '*Masse*' as 'group' in the essay's title and throughout its text. However, both the title and the first sections of Freud's monograph make it evident that he addressed a particular school of thought, known as 'crowd psychology' or 'mass psychology'.[16] Freud's short book starts with an extensive and on the whole approving discussion of Gustave Le Bon's *Psychologie des foules*, which was translated into German as *Psychologie der Massen*, and into English as *The Crowd: A Study of the Popular Mind*. Nevertheless the Standard Edition turned not only Freud's *Massen*, but also Gustave Le Bon's *foules* into 'groups', divesting thereby these terms of their historical and political connotations and removing them from their intellectual context. Consequently, I have modified the translation and – with the exception of the title of Freud's book – replaced Strachey's 'group' by 'crowd' wherever Freud spoke of *Masse*.

Le Bon – a racist, elitist and mysognist, and a physician who, like Freud, had attended Charcot's Tuesday lectures and witnessed his use of hypnotic suggestion – was probably the most prolific and influential exponent of crowd psychology. In fact, Le Bon often plagiarized and vulgarized other major authors in the field, such as the Italian criminologist Scipio Sighele – who had published his *La Folla Delinquente* (The Criminal Crowd) in Italian in 1891 and in French in 1892 – and his French colleague Gabriel Tarde, who in 1890 published *Les lois de l'imitation* (The Laws of Imitation) and in 1892 his paper on '*Les crimes des foules* (The Crimes of the Crowds)'.[17]

Crowd psychologists shared a deep mistrust of democratic politics, and devoted much of their efforts to pointing out their failings. Democratic theory, they argued, assumed that individual reason and judgement provided the basis for the political system, though in fact its dynamics were increasingly dominated by the irrational and spontaneous mechanisms of crowd behaviour, which reflected 'primordial sentiments' and were symptomatic of an evolutionary regression to an earlier, more primitive mentality.[18] What characterized a crowd in their eyes was a peculiar mental state, which turned its members into creatures with a decreased sense of responsibility, driven to unpredictable, exceptional and automatic behaviour. Thus, people became capable of committing extremely virtuous or immoral acts, which they would never have consciously chosen to undertake as individuals, such as martyrdom or looting. The mechanisms which elicited such psychological transformations were called 'imitation', 'suggestion' or 'contagion'. Nobody was immune to them; under appropriate conditions everybody could become part of a crowd, which was seen as a collective grouped around a leader.

In their representation of the leader–follower relationship, Sighele, Tarde and Le Bon were strongly influenced by Charcot's, Bernheim's and Liébeault's widely publicized experiments with hypnotic suggestion. The control which the hypnotist exercised over the hypnotized provided them with the prototype for the crucial role which they attributed to leaders in the formation and control of crowds.[19]

Contrary to the writings of Tarde and Sighele, which remained relatively obscure, Le Bon's *Psychologie des foules* became a bestseller and already ran into its twenty-sixth French edition by the time Freud discussed its second German edition. In his essay Freud devoted much space and attention to Le Bon and lauded him for his 'brilliantly executed picture of the crowd's psyche [*Massenseele*]'.[20] Though Freud generally agreed with Le Bon's descriptions, he found his approach wanting in terms of its explanatory scheme. In his view, Le Bon and other crowd psychologists failed to raise the question of how and why people succumbed to the suggestive or contagious influence of the crowd.[21] Moreover, Freud made 'a mild reproach against earlier writers for not having sufficiently appreciated the importance of the leader in the psychology of the crowd'.[22]

However, as a glance at Le Bon's book makes clear, by and large the oppositions which Freud's text set up between psychoanalysis and crowd psychology were artifice. Mikkel Borch-Jacobsen has emphasized that contrary to the impression which Freud created, Freud did not confront Le Bon with an antithetical perspective. Instead he appropriated crowd psychology for psychoanalysis, partly by translating its concepts into his own terminology and partly by grafting them onto a psychoanalytic support structure, while claiming to draw a clear boundary between the two.[23]

Like Freud, Le Bon emphasized the pivotal role of the leader as well as the psychology of what he called 'organized crowds'. While Le Bon devoted his attention to the psychology of court juries, parliaments and cabinets, Freud discussed the army and the Church as examples of 'highly organized, lasting and artificial crowds'.[24]

It is indicative of the all-encompassing tendency of Freud's theorizing that he included the latter two institutions in his psychology of masses. As he explained: 'Crowd psychology [*Massenpsychologie*] is . . . concerned with the individual man as a member of a race [*Stammes*], of a nation [*Volkes*], of a caste, of a profession, of an institution, or as a component part of a collection of people [*Menschenhaufens*] who have been organized into a crowd [*Masse*] at some particular time for some definite purpose.'[25] In other words, Freud conceived of any social unit in which members relate to one another as part of a community or organization of some kind, as a crowd.[26] In this way he continued the discussion which he had started in *Totem and Taboo*, concerning changes which are brought about in the psychic reality and behaviour of individuals when they conceive of themselves as members of a crowd rather than as antagonistic individuals.

As Freud emphasized in *Civilization and Its Discontents*, utilitarian considerations of interest and expediency are not strong enough to overcome what he called the 'primary mutual hostility of human beings'.[27] For even though he had admitted earlier on that people acquire value for one another by working together, he claimed that even 'the advantages of work in common, will not hold them together'.[28] In his words:

> The element of truth behind all this, which people are so ready to disavow, is that men are not gentle creatures who want to be loved, and who at most can defend themselves if they are attacked; they are, on the contrary, creatures among whose drive endowments is to be reckoned a powerful share of aggressiveness. As a result, their neighbour is for them not only a potential helper or sexual object, but also someone who tempts them to satisfy their aggressiveness on him, to exploit his capacity for work without compensation, to use him sexually without his consent, to seize his possessions, to humiliate him, to cause him pain, to torture and kill him. *Homo homini lupus.*[29]

Thus, a force is needed which can overcome the primary hostility among people, and bind them together in spite of it. What, then, could be the force which ties individuals into a crowd? According to Freud, this force is love. Continuing the line of thought which he had developed in the libido theory, Freud presented a complex picture of the interrelation between love and authority in *Group Psychology and the Analysis of the Ego.*

For him love constituted simultaneously the basis of authority, its instrument and effect. He claimed 'that love relationships . . . constitute the essence of the soul of the crowd [*Massenseele*]'.[30] In his words, 'if an individual gives up his distinctness in a crowd and lets its other members influence him by suggestion, it gives one the impression that he does it because he feels the need of being in harmony with them rather than in opposition to them – so that perhaps after all he does it *"ihnen zu Liebe"* '.[31]

Since Freud assumed human beings to be driven by a primary mutual hostility, he had to explain how such love could come about. Like in *Totem and Taboo,* he explained that the tie that binds members of a group to one another derives from their common submission to a father figure. Thus, Freud's explanatory scheme invokes the resurrected primal father as the ground of social cohesion which brings people together. According to Freud, it is because they share their love for the same father figure that members of a crowd feel similar and close to one another.[32] In his terms, a number of individuals see themselves as members of a crowd when they all relate to the same person – their leader – as their ideal. As he explained in an italicized passage, '*a primary crowd . . . is a number of individuals who have* put one and the same object in the place of their ego-ideal and have consequently identified themselves with one another in their ego'.[33] Crowd members not only share their love for their leader, but also the feeling that the object of their love, their collective father figure, is unavailable to all of them. He is a supreme being out of reach for regular humans.

Therefore, a feeling which could have been a reason for jealousy and competition becomes a foundation for cohesion and demands for justice: 'What appears later on in society in the shape of *Gemeingeist*, *esprit de corps*, "the spirit of the crowd" [*Massengeist*], etc., does not belie its derivation from what was originally envy. No one must want to put himself forward, every one must be the same and have the same. Social justice means that we deny ourselves many things so that others may have to do without them as well, or, what is the same thing, may not be able to ask for them.'[34]

As Freud clarified, this demand for mutuality and equality only concerns members of the crowd; the leader stands above them, and those who are outside the crowd experience the aggregate hostility of all those who are bound to each other by bonds of love. The crowd does not abolish the potential for hostility and hatred; instead it turns aggression against outsiders who are declared to be enemies. Freud commented: 'The dream of a German world-dominion called for anti-Semitism as its complement; and it is intelligible that the attempt to establish a new, communist civilization in Russia should find its psychological support in the persecution of the bourgeois. One only wonders, with concern, what the Soviets will do after they have wiped out their bourgeois.'[35] Religion, too, works in the same way; according to Freud, 'even if it calls itself the religion of love, [it] must be hard and unloving to those who do not belong to it. Fundamentally indeed every religion is in this same way a religion of love for all those whom it embraces; while cruelty and intolerance towards those who do not belong to it are natural to every religion.'[36] Freud claimed that the same was true for socialism; if it could succeed in replacing religion, 'there will be the same intolerance towards outsiders as in the age of the Wars of Religion'.[37]

What, then, are the attributes which endow a leader figure with charisma powerful enough to redirect the hostility of his followers? In *Moses and Monotheism* Freud mentioned the following traits as features of a 'great man' – that is, of a cultural father figure, whose influence can guide historical developments: 'The decisiveness of thought, the strength of will, the energy of action are part of the picture of a father – but above all the autonomy and independence of the great man, his divine unconcern which may grow into ruthlessness. One must admire him, one may trust him, but one cannot avoid being afraid of him too. We should have been led to realize this from the word itself: who but the father can have been the "great man" in childhood?'[38]

Most important, however, to gain the love of followers, is the illusion that the leader loves all of them 'equally and justly', as if he was their father. Freud discerned such fatherly love underneath the formal organizational structure of the Church and the army. As he explained, in both of them 'the same illusion holds good of there being a head – in the Catholic Church, Christ; in an army its Commander-in-Chief – who loves all the individuals in the crowd with an equal love. Everything depends on this illusion; if it were to be dropped, then both Church and army would dissolve ... There is no doubt that the tie which unites each individual with Christ is also the cause of the tie which unites them with one another. The like holds good of an army. The Commander-in-Chief is a father who loves all soldiers equally, and for that reason they are comrades among themselves.'[39]

Of course, this fatherly love is portrayed as an illusion in Freud's text: in reality, 'the leader himself need love no one else, he may be of a masterful nature [*Herrennatur*], absolutely narcissistic, self-confident and independent'.[40] But while the leader's love for his followers is an illusion and exists in the minds' of the followers only, their love for him provides the foundation for the crowd's cohesion.

The question remains, however, why people should want to admire, fear and submit to such a father figure. For Freud this longing for the father derived from an unconscious core, where people are still repentant brothers longing for the murdered primal father's return. As he explained: 'The leader of the crowd is still the dreaded primal father; the crowd still wishes to be governed by unrestricted force [*Gewalt*]; it has an extreme passion for authority [*autoritätssüchtig*]; in Le Bon's phrase, it has a thirst for obedience [*Unterwerfung*]'.[41] And in *Moses and Monotheism* he declared in a similar vein: 'We know that in the mass of mankind there is a powerful need for an authority who can be admired, before whom one bows down, by whom one is ruled [*beherrscht*] and perhaps even ill-treated ... It is a longing for the father felt by everyone from his childhood onwards'.[42]

In other words, members of a crowd are attached to their leader by a transference relationship. Driven by an unconscious fantasy whose origins lie in their collective childhood, they clothe him with authority, just as patients do with their analyst. Rather than relying on material means of power, such as military coercion, political terror or economic manipulation, Freud's discourse presents the rule of leaders as the result of a secretly wished-for and self-imposed dependence.

In *Totem and Taboo* longing for and submission to the dead father leads to the sons' renunciation of incestuous wishes and their submission to the totem as an imaginary father representative, that is, to the beginning of self-imposed authority, law and morality. However, the political resurrection of the father in the form of charismatic leaders sets in motion processes which contradict and override this development. Out of love for their leader followers renounce their moral autonomy and will. As we have seen, they all place the leader where their ego-ideal – that is, their conscience – was. Commands of leaders revive the paternal law and are introjected by the followers instead of their own ethical standards. Thus, a leader's pronouncements can decide on good and evil. As Freud put it: 'Conscience has no application to anything that is done for the sake of the [love] object; in the blindness of love remorselessness is carried to the pitch of crime.'[43]

Ridding his followers of the remorse and guilt which civilization has imposed on people, a leader without scruples can lead society into barbarism. Alternatively, an ethically motivated leader like Moses could impose new rules on them and lead a crowd of unruly Israelites to cultural achievements. In all instances followers are characterized by their emotional dependence on the leader's command and their total obedience to his rule. For better or worse, they have lost their autonomy.

Thomas Wartenberg has pointed out that 'according to Freud . . . the grouped individual lacks an internal agency with which to resist group pressure. S/he is therefore unable to say "No!" to demands upon her/him by the leader of a group. As a result groups discourage individuality and enforce conformity. It is this disability of group members to manifest independence from group norms that is the real focus of Freud's concern, although he formulates this issue in an inadequate manner.'[44]

To put it somewhat differently, what remains insufficiently formulated in Freud's essay is that his crowd psychology seeks to depict the origins of obedience in love. Freud was concerned with collective behaviour primarily as a manifestation of obedience. This is evident, for example, from the fact that he described the hypnotic relationship as literally being 'a crowd formation with two members'.[45] Although other crowd psychologists also related crowd behaviour to hypnosis, none of them went as far as to characterize the hypnotic dyad itself as a crowd. Undoubtedly, by including in his theory of collective behaviour a social formation which involved only two individuals, Freud stretched mass psychology beyond all limits. Moreover, his description of the hypnotic relationship as a crowd with *two* members is mistaken. In Freud's own terms, only the hypnotized person corresponds to the crowd members, while the hypnotist represents the leader standing above it – thus, the hypnotic relationship contains a crowd of one.

Such a transgression from large-scale social institutions to hypnotic suggestion is problematic if one regards Freud's *Group Psychology and the Analysis of the Ego* as dealing with collective behaviour; but it makes perfect sense if we consider the subject-matter of Freud's essay to be obedience to authority. By turning love into the explanatory factor of obedience, Freud demonstrated that in all social domains, private and public, small and large, political phenomena could be explained within a psychoanalytic frame of reference. By tracing the dynamics of authority and submission to the body, father-son relations, sexuality and love, Freud was capable of explaining their interplay in the family – where he dealt with it within the framework of the libido theory – as well as in large-scale stratified organizations such as the army and Church. From this vantage point, Freud maintained that only an authoritarian social order could provide a rational and feasible middle-way which avoids the fatal excesses of both (paternal) absolutism and (filial) anarchy, both of which are driven by the pleasure principle, and neither of which can ensure social stability. However, Freud also asserted that no social organization could completely ignore the pleasure principle. As he explained already a few years before he wrote *Totem and Taboo*: 'We ought not to exalt ourselves so high as completely to neglect what was originally animal in our nature. Nor should we forget that the satisfaction of the individual's happiness cannot be erased from among the aims of our civilization.'[46]

Whenever Freud advocated authoritarianism in the mind or society, he presented it as the only form of social and mental organization which allows human beings to gain pleasure; for in his view this is possible only under conditions of a tolerant, but also stable and efficacious dominion over drives and desires. Moreover, both in the psyche's internal world and in external social reality, Freud depicted authoritarian rule as the only form of government capable of pursuing a mediating middle-way between two opposed but dialectically interrelated extremes. For instance, in psychoanalytic discourse only the ego's rule over the mind can reconcile the harsh claims of the super-ego with the untamed passions of the id; and only a civilization built on self-imposed obedience to internalized authority figures can steer a middle course between fatherless chaos and paternal tyranny. In the same way Freud portrayed his advocacy for a freer sexual life as aiming at a mid-way between civilization's exaggerated demands for the suppression of drives, and the indiscipline and blind desire for satisfaction which he thought typical of the masses. Finally, Freud characterized cured patients as people capable of choosing on their own a middle way between sexual permissiveness and absolute asceticism.

Thus, Freud's models of the mind and his theories of therapy, history and society posit a tripartite dialectic, in which one pole is formed by absolutist types of rule, whose demands are excessively austere. By aiming at the complete suppression of drives, such strategies of domination inevitably lead to their antipode and bring about the situation which they want to prevent most: lawlessness and lack of control. In the mind the rigidity of the superego leads to mental illness and the production of symptoms, and in society despotism ends in various forms of parricide. At the same time, however, Freud's discourse also stresses that mental or social anarchy – which he portrayed as looming in the id or the unconscious, and as threatening society in the wake of parricides – can only lead to chaos, pain and violence. Since anarchy, like tyranny, fails to bring freedom and pleasure, disorders of the mind and society have to give way to a mediating hierarchical structure which can pursue a middle course between total satisfaction and complete renunciation. As I said earlier, for Freud liberation and real pleasure always demand a self-restraint which is predicated upon the internalization of authority.

* * *

Throughout this book I have focused on Freud's concern with the exercise of power and the role of authority in the mind, therapy, family and society. In this last part I have argued that in his discussions of social relations, Freud proposed a dialectical perspective on authority and obedience, which traces their dynamics to the antagonism between body and society, sexuality and civilization, and son and father – and ultimately defends authoritarianism.

This authoritarian bias contradicts the subversive, critical tendency of Freud's writings on hysteria, the psyche and therapy, to which I have pointed in the first three parts. There seem to be two faces to Freud's politics, as it were. On the one hand, he undermined hierarchies established by the medical discourse of his age, decentred the subject by a repertoire of political metaphors, and initiated an emancipatory therapeutic practice. On the other hand, he defended patriarchy and admired leaders capable of controlling crowds. In fact, these two faces represent two sides of one analogical process of reasoning, which led him not only to structure the private realm by means of categories borrowed from society, but also to portray collective behaviour by means of concepts from the private sphere. In this way Freud aimed to present psychology – and thereby, obviously, psychoanalysis – as the most important of all social sciences, and to establish its primacy over all other aspects and modes of social analysis. Thus, in his *New Introductory Lectures* he dismissed sociology as nothing 'but applied psychology'.[47]

I believe that Freud overexpanded the psychoanalytic framework in order to demonstrate its all-encompassing inclusiveness and to apply to large-scale social processes and institutions the concepts and categories which he had developed in his writings on the private realm. He not only dissected the mind as a microcosm in analogy to the social macrocosm, but also approached the latter as if it was an individual writ large – an eternal son, as it were. Emancipation of the human race could be said to be achieved, therefore, when a rational part – the ego of humanity, so to speak – gained dominance; that is, when crowds were ruled by rational leaders.

As a political theorist, I consider the tendency of psychoanalytic discourse to 'politicize' the family, mind and therapy to be salutary. However, psychoanalytic discourse becomes problematic when it turns large-scale political processes into epiphenomena of psychology. Such a perspective transforms society into an empire of passion and portrays it almost exclusively as a realm where desires, love and hate are evoked, exchanged, transformed and consumed, while processes in which material goods are produced and distributed are relegated to a secondary or negligible position. An approach that consistently turns away from external reality, marginalizes material resources of power and represents authority figures primarily as objects of the fantasies and desires of those subject to their power, cannot provide a self-contained method for the analysis of politics.

Nevertheless, I regard many of the categories which Freud developed in the process of theorizing on the private domains of mind, family and therapy as valuable assets which can be used with benefit in a sociologically grounded, non-reductionist analysis of social relations. Indeed, not only neo-Marxist theories, but also much of contemporary feminist thinking, as well as the work of Michel Foucault would have been unthinkable without Freud's analysis of the dialectics of sexuality and politics. For instance, when Foucault states in *The History of Sexuality* that his purpose is 'to show how deployments of power are directly connected to the body – to bodies, functions, physiological processes, sensations, and pleasures', his declaration can be read as acknowledging his project to be not only a critique, but also a continuation of Freud's work.[48]

Ironically, while Freud stressed the importance of leader figures in his depiction of social relations, no other twentieth-century thinker has contributed more to contemporary ways of unmasking leaders and their postures by drawing attention to unconscious wishes, fantasies, fears and anxieties, which are part of all human nature. I suggest therefore that despite the authoritarian bias inherent in his writings on social relations, Freud provided a useful vocabulary in which hidden motives, mechanisms and strategies of repression, domination and subjugation can be unmasked and articulated. It allows the conceptualization of the intrusion of society into the individual and the formulation of critiques of alienation, discontent, guilt, shame, frustration, exploitation and inequality – not the least gender inequality. Freud's true contribution to critical political analysis lies in forging these categories.

Conclusions

The aim of this study has been to present a political reading of Freud's writings. I have found politics on the 'surface' of Freud's texts, as well as in their 'underlying' logic. I have established that politics provides the largest single repertoire of Freud's metaphors and analogies and structures his depiction of the family and sexuality, his hypotheses on the development of the psychic and social structures, and the groundwork of his therapeutic practice. Nevertheless, I do not claim that Freud saw himself as a political theorist or intended his writings to be contributions to political theory. On the contrary, I have stressed repeatedly that his work was not motivated by political considerations, and I assume that Freud would have rejected my claim that his theory is inherently political. Thus, by presenting a strong thesis concerning the political character of psychoanalysis, my reading opposes Freud's conscious intentions and self-conception as a non-political scientist.

Of course, the conscious self-understanding and self-presentation of an author cannot set absolute boundaries to the range of possible meanings of his or her texts (Freud could hardly have objected to this claim). Rather, it is the reader's task to distinguish meanings which were consciously intended by the author from others, which are produced by the logic and language of his work.[1] As Frank Kermode has pointed out, a classic 'would not be read, and so would not be a classic, if we could not in some way believe it to be capable of saying more than its author meant'.[2] However, even though the self-image of an author cannot limit the meaning of his or her texts, it cannot be dismissed as irrelevant to an understanding of these texts.

How, then, is the political content of psychoanalysis related to Freud's understanding of what he was doing? In short, I contend that what led Freud to privilege political language and logic in his discourse, was his endeavour to create an interdisciplinary science of the mind and human behaviour, which merges interpretation of meaning and causal explanation into one universe of discourse.[3]

Let me explain: Freud persistently refused to observe phenomena from only one point of view or to ask only one type of question. As is well known, he always regarded the workings of the psyche, individual action and social processes as 'overdetermined'. For him, they inevitably were the effect of many causes, carried a variety of often contradictory meanings, expressed several and sometimes incompatible intentions, and fulfilled multiple functions. To cope with this complexity, Freud developed a pluralistic and interdisciplinary science, which he organized around four interrelated but nevertheless distinct perspectives. He always discerned *meaning* in mental phenomena and human action, taking them to be expressions similar to those of a language. He revealed hidden dynamic *forces* – drives and energies – which were supposed to be akin to blind, impersonal physical entities, and to occupy and propel ideas. He delineated the contours of psychic *structures* in and across which the flow of psychic energy is said to take place. Lastly, his enquiry led him to look for origins in the early childhood of individuals and of the human race, that is, for the *history* of observable phenomena as well as for the developmental sequence of the forces and structures which he could not approach directly.

These four types of questions belong to two categories of inquiry which Freud aimed to unite within the psychoanalytic framework. On the one hand there are questions which refer to intention, meaning and history. They belong to what is commonly known as interpretive or hermeneutic discourse and are usually relegated to the humanities. On the other hand, there are hypotheses on causal connections, forces, and boundaries of psychic structures, which are characteristic of the mechanistic discourse which we know from the natural sciences.

I suggest that Freud structured the psyche in analogy to a polity, because it is in the nature of political discourse to combine references to causal forces over which actors have no control, with references to the self-conceptions and intentions of actors. As I have stated in the preface, political discourse is concerned with the distribution and exercise of power; and even though power can be pictured as a quasi-mechanical force operating causally in and through social structures, it is always also embedded in the historically evolved pattern of symbols and rules characteristic of all human affairs. That is, political power has not only to do with material assets and resources, such as territory, money and arms, but is also related to the human capacity of symbolization, to signalling and the obedience to signals, and based on an understanding of purposes and meaning.

In my view, Freud was insufficiently aware of the fact that his attempt at an integration of causal explanations and interpretations of meaning turned his project into a political science of the mind, individual action and social institutions and processes. Nevertheless, the political logic and language of Freud's discourse are neither accidental features nor the consequence of extraneous interests and motivations. Rather, they result organically from Freud's attempt to synthesize disparate languages of inquiry into one theoretical universe and they form the thread which holds the tapestry of psychoanalysis together, despite the fact that its fabric is woven of a variety of colours and materials.

A number of commentators have paid attention to the fact that Freud's discourse unites mechanics and meaning, but as a rule they posit incompatibility between these two fabrics of the theoretical tapestry which Freud wove into one another. Charles Rycroft has articulated this position succinctly by stating that 'if dreams have meaning and can be interpreted they must be creations of a person or an agent who endows them with meaning, while, if they are phenomena with causes they must be explicable in terms of prior events without reference to an agent. One cannot really have it both ways and the attempt to do so leads only to confusion.'[4]

On the basis of this assumption commentators and translators have continually sought to restrict Freud's interdisciplinary work to either its hermeneutic or causal dimension. For instance, in order to enhance the natural-scientific appearance of Freud's work, James Strachey eliminated from the *Standard Edition* all instances in which Freud linked psychoanalysis to the *Geisteswissenschaften* (humanities). By rendering this German term wrongly as 'mental sciences', Strachey obscured the significance of crucial statements in which Freud stated his aim to establish a new science through a synthesis of the natural sciences and the humanities. Thus, the *Standard Edition* distorts a declaration of 1910, which proclaimed the purpose of the International Psychoanalytic Association 'to foster and to further the science of psycho-analysis founded by Freud, both as pure psychology and in its application to medicine and the *Geisteswissenschaften* ["humanities", mistranslated as "mental sciences"]'.[5] Almost two decades later Freud argued that the training most suitable for analysts was not available in the traditional university curriculum, since it would have to 'include *geisteswissenschaftlichen Stoff* ["elements from the humanities", mistranslated as "elements from the mental sciences"], . . . from psychology, the history of civilization and sociology, as well as from anatomy, biology and the study of evolution'.[6] In the same passage Freud maintained that as long as there were no independent psychoanalytic institutes in which such comprehensive training could be made possible, a 'preliminary education in medicine' was recommended. He warned, however: 'It should not be forgotten . . . that this is not the whole of psycho-analysis, and that for its other aspect we can never do without the co-operation of people who have had preliminary education in the *Geisteswissenschaften* ["humanities", again mistranslated as "mental sciences"]'.[7]

A number of historians and philosophers of science critical of Freud have also tried to turn him into an aspiring – but ultimately misguided – natural scientist of the mind, whom they then take to task for not living up to natural-scientific criteria of theory construction and corroboration. Probably the most scholarly attempt to do so has been undertaken by Frank Sulloway. In Sulloway's reading Freud appears as an heir to Darwin and a 'crypto-biologist', employing 'a highly hypothetico-deductive methodology'.[8] Since Sulloway aims to reduce psychoanalysis to quasi-biology, his book hardly refers to Freud's clinical practice. Even though it is mainly a study of Freud's early work, seminal concepts which have to do with interpretation, such as the 'talking-cure', are hardly touched upon and have found no place in the detailed 45-page index.[9]

As we see, in order to assimilate Freud to a natural-scientific paradigm one has to recast some elements of his texts and remain silent about others. After all, Freud's work systematically transcends the boundaries of methods and procedures which are typical of the natural sciences. For instance, in his *Introductory Lectures* Freud stated that his insights into the unconscious meaning of dream symbols had many sources and that they were gained 'from fairy tales and myths, from buffoonery and jokes, from folklore (that is, from knowledge about popular manners and customs, sayings and songs) and from poetic and colloquial linguistic usage'.[10] Reliance on evidence from these fields brings psychoanalysis closer to textual and cultural disciplines, such as philology or literature. Moreover, as is well-known, Freud's writings include not only lectures, case studies, clinical guidelines and theoretical treatises on mental illness, dreams, sexuality and mental processes in general, but also a confusing mixture of literary analyses, biographical comments on writers, as well as quasi-literary texts.

Aware of these aspects of Freud's work, some commentators have placed Freud in the history of hermeneutics. They belittle his debt to the natural sciences in comparison to that which he owed to disciplines concerned with the study of language. John Forrester, for instance, claims that 'it was the field of philological sciences that acted as a source of inspiration for Freud's and psychoanalysis' preoccupation with language'.[11] Forrester seems to concur with Michel Foucault's claim that 'Freud more than anyone else brought the knowledge of man closer to its philological and linguistic model'.[12] Jacques Lacan, too, conceives psychoanalysis primarily in linguistic or hermeneutic terms. In Lacan's words: 'If psychoanalysis is to become instituted as the science of the unconscious, one must set out with the notion that the unconscious is structured like a language.'[13]

In contrast to these commentators, Paul Ricoeur has recognized Freud's attempted union of hermeneutics and causal explanation as constituting not only the 'central difficulty in psychoanalytic epistemology', but also its *raison d'être*.[14] Throughout his discussion of Freud's writings, Ricoeur refers to them as forming a 'mixed discourse that falls outside the motive–cause alternative'.[15] However, he argues that in terms of the procedures which can be used to establish their validity, psychoanalytic interpretations are located within the hermeneutic realm of meaning alone, and subject 'to the same kind of questions as the validity of a historical or exegetical interpretation'.[16]

Jürgen Habermas also stresses the cause–intention merger in psychoanalysis and declares Freud's science to be 'the only tangible example of a science incorporating methodical self-reflection' because it 'joins hermeneutics with operations that genuinely seemed to be reserved to the natural sciences'.[17] Yet Habermas also criticizes Freud for failing to recognize psychoanalysis as the self-reflective depth hermeneutics which he, Habermas, proclaims it to be, and for undergirding it with misleading scientistic models of energy-distribution. In order to develop psychoanalysis in what he takes to be its proper direction, Habermas, too, suggests replacing causal aspects in Freud's discourse by a hermeneutics 'which explicates the conditions of the possibility of psychoanalytic knowledge'.[18]

Thus, what commentators on both sides of the science-or-hermeneutics divide have in common, is that they seek to restrict Freud's interdisciplinary work to one discursive dimension, which they make dominant as representing the 'true' Freud.[19] In contrast to these one-dimensional reductions of Freud's work to either hermeneutics or science, a political reading, such as has been suggested here, does not 'discipline' psychoanalysis by imposing on it a stringent interpretive regime which excludes fundamental components from its domain. Instead, a political reading of Freud explains how and why facets of psychoanalysis which *prima facie* may appear to be incompatible with each other, form part of this complex but coherent interdisciplinary science.

As I have shown, such a reading is plausible in terms of the textual and contextual evidence available. It is parsimonious, comprehensive and internally consistent, in that it can be used throughout Freud's texts. It is applicable both to Freud's individual psychology and his theory of large-scale social formations. It can make sense of some aspects of his writings which hitherto have seemed to be confused or mistaken, such as his notions of psychic energy and representation. It provides insights both into Freud's theory-formation and the dynamics of psychoanalytic practice, as well as into the relationship between the two. Therefore I suggest that a political reading of psychoanalysis constitutes an alternative which is preferable to the two dominant traditions of commentary on Freud.

Moreover, a political reading of Freud is fruitful in that it can serve to keep psychoanalytic discourse alive as a language for the articulation of internal and interpersonal conflicts. Obviously, this does not mean that I hold Freud's concepts and categories to be sacred and beyond criticism. Rather, my position implies that Freud's work should provoke critical thinking about the mind's hidden dynamics, forces and structures. Thus, I suggest that both one's understanding of the psyche and of politics may benefit from an attempt to develop a discourse on power which is applicable not only to the external world but also to the mind's internal reality, intertwines the interpretation of meaning with causal explanation, and thereby continues a project which Freud initiated about a century ago.

Notes

All references which indicate only year of publication, volume (in Roman numbers) and page (in Latin numbers), are to Freud's books and articles in *The Standard Edition of the Complete Psychological Works of Sigmund Freud*, 24 vols, ed. J. Strachey (London: The Hogarth Press, 1953–74). The translation of some passages has been modified; such modifications have been indicated in the notes. All titles of items from the *Standard Edition* can be found in the list of 'References to the Standard Edition' in the references section below. In all instances translations from German sources are my own.

Preface

1 e.g. W. J. M. McGrath, 'Freud as Hannibal: The politics of the brother band', *Central European History* 7 (1974): 31–57; W. J. M. McGrath, *Freud's Discovery of Psychoanalysis: The Politics of Hysteria* (Ithaca: Cornell University Press, 1986); S. Rothman and P. Isenberg, 'Sigmund Freud and the politics of marginality', *Central European History* 7 (1974): 58–78; C. E. Schorske, *Fin-de-siècle Vienna: Politics and Culture* (Cambridge: Cambridge University Press, 1981).

2 e.g. R. Jacoby, *The Repression of Psychoanalysis: Otto Fenichel and the Political Freudians* (New York: Basic Books, 1983); F. Roustang, *Dire Mastery: Discipleship from Freud to Lacan* (Baltimore: Johns Hopkins University Press, 1982); P. Roazen, *Freud and His Followers* (Harmondsworth: Penguin, 1976); M. Rustin, 'The social organization of secrets: Towards a sociology of psychoanalysis', *International Review of Psycho-Analysis* 12 (1985): 143–59; S. Turkle, *Psychoanalytic Politics: Freud's French Revolution* (New York: Basic Books, 1978); G. Weisz, 'Scientists and sectarians: The case of psychoanalysis', *Journal of the History of the Behavioral Sciences* 11 (1975): 350–64.

3 e.g. C. F. Alford, *The Self in Social Theory: A Psychoanalytic Account of Its Construction in Plato, Hobbes, Locke, Rawls, and Rousseau* (New Haven: Yale University Press, 1991); I. Craib, *Psychoanalysis and Social Theory: The Limits of Sociology* (Amherst: The University of Massachusetts Press, 1990); J. M. Glass, 'Hobbes and narcissism: Pathology in the state of nature', *Political*

Theory 8 (1980): 335–63; J. M. Glass, 'Notes on the paranoid factor in political philosophy: Fear, anxiety, and domination', *Political Psychology* 9 (1988): 209–28; F. Weinstein and G. M. Platt, *The Wish to be Free: Society, Psyche and Value Change* (Berkeley: University of California Press, 1969); F. Weinstein and G. M. Platt, *Psychoanalytic Sociology* (Baltimore: Johns Hopkins University Press, 1973).

4   e.g. I. H. Cohen, *Ideology and Unconsciousness: Reich, Freud, and Marx* (New York: New York University Press, 1982); E. Fromm, *The Crisis of Psychoanalysis* (Harmondsworth: Penguin, 1978); G. Horowitz, *Basic and Surplus Repression in Psychoanalytic Theory: Freud, Reich and Marcuse* (Toronto: University of Toronto Press, 1977); J. Kovel, *The Radical Spirit: Essays on Psychoanalysis and Society* (London: Free Association Books, 1988); R. Lichtman, *The Production of Desire: The Integration of Psychoanalysis into Marxist Theory* (New York: The Free Press, 1982); W. Reich, *The Mass Psychology of Fascism* (Harmondsworth: Penguin, 1978); W. Reich, *Sex-Pol, Essays 1929–1934*, ed. L. Baxandall (New York: Random House, 1972).

5   e.g. R. Boyers (ed.), *Psychological Man* (New York: Harper and Row, 1975); N. Hale, *Freud and the Americans* (New York: Oxford University Press, 1971); B. Richards, *Images of Freud: Cultural Responses to Psychoanalysis* (London: J. M. Dent, 1989); P. Rieff, *The Triumph of the Therapeutic* (Harmondsworth: Penguin, 1966).

6   e.g. J. Benjamin, *The Bonds of Love: Psychoanalysis, Feminism, and the Problem of Domination* (New York: Pantheon, 1988); T. Brennan, *The Interpretation of the Flesh: Freud and Femininity* (London: Routledge, 1992); N. Chodorow, *The Reproduction of Mothering: Psychoanalysis and the Sociology of Gender* (Berkeley: University of California Press, 1982); N. Chodorow, *Feminism and Psychoanalytic Theory* (New Haven: Yale University Press, 1989); J. Mitchell, *Psychoanalysis and Feminism* (Harmondsworth: Penguin, 1975); M. Sprengnether, *The Spectral Mother: Freud, Feminism and Psychoanalysis* (Ithaca: Cornell University Press, 1990).

7   J. B. Abramson, *Liberation and Its Limits: The Moral and Political Thought of Freud* (New York: Free Press, 1984); S. Frosh, *The Politics of Psychoanalysis: An Introduction to Freudian and Post-Freudian Theory* (Houndmills: Macmillan, 1987); Y. Gabriel, *Freud and Society* (London: Routledge and Kegan Paul, 1983); J. Habermas, *Knowledge and Human Interest* (London: Heinemann, 1978); R. Jacoby, *Social Amnesia: A Critique of Conformist Psychology From Adler to Laing* (Hassocks: Harvester Press, 1975); H. Marcuse, *Eros and Civilization: A Philosophical Inquiry into Freud* (Boston: Beacon Press, 1966); H. Marcuse, *Five Lectures: Psychoanalysis, Politics, and Utopia* (Boston: Beacon Press, 1970); P. Rieff, *Freud: The Mind of the Moralist* (London: Methuen, 1965); P. Roazen, *Freud: Political and Social Thought* (New York, 1970); E. V. Wolfenstein, *Psychoanalytic-Marxism: Groundwork* (London: Free Association Books, 1993).

8   R. A. Dahl, *Modern Political Analysis* (New Jersey: Prentice-Hall, 1963), p. 6.

9   My discussion of the concept of power draws on the following sources: T. Ball, 'Power, causation and explanation', *Polity* 8 (1975): 189–214; T. Ball,

Transforming Political Discourse: Political Theory and Critical Conceptual History (Oxford: Basil Blackwell, 1988), pp. 80–105; W. E. Connolly, *The Terms of Political Discourse* (Oxford: Oxford University Press, 1983), pp. 9–44, 85–137; M. Foucault, *Power/Knowledge: Selected Interviews and Other Writings 1972–1977*, ed. C. Gordon (New York: Pantheon, 1980); J. C. Isaac, *Power and Marxist Theory: A Realist View* (Ithaca: Cornell University Press, 1987); S. Lukes, *Power: A Radical View* (London: Macmillan, 1972); T. E. Wartenberg, *The Forms of Power: From Domination to Transformation* (Philadelphia: Temple University Press, 1990).

Part I

1 Cf. Q. Skinner, *The Foundations of Modern Political Thought* (Cambridge: Cambridge University Press, 1978), vol. 1, p. xiii. Cf. J. Tully (ed.), *Meaning and Context: Quentin Skinner and his Critics* (Princeton: Princeton University Press, 1988), which contains a comprehensive collection of Skinner's methodological articles, an excellent introduction by James Tully, and a number of essays written by Skinner's critics.

Chapter 1

1 B. A. Morel, *Traité des dégénérences physiques, intéllectuelles et morales de l'espèce humaine et des causes qui produisent ces variétés maladives* (Paris: Ballière, 1857).

2 e.g. L. Löwenfeld, *Die nervösen Störungen sexuellen Ursprungs* (Wiesbaden: J. F. Bergmann, 1891), pp. 61, 75–6; cf. D. Pick, *Faces of Degeneration: A European Disorder, c.1848–c.1918* (Cambridge: Cambridge University Press, 1989); J. E. Chamberlin and S. L. Gilman (eds), *Degeneration: The Dark Side of Progress* (New York: Columbia University Press, 1985); R. A. Nye, 'Degeneration and the medical model of cultural crisis in the French *Belle Epoque*', in S. Drescher, S. Sabean and S. Sharlin (eds), *Political Symbolism in Modern Europe: Essays in Honor of G. L. Mosse* (New Brunswick: Transaction, 1982); G. L. Mosse, 'Nationalism and respectability: Normal and abnormal sexuality in the nineteenth century', *Journal of Contemporary History* 17 (1982): 221–46; S. L. Gilman, *Difference and Pathology: Stereotypes of Sexuality, Race, and Madness* (Ithaca: Cornell University Press, 1985), especially pp. 150–62, 191–216.

3 Cited in H. F. Ellenberger, *The Discovery of the Unconscious: The History and Evolution of Dynamic Psychiatry* (London: Allen Lane, 1970).

4 M. S. Micale, 'Charcot and the idea of hysteria in the male: a study of gender, mental science and medical diagnostics in late nineteenth century France', *Medical History* 34 (1990): 363–411; E. Showalter, 'Hysteria, feminism, and gender', in S. L. Gilman et al., *Hysteria Beyond Freud* (Berkeley, University of California Press, 1993), pp. 307, 313–14.

5 T. Lutz, *American Nervousness, 1903: An Anecdotal History* (Ithaca: Cornell University Press, 1991); G. F. Drinka, *The Birth of Neurosis: Myth, Malady and*

the Victorians (New York: Simon and Schuster, 1984), pp. 184–97; Ellenberger, *Discovery of the Unconscious*, pp. 242–4.

6   All these elements can be found in two then widely-read works: R. Krafft-Ebing, *Nervosität und neurasthenische Zustände* (Vienna: Hödler, 1895) and F. C. Müller's *Handbuch der Neurasthenie* (Leipzig: Vogel, 1893), which declared neurasthenia to be the *'Signatur unserer Culturepoche'* ('the mark of our cultural era'). Cf. pp. 1–17, where Müller's comprehensive bibliography lists several hundred items.

7   W. James, 'Degeneration. Max Nordau', *The Psychological Review* 2 (1895): 289–90; G. B. Shaw, *The Sanity of Art* (New York: Boni and Liveright, 1918); cf. L. L. Maik, 'Nordau's *Degeneration*: The American controversy', *Journal of the History of Ideas* 50 (1989): 607–23.

8   M. Nordau, *Degeneration* (London: Heinemann, 1920), p. 18.

9   Ibid., p. 40.

10 Cf. Pick, *Faces of Degeneration*, pp. 109–52.

11 C. Lombroso, *Genie und Irrsinn in ihren Beziehungen zum Gesetz, zur Kritik und zur Geschichte* (Leipzig: Reclam, 1887), p. 78.

12 R. Krafft-Ebing, *Psychopathia Sexualis: A Medico-Forensic Study*, trans. H. E. Wedeck (New York: Putnam, 1965), p. 27.

13 S. L. Gilman, *Freud, Race, and Gender* (Princeton: Princeton University Press, 1993), pp. 104–5.

14 Ibid., pp. 209–39; D. Pick, 'The faces of anarchy: Lombroso and the politics of criminal science in post-unification Italy', *History Workshop Journal* 21 (1986): 60–86; I. Dowbiggin, 'Degeneration and hereditarianism in French mental medicine 1840–90: Psychiatric theory as ideological adaptation', in W. F. Bynum, R. Porter and M. Shepherd (eds) *The Anatomy of Madness: Essays in the History of Psychiatry*, vol. 1 (London: Tavistock, 1985), pp. 188–232; W. Schneider, 'Toward the improvement of the human race: The History of eugenics in France', *Journal of Modern History* 54 (1982): 268–91; R. A. Nye, *Crime, Madness and Politics in Modern France: The Medical Concept of National Decline* (Princeton: Princeton University Press, 1984).

15 J. Goldstein, 'The hysteria diagnosis and the politics of anticlericalism in late nineteenth-century France', *Journal of Modern History* 54 (1982): 239.

16 J. Goldstein, *Console and Classify: The French Psychiatric Profession in the Nineteenth Century* (Cambridge: Cambridge University Press, 1987), p. 368.

17 Ibid., p. 372.

18 H. S. Decker, *Freud in Germany: Revolution and Reaction in Science 1893–1907* (New York: International Universities Press, 1977; *Psychological Issues*, vol. XI), p. 80.

19 Cited ibid., p. 80.

20 Cited in Gilman, *Freud, Race, and Gender*, p. 94.

21 J. Goldstein, 'The Wandering Jew and the problem of psychiatric anti-Semitism in *fin-de-siècle* France', *Journal of Contemporary History* 20 (1985): 526–7; C. G. Goetz, 'Commentary', in *Charcot, the Clinician: The Tuesday Lessons*, trans. C. G. Goetz (New York: Raven Press, 1987), pp. 23–4. Cf. S. L. Gilman, 'The image of the hysteric', in S. L. Gilman et al.,

Hysteria Beyond Freud (Berkeley, University of California Press, 1993), pp. 411–14.

22 T. Gelfand, 'Charcot's response to Freud's rebellion', *Journal of the History of Ideas* 50 (1989): 295, 298–300. For a comprehensive analysis of the literature cf. Gilman, *Freud, Race, and Gender*, pp. 93–113.

23 A. Pilcz, *Beitrag zur vergleichenden Rassenpsychiatrie* (Leipzig und Wien: Deuticke, 1906); H. Hoppe, *Krankheiten und Sterblichkeit bei Juden und Nichtjuden: Mit besonderer Berücksichtigung der Alkoholfrage* (Berlin: Calvary, 1903); M. Sichel, *Die Geistesstörungen bei den Juden* (Leipzig: Kaufmann, 1909); M. Sichel, 'Die progressive Paralyse bei den Juden', *Archiv für Psychiatrie* 52 (1913): 1030–42.

24 Cf. S. L. Gilman, 'Jews and mental illness: Medical metaphors, anti-Semitism and the Jewish response', *Journal of the History of the Behavioral Sciences* 20 (1984): 150–9. For the Jewish Response in France, cf. Goldstein, 'Wandering Jew', p. 534.

25 C. Lombroso, *Der Antisemitismus und die Juden im Lichte der modernen Wissenschaft* (Leipzig: Wigand, 1894), pp. 68–72.

26 Ibid., pp. 30–1, 36, 43.

27 Ibid., pp. 73–5.

28 Sichel, *Geistesstörungen bei den Juden*, p. iii.

29 Hoppe, *Krankheiten und Sterblichkeit*, pp. 55–7.

30 Ibid., pp. 58–9.

31 L. Pinsker, *Autoemanzipation!* (Berlin: Jüdischer Verlag, 1936), p. 9.

32 Nordau, *Degeneration*, p. 209.

33 For further illustrations of the discourse of Jewish doctors on hysteria among Jews, cf. Gilman, 'The image of the hysteric', pp. 405–6.

34 R. Becker, *Die Nervosität bei den Juden: Ein Beitrag zur Rassenpsychiatrie* (Zürich: Orell Füssli, 1919), pp. 5, 30.

Chapter 2

1 Cf. 1888b, I : 50.

2 1892–4, I : 143.

3 Ibid., p. 139.

4 1895d, II : 103–4.

5 Ibid., p. 294; cf. p. 233.

6 Ibid., p. 102.

7 Ibid., p. 122.

8 1896a, III : 143–9.

9 1895d, II : 104.

10 1893a, II : 13.

11 1908d, IX : 195.

12 1895d, II : 123.

13 1893h, III : 37; cf. 1893a, II : 8.

14 1892–3, I : 126.

15 1895d, II : 89.

16 Ibid., p. 170.
17 Ibid., p. 161.
18 Ibid., p. 152.
19 Ibid., p. 143.
20 Ibid., p. 155.
21 Ibid., p. 176.
22 Ibid., p. 166 (original emphasis).
23 1895d, II : 257–60.
24 For two enlightening surveys and critical discussions of the feminist interpretation and historiography of hysteria, cf. E. Showalter, 'Hysteria, feminism, and gender', in Gilman et al., *Hysteria Beyond Freud*, pp. 286–344; M. S. Micale, 'Hysteria and its historiography: A review of past and present writings (II)', *History of Science* 27 (1989): 319–31. Cf. also my discussion of feminist interpretations of hysteria in chapter 11.
25 M. Foucault, *Mental Illness and Psychology* (New York: Harper and Row, 1976), pp. 39–40.
26 1908d, IX : 191–2.
27 1895d, II : 233.
28 1908d, IX : 194.
29 Ibid., p. 182.
30 Ibid., pp. 145–6.
31 1895c, III : 74; 1895f, III : 123–39; 1896a, III : 143–56; 1896b, III : 163.
32 1898a, III : 274.
33 1905d, VII : 138.
34 H. Nunberg and E. Federn (eds), *Minutes of the Vienna Psychoanalytic Society*, vol. 1: 1906–8 (New York: International Universities Press, 1962), p. 186.
35 M. Foucault, *The History of Sexuality, Volume One: An Introduction* (Harmondsworth: Penguin, 1981), p. 119. Cf. S. L. Gilman, 'Sexology, psychoanalysis, and degeneration: From a theory of race to a race of theory', in Chamberlin and Gilman (eds) *Degeneration*, pp. 72–96. Gilman provides a comprehensive collection of Freud's comments on degeneracy.
36 1905e, VII : 50.
37 1908d, IX : 198, 203.
38 1908b, IX : 172.
39 1916–17, XVI : 434.
40 E. Fromm, *The Crisis of Psychoanalysis: Essays on Freud, Marx and Social Psychology* (Harmondsworth: Penguin, 1978), p. 15.

Chapter 3

1 É. Drumont, *La France Juive*, vol. 1 (Paris: Marpon & Flammarion, 1886), p. 107.
2 L. Stewart, 'Freud before Oedipus: Race and heredity in the origins of psychoanalysis', *Journal of the History of Biology* 9 (1976): 222.

3 F. J. Sulloway, *Freud, Biologist of the Mind: Beyond the Psychoanalytic Legend* (London: Burnett/André Deutsch, 1979), p. 423; W. J. M. McGrath, *Freud's Discovery of Psychoanalysis* (Ithaca: Cornell University Press, 1986), pp. 161–2. Sander Gilman has praised Stewart's article as 'the best essay written on the question of Freud's use and reaction to the science of race'. S. L. Gilman, *Freud, Race, and Gender* (Princeton: Princeton University Press, 1993), p. 205.

4 D. Bakan, *Sigmund Freud and the Jewish Mystical Tradition* (Princeton: Princeton University Press, 1958), p. 170.

5 J. M. Cuddihy, *The Ordeal of Civility: Freud, Marx, Lévi-Strauss, and the Jewish Struggle with Modernity* (New York: Basic Books, 1974), pp. 18–19, 25–6, 101, 30.

6 M. Robert, *From Oedipus to Moses: Freud's Jewish Identity* (Garden City: Anchor/Doubleday, 1976); cf. M. Bergman, 'Moses and the evolution of Freud's Jewish identity', *Israel Annals of Psychiatry and Related Disciplines* 14 (1976): 3–26; W. J. M. McGrath, 'Freud as Hannibal', *Central European History* 7 (1974): 31–57; S. Rothman and P. Isenberg, 'Sigmund Freud and the politics of marginality', *Central European History* 7 (1974): 58–78.

7 D. S. Blatt, 'The development of the hero: Sigmund Freud and the reformation of the Jewish tradition', *Psychoanalysis and Contemporary Thought* 11 (1988): 639–703.

8 E. Rice, *Freud and Moses: The Long Journey Home* (New York: State University of New York Press, 1990).

9 Y. H. Yerushalmi, *Freud's Moses: Judaism Terminable and Interminable* (New Haven: Yale University Press, 1991), p. 99.

10 E. Roith, *The Riddle of Freud: Jewish Influences on his Theory of Female Sexuality* (London: Tavistock, 1987).

11 Gilman, *Freud, Race, and Gender*, pp. 48.

12 It is impossible to provide here a comprehensive bibliography of this extensive body of literature. However, for an overview of the first 50 years of writings on Freud and Judaism cf. J. Miller, 'Interpretations of Freud's Jewishness, 1924–1974', *Journal of the History of the Behavioral Sciences* 17 (1981): 357–74. For a more up-to-date summary cf. I. Oxaal, 'The Jewish origins of psychoanalysis reconsidered', in E. Timms and N. Segal (eds), *Freud in Exile: Psychoanalysis and its Vicissitudes* (New Haven: Yale University Press, 1988), pp. 37–53. For the most recent and exhaustive list of the literature I have come across, cf. Gilman, *Freud, Race, and Gender*, pp. 201–4.

13 C. Schorske, *Fin-de-Siècle Vienna: Politics and Culture* (Cambridge: Cambridge University Press, 1981).

14 D. B. Klein, *Jewish Origins of the Psychoanalytic Movement* (New York: Praeger, 1981), p. ix.

15 Ibid., pp. 150–1.

16 Ibid., p. 139.

17 P. Gay, *A Godless Jew: Freud, Atheism, and the Making of Psychoanalysis* (New Haven: Yale University Press, 1987), p. 48.

18 Ibid., p. 147; cf. P. Gay, *Freud, Jews and Other Germans: Masters and Victims in Modernist Culture* (New York: Oxford University Press, 1978), p. 77.

19 D. B. Klein, 'Assimilation and dissimilation', *New German Critique* 19 (Winter 1980): 162.

20 W. J. M. McGrath, 'Oedipus at Berggasse 19', *New York Review of Books*, 18 August 1988, p. 27.

21 J. Tully, 'The pen is a mighty sword', in Tully (ed.), *Meaning and Context: Quentin Skinner and his Critics* (Princeton: Princeton University Press, 1988), p. 12.

22 4 September 1883, Freud, *The Letters of Sigmund Freud*, ed. E. L. Freud (New York, Basic Books, 1975), p. 54. Cf. Yerushalmi, *Freud's Moses*, p. 39.

23 6 May 1926, Freud, *Letters of Sigmund Freud*, p. 367; cf. 1925d, XX : 9; 1925e, XIX : 222.

24 M. Graf, 'Reminiscences of Professor Sigmund Freud', *The Psychoanalytic Quarterly* 11 (1942): 473.

25 26 December 1908, 20 July 1908, S. Freud and K. Abraham, *A Psycho-Analytic Dialogue: The Letters of Sigmund Freud and Karl Abraham 1907–1926*, eds H. C. Abraham and E. L. Freud (London: Hogarth Press, 1965), pp. 63, 46 (hereafter *Freud/Abraham*).

26 26 December 1908, ibid., p. 64.

27 5 May 1908, ibid., p. 34.

28 26 December 1908, ibid., p. 64.

29 23 July 1908, ibid., p. 46. For a more complete account of Freud's epistolary comments on his and his followers' Jewish identity, cf. Gilman, *Freud, Race, and Gender*, pp. 30–4.

30 1912–13, XIII : xv; cf. 1928a, XXI : 170.

31 6 May 1926, Freud, *Letters of Sigmund Freud*, pp. 366–7.

32 1905c, VIII : 72.

33 Ibid., p. 49; cf. Gay, *Godless Jew*, p. 129. For a different view of Freud's preoccupation with Jewish jokes, cf. S. L. Gilman, 'Jewish jokes: Freud and the hidden language of the Jews', *Psychoanalysis and Contemporary Thought* 7 (1984): 591–614.

34 11 December 1938, cited in Gay, *Godless Jew*, p. 152.

35 1939a, XXIII : 7.

36 Ibid., p. 113.

37 Ibid., p. 51.

38 Cited in Yerushalmi, *Freud's Moses*, p. 43.

39 Cited in Gilman, *Freud, Race, and Gender*, p. 29.

40 I. Deutscher, *The Non-Jewish Jew and Other Essays*, ed. T. Deutscher (London: Oxford University Press, 1968), pp. 34–5.

Chapter 4

1 1893c, I : 162–3.

2 Ibid., pp. 169–70.

3 G. Zilboorg, *History of Medical Psychology* (New York: W. W. Norton, 1941), p. 345.

4 H. S. Decker, *Freud in Germany: Revolution and Reaction in Science 1893–1907* (New York: International Universities Press, 1977), pp. 69–70.

5 K. Levin, *Freud's Early Psychology of the Neuroses* (Hassocks: Harvester Press, 1978), pp. 19, 29–33; Zilboorg, *History of Medical Psychology*, p. 423.

6 1916–17, XV : 20. Cf. R. Porter, 'The body and the mind, the doctor and the patient: Negotiating hysteria', in S. L. Gilman et al. (eds), *Hysteria Beyond Freud* (Berkeley: University of California Press, 1993), p. 237.

7 1896c, III : 200–1.

8 Ibid., p. 202.

9 Ibid., p. 209.

10 1896b, III : 164; 1896c, III : 208.

11 28 April 1897 and 12 December 1897, S. Freud, *The Complete Letters of Sigmund Freud to Wilhelm Fliess, 1887–1904*, ed. and trans. J. M. Masson (Cambridge, Mass.: Harvard University Press, 1985), p. 237; p. 286 (hereafter *Freud/Fliess*).

12 21 September 1897, ibid., p. 264.

13 11 January 1897, ibid., p. 222.

14 2 November 1896, ibid., p. 212.

15 1896a, III : 154.

16 The word '*Urszenen*' appears in Draft L, attached to Freud's letter to Fliess, 2 May 1897, *Freud/Fliess*, p. 240.

17 1896c, III : 211.

18 Ibid., p. 215; cf. J. Forrester, 'Rape, seduction and psychoanalysis', in S. Tomaselli and R. Porter (eds), *Rape* (Oxford: Oxford University Press, 1986), p. 71.

19 1896c, III : 215.

20 26 April 1896, *Freud/Fliess*, p. 184.

21 1905d, VII : 190.

22 F. J. Sulloway, *Freud, Biologist of the Mind: Beyond the Psychoanalytic Legend* (London: Burnett/André Deutsch, 1979), p. 447.

23 1914d, XIV : 17.

24 1933a, XXII : 120.

25 1925d, XX : 33; cf. 1914d, XIV : 17.

26 10 September 1981, cited in J. M. Masson, *Freud: The Assault on Truth: Freud's Suppression of the Seduction Theory* (London: Faber, 1984), p. 113.

27 Masson, *Freud: The Assault on Truth*, p. xxiii; cf. pp. 134, 189.

28 Ibid., p. 11; cf. pp. 131–3.

29 E. Fromm, *The Crisis of Psychoanalysis: Essays on Freud, Marx and Social Psychology* (Harmondsworth: Penguin, 1978), p. 63; A. Miller, *Thou Shalt not Be Aware: Society's Betrayal of the Child* (London: Pluto Press, 1984; originally published in German in 1981).

30 Fromm, *The Crisis of Psychoanalysis*, pp. 62–3.

31 My discussion here draws on A. Davidson, 'Assault on Freud', *London Review of Books*, 5–19 July 1984, pp. 9–11; R. A. Paul, 'Freud and the

seduction theory: A critical examination of Masson's *Freud: The Assault On Truth'*, *Journal of Psychoanalytic Anthropology* 8 (1985): 161–87; P. Robinson, *Freud and His Critics* (Berkeley: University of California Press, 1993), pp. 101–78.

32 Robinson, *Freud and His Critics*, p. 115.

33 1896a, III : 153.

34 1896c, III : 204.

35 21 September 1897, *Freud/Fliess*, p. 264.

36 H. Israels and M. Schatzman, 'The seduction theory', *History of Psychiatry* 4 (1991): 53–6. Cf. J. G. Schimek, 'Fact and fantasy in the seduction theory: A historical review', *Journal of the American Psychoanalytic Association* 35 (1987): 937–65.

37 5 July 1907, *Freud/Abraham*, p. 2.

38 1 January 1913, S. Freud and O. Pfister, *Psycho-Analysis and Faith: The Letters of Sigmund Freud and Oskar Pfister*, eds E. L. Freud and H. Meng (London: Hogarth Press, 1963), p. 59. Cf. 1931b, XXI : 232; 1895d, II : 134n. (footnote dates from 1924); 1939a, XXIII : 75; 1940a, XXIII : 187.

39 1931b, XXI : 232.

40 1940a, XXIII : 187.

41 1916–17, XVI : 367–70.

42 3 January 1899, *Freud/Fliess*, p. 338.

43 1900a, V : 491.

44 1914d, XIV : 18.

45 Masson, *Freud: The Assault on Truth*, p. 144.

46 Fromm, *Crisis of Psychoanalysis*, pp. 98–110; W. G. Niederland, *The Schreber Case: Psychoanalytic Profile of a Paranoid Personality* (New York: Quadrangle, 1974); M. Schatzman, *Soul Murder: Persecution in the Family* (New York: Random House, 1973); L. Sheleff, *Generations Apart: Adult Hostility to Youth* (New York: McGraw-Hill, 1981), pp. 53–70.

47 1900a, IV : xxiii.

48 1925d, XX : 47.

49 1900a, V : 342.

50 1939a, XXIII : 132; Freud's conception of an unconscious phylogenetic inheritance is discussed in more detail in chapter 16.

51 1929a, XXI : 249 (translation modified).

52 1905d, VII : 171.

53 C. Taylor, 'Interpretation and the sciences of man', *Review of Metaphysics* 25 (1971): 3–51; Z. Bauman, *Hermeneutics and Social Science: Approaches to Understanding* (London: Hutchinson, 1978), p. 31.

Part II

1 D. E. Carlston, 'Turning psychology on itself: The rhetoric of psychology and the psychology of rhetoric', in J. S. Nelson, A. Megill and D. N. McCloskey (eds), *The Rhetoric of the Human Sciences: Language and Argument in Scholarship and Public Affairs* (Madison: University of Wisconsin Press,

1987), p. 153; cf. S. E. Leary (ed.), *Metaphors in the History of Psychology* (Cambridge: Cambridge University Press, 1990).

2 1926e, XX : 195.

3 1933a, XXII : 72.

4 1916–17, XVI : 246.

5 1900a, V : 536.

6 M. Black, *Models and Metaphors* (Ithaca: Cornell University Press, 1962), pp. 39–42.

7 Although it is sufficient for my purpose here to make the case for the metaphorical nature of psychological theories, I should add, perhaps, that I hold all theories in the human sciences to be metaphorically constituted. On the role of metaphors in the human sciences, cf. R. H. Brown, *A Poetic for Sociology: Toward a Logic of Discovery for the Human Sciences* (London: Cambridge University Press, 1977); H. M. Drucker, 'Just analogies?: The place of analogies in political thinking', *Political Studies* 18 (1970): 448–60; E. F. Miller, 'Metaphor and political knowledge', *American Political Science Review* 73 (1979): 155–70; Nelson, Megill and McCloskey (eds) *Rhetoric of the Human Sciences*; E. Zashin and P. C. Chapman, 'The uses of metaphor and analogy: Toward a renewal of political language', *Journal of Politics* 36 (1974): 290–326.

8 1915e, XIV : 181 (original emphasis).

9 1926f, XX : 265.

10 1915e, XIV : 181.

11 Ibid., pp. 173–5.

12 1916–17, XV : 67.

13 1920g, XVIII : 60.

14 Ibid., pp. 30–1.

15 1937c, XXIII : 225.

16 D. P. Spence, *The Freudian Metaphor: Toward Paradigm Change in Psychoanalysis* (New York: W. W. Norton, 1987), p. 7.

17 S. Fisher and R. P. Greenberg, *The Scientific Credibility of Freud's Theories and Therapy*, vol. 1 (Brighton: Harvester Press, 1977), p. 414; P. Kline, *Fact and Fantasy in Freudian Theory* (London: Methuen, 1972), pp. 351–3.

18 Cf. J. T. Edelson, 'Freud's use of metaphor', *The Psychoanalytic Study of the Child* 38 (1983): 17–60; B. D. Lewin, 'Metaphor, mind and manikin', *The Psychoanalytic Quarterly* 40 (1971): 6–39; L. Wurmser, 'A defense of the use of metaphor in analytic theory formation', *The Psychoanalytic Quarterly* 46 (1977): 466–98; P. Mahony, *Freud as a Writer* (New York: International Universities Press, 1982).

19 Cf. M. M. Gill, 'Metapsychology is not psychology', in M. M. Gill and P. S. Holzman (eds), *Psychology Versus Metapsychology* (New York: International Universities Press, 1976; *Psychological Issues*, vol. IX). For concise and critical histories of psychoanalytic opposition to metapsychology, cf. M. H. Klein, 'Throwing out the baby with the bathwater: A historical analysis of the antimetapsychology movement', *Psychoanalysis and Contemporary Thought* 12 (1989): 565–98; J. Kovel, *The Radical Spirit: Essays on*

Psychoanalysis and Society (London: Free Association Books, 1988), pp. 80–115.

20 M. N. Eagle, *Recent Developments in Psychoanalysis: A Critical Evaluation* (Cambridge, Mass.: Harvard University Press, 1984), p. 149.

21 S. Weber, *Institution and Interpretation* (Minneapolis: University of Minnesota Press, 1987), p. 73.

Chapter 5

1 1900a, V : 613.
2 1916–17, XV : 138–9.
3 22 December 1897, S. Freud, *The Complete Letters of Sigmund Freud to Wilhelm Fliess, 1887–1904*, ed. and trans. J. M. Masson (Cambridge, Mass.: Harvard University Press, 1985), p. 289 (hereafter *Freud/Fliess*); cf. 1895d, II : 269; 1896b, III : 182–5.
4 1900a, IV : 141–3.
5 E. Gellner, *The Psychoanalytic Movement or the Cunning of the Unreason* (London: Paladin, 1985), p. 112.
6 R. Rorty, *Essays on Heidegger and Others, Philosophical Papers*, vol. 2 (Cambridge: Cambridge University Press, 1991), p. 149.
7 M. G. Levine, 'Censorship's self-administration', *Psychoanalysis and Contemporary Thought* 9 (1986): 609–14.
8 1900a, IV : 307 (translation modified).
9 Ibid., p. 284.
10 1900a, V : 489.
11 Ibid., p. 516.
12 1916–17, XV : 141 (emphasis added).
13 Levine, 'Censorship's self-administration', pp. 605–40.
14 1916–17, XV : 140.

Chapter 6

1 1916–17, XVI : 295.
2 1895d, II : 225n.
3 1900a, V : 537n.
4 Ibid., p. 191.
5 1917a, XVII : 141.
6 1933a, XXII : 72–73.
7 Ibid., p. 72.
8 1926e, XX : 195.
9 1924d, XIX : 176.
10 J. Laplanche and J.-B. Pontalis, *The Language of Psycho-Analysis* (London: The Hogarth Press, 1980), pp. 364–5; cf. H. F. Pitkin, *The Concept of Representation* (Berkeley: University of California Press, 1967), p. 154.
11 1930a, XXI : 124.
12 Ibid., p. 136.

13 1933a, XXII : 60.

14 1924c, XIX : 167.

15 1933a, XXII : 61.

16 1940a, XXIII : 148.

17 1933a, XXII : 75 (translation modified); cf. 1926e, XX : 196.

18 1923b, XIX : 36; cf. 1940a, XXIII : 146.

19 1940a, XXIII : 199.

20 1923b, XIX : 17 (original emphasis).

21 1926e, XX : 201.

22 Ibid., p. 201.

23 1923b, XIX : 55.

24 Ibid., p. 56.

25 1933a, XXII : 78.

26 1940a, XXIII : 172–3.

27 1926e, XX : 221.

28 1932c, XXII : 221 (emphasis added).

29 1917a, XVII : 143.

30 Ibid., p. 142.

Chapter 7

1 A. Rabinbach, *Human Motor: Energy, Fatigue and the Origins of Modernity* (Berkeley: University of California Press, 1992), p. 53.

 2 Cited ibid., p. 55.

 3 1894a, III : 60–61.

 4 1950a, I : 295.

 5 1900a, V : 538.

 6 1950a, I : 298, 301, 312, 336; 1900a, V : 579; 1912c, XII : 231; 1916–17, XVI : 345; 1923b, XIX : 45.

 7 1915d, XIV : 149.

 8 D. R. Swanson, 'A critique of psychic energy as an explanatory concept', *Journal of the American Psychoanalytic Association* 25 (1977): 630.

 9 Panel Report, 'The concept of psychic energy', *Journal of the American Psychoanalytic Association* 11 (1963): 605–18; Panel Report, 'Psychic energy reconsidered', *Journal of the American Psychoanalytic Association* 25 (1976): 647–57.

10 Y. Elkana, 'Borrowing the concept of energy in Freudian psychoanalysis', in E. Cohen, M. Lissak and U. Almagor (eds) *Comparative Social Dynamics: Essays in Honor of S. N. Eisenstadt* (Boulder, Co. Westview Press, 1985), p. 229.

11 Ibid., p. 228.

12 Cf. E. Fromm, *The Crisis of Psychoanalysis* (Harmondsworth: Penguin, 1978), p. 49.

13 1911b, XII : 222.

14 1930a, XXI : 103.

15 1900a, V : 561 (original emphasis).

16 Freud called this quality *'das Drängende'*: 1909b, X : 140–1; cf. 1910a, XI : 136; 1914c, XIV : 78, 1933a, XXII : 96; 1940a, XXIII : 145; J. Strachey, 'Editor's introduction', XIV : 111; J. C. Burnham, 'The medical origins and cultural uses of Freud's instinctual drive theory', *Psychoanalytic Quarterly* 43 (1974): 196–7.

17 1915c, XIV : 117, cf. p. 123; 1910c, XI : 136; 1910i, XI : 217; 1926e, XX : 200.

18 1900a, V : 536. For Freud's repeated emphasis on this point cf. 1915e, XIV : 174; 1916–17, XV : 21; 1916–17, XVI : 393; 1925d, XX : 32–3; 1926e, XX : 194.

19 1937c, XXIII : 242.

20 Cf. Strachey, 'Editor's introduction', XIV : 112–13. Strachey remarks on this duality as if it were an irresolvable contradiction in Freud's writings. But rather than a confusion on Freud's part, it is another instance in which Freud's discourse both posits and transcends boundaries by means of a political metaphor. For Paul Ricoeur's difficulties with the same problem, cf. Ricoeur, *Freud and Philosophy: An Essay on Interpretation* (New Haven: Yale University Press, 1970), pp. 116 n. 2, 137.

21 1915c, XIV : 122 (emphasis added).

22 1905d, VII : 168 (emphasis added).

23 1915e, XIV : 177 (translation modified). As Darius Ornston shows, Strachey was rather fond of the verb 'to represent'. He used it not only to translate *repräsentieren*, but also *entsprechen, wiedergeben, vertreten, darstellen* and *hinstellen*. Cf. D. Ornston, 'Strachey's influence: A preliminary report', *International Journal of Psycho-Analysis* 63 (1982): 416.

24 1910i, XI : 214–15.

25 1915c, XIV : 122 (translation modified); cf. 1940a, XXIII : 148.

26 One of Freud's metapsychological papers is entitled *'Triebe und Triebschicksale'*, which could be translated as 'Drives and their destinies', though Strachey chose 'Instincts and their vicissitudes'. 1915c, XIV : 117.

27 Cf. Laplanche and Pontalis, *Language of Psycho-Analysis*, p. 216.

28 1915c, XIV : 122 (translation modified).

29 1916–17, XVI : 328 (translation modified).

30 Ibid., p. 323, cf. p. 305; 1905e, VII : 50; 1908d, IX : 191.

31 1916–17, XVI : 323 (translation modified).

32 1905d, VII : 235.

33 1910a, XI : 49.

34 1916–17, XVI : 341.

Chapter 8

1 1916–17, XVI : 356.

2 1900a, V : 596–9; 1920g, XVIII : 34; 1940a, XXIII : 168.

3 1917d, XIV : 234 n. 1.

4 J. Strachey, 'Appendix', in Freud, *Standard Edition*, III : 63n.

5 1925h, XIX : 237.

6 1900a, V : 599.

7 Ibid., p. 567, cf. pp. 603–4; 1920g, XVIII : 19.

8 1915e, XIV : 201–2 (translation modified).
9 1900a, V : 613.
10 1926d, XX : 92.
11 1900a, V : 616–17.
12 1933a, XXII : 89.
13 1950a, I : 360–1, cf. p. 370.
14 1911b, XII : 223.
15 1900a, V : 567.
16 1940a, XXIII : 198.
17 1933a, XXII : 33.
18 1926e, XX : 196.
19 1920g, XVIII : 63 (translation modified).
20 1940a, XXIII : 149; 1930a, XXI : 118.
21 1920g, XVIII : 38 (original emphasis).
22 Ibid., pp. 55–6.
23 1930a, XXI : 119.
24 Ibid., p. 122 (translation modified).
25 1933a, XXII : 95.
26 I have chosen not to elaborate on the notion of aggression in Freud's work. However, it has been extensively treated by other authors; for two particularly lucid and comprehensive examples, cf. E. Fromm, *The Anatomy of Human Destructiveness* (Harmondsworth: Penguin, 1977), pp. 581–631; P. Stepansky, *A History of Aggression in Freud* (New York: International Universities Press, 1977; *Psychological Issues*, vol. X).
27 7 February 1930, S. Freud and O. Pfister, *Psycho-Analysis and Faith: The Letters of Sigmund Freud and Oskar Pfister*, eds. H. Meng and E. L. Freud, (London: Hogarth Press, 1963), p. 133.

Chapter 9

1 1933a, XXII : 73; cf. 1913j, XIII : 184.
2 1900a, V : 603; cf. p. 598; 1911b, XII : 220 n. 4.
3 C. B. Macpherson, *The Political Theory of Possessive Individualism* (Oxford: Clarendon Press, 1962), p. 21.
4 Cited in M. Oakeshott, *Hobbes on Civil Association* (Oxford: Clarendon Press, 1975), p. 72.
5 Cited ibid., p. 81.
6 1914d, XIV : 16; cf. 1925d, XX : 30.
7 1900a, V : 610.
8 1933a, XXII : 57.
9 1939a, XXIII : 76.
10 1926d, XX : 146; 1900a, V : 600–1; 1939a, XXIII : 76.
11 1915e, XIV : 181 (translation modified). cf. 1907b, IX : 124; 1905d, VII : 177; 1937c, XXIII : 226.
12 1915d, XIV : 149.
13 1924e, XIX : 185; 1913j, XIII : 181; cf. 1917a, XVII : 142.

14 1940a, XXIII : 173.
15 1926e, XX : 205.
16 1933a, XXII : 80.
17 1900a, V : 580–1.
18 1916–17, XVI : 435.
19 H. Nunberg and E. Federn (eds), *Minutes of the Vienna Psychoanalytic Society*, vol. 2 (New York: International Universities Press, 1962–74), p. 89.
20 1937c, XXIII : 225.
21 1916–17, XVI : 455.
22 1908d, IX : 187; 1914c, XIV : 94; 1916–17, XVI : 345.
23 1914c, XIV : 95.
24 1930a, XXI : 80.
25 1909b, X : 145 (original emphasis; translation modified).
26 1916–17, XVI : 433.
27 1895d, II : 305.
28 1937c, XXIII : 250.
29 1923b, XIX : 50n.
30 1916–17, XVI : 434.
31 Cited in E. Jones, *The Life and Work of Sigmund Freud*, 3 vols, (New York: Basic Books, 1953–7), vol. 2, p. 182 (original emphasis).

Chapter 10

1 1916–17, XVI : 285; cf. 1917a, XVII : 139–44.
2 I. Berlin, *Four Essays on Liberty* (London: Oxford University Press, 1969), pp. xliii–xliv, 132–3.
3 G. Lakoff and M. Johnson, *Metaphors We Live By* (Chicago: Chicago University Press, 1980), p. 158.
4 Berlin, *Four Essays on Liberty*, pp. xliii, 130.
5 Ibid., p. 152.
6 Ibid., pp. xliii–xliv, 131–2, 152.
7 Ibid., pp. xliii–xliv, xxxvii–xxxix, 122–3, 126.
8 P. Gay, 'Freud and freedom: On a fox in a hedgehog's clothing', in A. Ryan (ed.), *The Idea of Freedom: Essays in Honour of Isaiah Berlin* (Oxford: Oxford University Press, 1979), pp. 56–9.
9 R. Rorty, *Essays on Heidegger and Others* (Cambridge: Cambridge University Press, 1991), p. 157.
10 1925i, XIX : 133.
11 1933a, XXII : 171.
12 1925e, XIX : 220 (translation modified).
13 M. J. Adler, *The Idea of Freedom: A Dialectical Examination of Conceptions of and the Controversies about Freedom*, vol. 2 (Garden City: Doubleday, 1961), pp. 548–9.
14 R. Jacoby, *Social Amnesia: A Critique of Conformist Psychology from Adler to Laing* (Hussocks: Harvester Press, 1975), p. 26.
15 Adler, *Idea of Freedom*, vol. 2, pp. 265–6.

16 1915b, XIV : 299.

17 1930a, XXI : 76–7.

18 Y. Gabriel, *Freud and Society* (London: Routledge and Kegan Paul, 1983), p. 101.

19 B. Richards, *Images of Freud: Cultural Responses to Psychoanalysis* (London: J. M. Dent, 1989), p. 21.

20 1916–17, XVI : 434.

21 P. Rieff, *Freud: The Mind of the Moralist* (London: Methuen, 1965), pp. 315–34; cf. J. B. Abramson, *Liberation and Its Limits: The Moral and Political Thought of Freud* (New York: Free Press, 1984), pp. 220–1; P. Ricoeur, *Freud and Philosophy: An Essay on Interpretation* (New Haven: Yale University Press, 1970), p. 280.

Part III

1 P. Laslett, 'The face to face society', in P. Laslett (ed.), *Philosophy, Politics and Society* (Oxford: Basil Blackwell, 1963), p. 158.

2 For the notion of situated social power, cf. T. E. Wartenberg, 'Situated social power', in T. E. Wartenberg (ed.), *Rethinking Power* (Albany, N.Y.: New York State University Press, 1992).

Chapter 11

1 E. Showalter, *The Female Malady: Women, Madness and English Culture, 1830–1980* (London: Virago, 1987), p. 154.

2 G. Didi-Huberman, *Invention de l'hystérie: Charcot et l'iconographie photographique de la Salpêtrière* (Paris: Macula, 1982), p. 32. Cf. Showalter, *Female Malady*, pp. 148–50. For a critique of Didi-Huberman cf. M. S. Micale, 'Hysteria and its historiography: A review of past and present writings (II)', *History of Science* 27 (1989): 337–8. For a fascinating history of the pictorial representation of hysteria cf. S. L. Gilman, 'The image of the hysteric', in S. L. Gilman et al., *Hysteria Beyond Freud* (Berkeley: University of California Press, 1993), pp. 345–452.

3 H. S. Decker, 'Freud and Dora: Constraints on medical progress', *Journal of Social History* 14 (1980–1), p. 451.

4 C. Smith-Rosenberg, 'The hysterical woman: Sex roles and role conflict in 19th-century America', *Social Research* 39 (1972): 674–5.

5 P. Flechsig, 'On the gynecological treatment of hysteria', in J. M. Masson (ed.), *A Dark Science: Women, Sexuality and Psychiatry in the Nineteenth Century* (New York: Farrar, Straus, and Giroux, 1986), p. 57. Originally published in *Neurologisches Centralblatt* 19/20 (1884).

6 A. Hegar, 'On the sham castration performed by Dr. Israel', in Masson (ed.), *A Dark Science*, p. 155. Originally published in *Berliner klinische Wochenschrift* 48 (1880): 680–4.

7 G. F. Drinka, *The Birth of Neurosis: Myth, Malady and the Victorians* (New York: Simon and Schuster, 1984), p. 198.

8   S. W. Mitchell, *Fat and Blood: An Essay on the Treatment of Certain Forms of Neurasthenia and Hysteria*, 3rd edn (Philadelphia: J. B. Lippincott, 1884), p. 61.

9   Ibid., p. 41.

10 Ibid., p. 47.

11 Ibid., p. 49.

12 Ibid., p. 55.

13 Ibid., pp. 57–8. For a comprehensive discussion of Weir Mitchell's treatment of female patients, cf. S. Poirier, 'The Weir Mitchell rest cure: Doctor and patients', *Women's Studies* 10 (1983): 15–40; cf. E. Showalter, 'Hysteria, feminism, and gender', in Gilman et al., *Hysteria Beyond Freud*, pp. 297–300.

14 1895d, II : 138, 267; cf. J. Strachey, 'Editor's Introduction' II : xi–xii.

15 1888b, I : 55.

16 1890a, VII : 298 (translation modified).

17 Cited in F. J. Sulloway, *Freud, Biologist of the Mind* (London: Burnett/ André Deutsch, 1979), p. 42.

18 1889a, I : 94; cf. J. Forrester, 'Contracting the disease of love: Authority and freedom in the origins of psychoanalysis', in W. F. Bynum, R. Porter and M. Shepherd (eds), *The Anatomy of Madness: Essays in the History of Psychiatry*, vol. 2 (London: Tavistock, 1985), p. 257.

19 1889a, I : 95. For racial conflicts in German-speaking science during the second half of the nineteenth century, cf. S. L. Gilman, *Freud, Race, and Gender* (Princeton: Princeton University Press, 1993), pp. 17–18.

20 H. F. Ellenberger, *The Discovery of the Unconscious* (London: Allen Lane, 1970), pp. 759–62, cf. 85–102; Sulloway, *Freud, Biologist of the Mind*, p. 286.

21 Ellenberger, *Discovery of the Unconscious*, p. 86.

22 1925d, XX : 17.

23 Ibid., p. 18.

24 Ellenberger, *Discovery of the Unconscious*, p. 87; cf. A. Carotenuto, *Kant's Dove: The History of Transference in Psychoanalysis* (Wilmette, Ill.: Chiron Publications, 1991), pp. 51–2; Forrester, 'Contracting the disease of love', p. 257.

25 Showalter, *Female Malady*, p. 150.

26 Forrester, 'Contracting the disease of love', p. 258; cf. A. de Swaan 'Zur Soziogenese des psychoanalytischen "Settings" ', *Psyche* 32 (1978): 793–825.

27 1895d, II : xxix.

28 1905e, VII. C. Bernheimer and C. Kahane (eds), *In Dora's Case: Freud – Hysteria – Feminism* (New York: Columbia University Press, 1985), contains a representative collection of articles and a comprehensive bibliography listing over 60 items, mostly written from a feminist angle.

29 1905e, VII : 28.

30 Showalter, *Female Malady*, p. 147.

31 Cited in Bernheimer and Kahane (eds), *In Dora's Case*, p. 1.

32 T. Moi, 'Representation of patriarchy: Sexuality and epistemology in Freud's Dora', in Bernheimer and Kahane (eds) *In Dora's Case*, pp. 192–3.

33 P. J. Swales, 'Freud, his teacher and the birth of psychoanalysis', in P. E. Stepansky (ed.), *Freud: Appraisals and Reappraisals, Contributions to Freud Studies*, vol. 1 (Hillsdale, N.J., Analytic Press, 1986), p. 27.

34 1895d, II : 69n.

35 Ibid., p. 76n.

36 8 February 1897, S. Freud, *The Complete Letters of Sigmund Freud to Wilhelm Fliess, 1887–1904*, ed. and trans. J. M. Masson (Cambridge, Mass.: Harvard University Press, 1985), p. 229; cf. Swales, 'Freud, his teacher', p. 12.

37 Swales, 'Freud, his teacher', p. 22.

38 1895d, II : 177.

39 1910a, XI : 22; 1895d, II : 108; 1916–17, XVI : 448–50; 1925d, XX : 16–17.

40 1895d, II : 21.

41 Ibid., p. 22.

42 Ibid., p. 30.

43 E. Jones, *Life and Work of Sigmund Freud*, vol. 1 (New York: Basic Books, 1953–7), p. 223n.

44 Cf. H. F. Ellenberger. 'The story of "Anna O.": A critical review with new data', *Journal of the History of the Behavioral Sciences* 8 (1972): 267–79.

45 1895d, II : 282.

46 Ibid., p. 110n.

47 Ibid., p. 281.

48 Ibid., pp. 153–4.

49 Ibid., p. 270.

50 1913c, XII : 133.

51 Cf. E. V. Wolfenstein, *Psychoanalytic-Marxism: Groundwork* (London: Free Association Books, 1993), p. 351.

52 1913c, XII : 131. For the way in which physicians of Freud's period related to remuneration, cf. de Swaan, 'Zur Soziogenese des psychoanalytischen "Settings" ', pp. 793–825.

53 1913c, XII : 131.

54 1919a, XVII : 166.

55 Cf. 1916–17, XVI : 353–4.

56 1913c, XII : 133.

57 Ibid., p. 132.

58 1916–17, XVI : 432.

Chapter 12

1 Cf. E. Fischer-Homberger, *Die traumatische Neurose: Vom somatischen zum sozialen Leiden* (Bern: Huber, 1975), pp. 29–32.

2 J. Keegan, *The Face of Battle: A Study of Agincourt, Waterloo and the Somme* (Harmondsworth: Penguin, 1978), p. 334.

3 M. Nonne, 'Therapeutische Erfahrungen an den Kriegsneurosen in the Jahren 1914–1918', in O. von Schjerning (ed.), *Handbuch der Ärztlichen Erfahrungen im Weltkriege 1914/1918* (Leipzig, 1922/34), p. 104.

4   A. J. P. Taylor, *Illustrated History of the First World War* (New York: Putnam, 1964), pp. 91–4.

5   Ibid., p. 96.

6   Ibid., p. 105.

7   Keegan, *Face of Battle*, p. 334. According to Elaine Showalter, already by 1916 40 per cent of English casualties in the combat zone were due to nervous disorders. E. Showalter, 'Hysteria, feminism, and gender', in S. L. Gilman et al., *Hysteria Beyond Freud* (Berkeley: University of California Press, 1993), p. 321.

8   P. Büttner, *Freud und der erste Weltkrieg* (D. Phil. thesis, unpubl., Heidelberg, 1975), pp. 28–9; cf. Fischer-Homberger, *Traumatische Neurose*, pp. 136–43.

9   Fischer-Homberger, *Traumatische Neurose*, p. 144.

10 M. Nonne, 'Therapeutische Erfahrungen', p. 103.

11 Cf. R. Gaupp, 'Schreckneurose und Neurasthenie', in Schjerning (ed.) *Handbuch der Ärztlichen Erfahrungen*, p. 88.

12 Fischer-Homberger, *Traumatische Neurose*, p. 136.

13 These two terms recur throughout the literature; e.g. H. Vogt, 'Die Neurosen im Kriege', in O. Hezel, et. al. *Die Kriegsbeschädigungen des Nervensystems* (Wiesbaden: Bergmann, 1917), p. 197.

14 Ibid., pp. 197–200. Twenty years later the fear of malingerers is still evident throughout H. Wietfeldt's *Kriegsneurose als psychisch-soziale Mangelkrankheit* (Leipzig: Thieme, 1936).

15 Cited in Büttner, *Freud und der erste Weltkrieg*, p. 33. For English attitudes cf. Showalter, *Female Malady*, p. 170.

16 Cited in Büttner, *Freud und der erste Weltkrieg*, p. 27.

17 Ibid., p. 36.

18 Cited in Fischer-Homberger, *Traumatische Neurose*, pp. 139–40; cf. Büttner, *Freud und der erste Weltkrieg*, pp. 30–3.

19 Cited in Fischer-Homberger, *Die traumatische Neurose*, p. 191. In Britain the debate was similar to the one dividing the German camp. Some psychiatrists assembled data in order to uncover hereditary causes of the illness, while others countered this research with the argument that it represented 'a slur on the noblest of our race'. Cf. M. Stone, 'Shellshock and the psychologists', in Bynum, Porter and Shepherd (eds) *Anatomy of Madness*, vol. 2 (London: Tavistock, 1985), p. 252; cf. Showalter, *The Female Malady*, p. 170.

20 Cited in Fischer-Homberger, *Traumatische Neurose*, p. 150.

21 Cf. Nonne, 'Therapeutische Erfahrungen', p. 105.

22 Ibid. pp. 109–10.

23 K. Pönitz, *Die klinische Neuorientierung zum Hysterieproblem unter dem Einflusse der Kriegserfahrungen* (Berlin: J. Springer, 1921), pp. 26–7; cf. Nonne, 'Therapeutische Erfahrungen', pp. 106–13. For coercion and brutality in English psychiatry, cf. Showalter, *Female Malady*, pp. 176–80.

24 Nonne, 'Therapeutische Erfahrungen', pp. 106–10. Shell-shocked soldiers in other countries did not fare any better. Cf. Showalter, 'Hysteria, feminism and gender', pp. 322–3.

25 W. Stekel, *The Autobiography of Wilhelm Stekel: The Life Story of a Pioneer Psychoanalyst*, ed. E. A. Gutheil (New York: Liveright, 1950), p. 159.

26 Ibid., p. 115. Büttner, *Freud und der erste Weltkrieg*, p. 34. K. R. Eissler, *Freud und Wagner-Jauregg vor der Kommission zur Erhebung militärischer Pflichtverletzungen* (Wien: Löcker, 1979), p. 309 n. 37.

27 26 July 1914; 2 August 1914, S. Freud and K. Abraham, *A Psycho-Analytic Dialogue* (London: Hogarth Press, 1965), pp. 180, 184 (*hereafter Freud/ Abraham*).

28 E. Jones, *Life and Work of Sigmund Freud*, vol. 2 (New York: Basic Books, 1953–7), p. 171.

29 3 July 1915, *Freud/Abraham*, p. 215.

30 1915b, XIV : 275. Despite its detached tone, a muted pro-German sentiment can be discerned even in this essay: cf. p. 279.

31 4 March 1915, *Freud/Abraham*, p. 205.

32 1916a, XIV : 307.

33 20 May 1917, *Freud/Abraham*, p. 238. Cf. Jones, *Life and Work of Sigmund Freud*, vol. 2, p. 191.

34 9 November 1918, Jones, *Life and Work of Sigmund Freud*, vol. 2, p. 201. Cf. 11 November 1917; 10 December 1917; 22 March 1918, in *Freud/Abraham*, pp. 261, 263–4, 272.

35 M. Grotjahn, 'Karl Abraham', in F. Alexander, S. Eisenstein and M. Grotjahn (eds) *Psychoanalytic Pioneers* (New York: Basic Books, 1966), p. 3.

36 K. Abraham, 'Erstes Korreferat', in S. Freud et al., *Zur Psychoanalyse der Kriegsneurosen* (Leipzig and Vienna: Internationaler psychoanalytischer Verlag, 1919), pp. 40–1.

37 S. Lorand, 'Sandor Ferenczi', in Alexander, Eisenstein and Grotjahn (eds.) *Psychoanalytic Pioneers*, p. 18; cf. Büttner, *Freud und der erste Weltkrieg*, pp. 63–5.

38 S. Ferenczi, *Further Contributions to the Theory and Technique of PsychoAnalysis* (London: Hogarth Press, 1950), p. 124.

39 Büttner, *Freud und der erste Weltkrieg*, p. 64.

40 P. Roazen, *Freud and His Followers* (Harmondsworth: Penguin, 1979), p. 322; cf. P. Roazen, *Brother Animal: The Story of Freud and Tausk* (New York: A. A. Knopf, 1969), p. 61.

41 1919f, XVII : 274.

42 V. Tausk, 'On the psychology of the war deserter', *Psychoanalytic Quarterly* 38 (1969): 354. Originally the article appeared in *Internationale Zeitschrift für ärztliche Psychoanalyse* 4 (1916): 193–204, 229–40.

43 J. S. Peck, 'Ernst Simmel', in Alexander, Eisenstein and Grotjahn (eds), *Psychoanalytic Pioneers*, p. 373.

44 Jones, *Life and Work of Sigmund Freud*, vol. 2, pp. 197–8; cf. Büttner, *Freud und der erste Weltkrieg*, pp. 88–91; R. W. Clark, *Freud, the Man and the Cause* (London: Jonathan Cape., 1980), pp. 386–8. For parallel developments on the British side, cf. Stone, 'Shellshock and the psychologists', pp. 255–6.

45 S. Ferenczi, 'Die Psychoanalyse der Kriegsneurosen', in Freud et al., *Zur Psychoanalyse der Kriegsneurosen*, p. 19.

46 E. Simmel, 'Zweites Korreferat', in Freud et al., *Zur Psychoanalyse der Kriegsneurosen*, p. 45.

47 Ibid., pp. 42–60.

48 L. E. Hoffman, 'War, revolution, and psychoanalysis: Freudian thought begins to grapple with social reality', *Journal of the History of the Behavioral Sciences* 17 (1981): 257.

49 Ibid., p. 264 n. 8.

50 1919a, XVII : 168.

51 Ibid., p. 167.

52 Ibid., p. 168.

53 Ibid., p. 162.

54 Ibid., p. 164.

55 Ibid., p. 165.

56 27 October 1918, *Freud/Abraham*, p. 279.

57 Wagner-Jauregg was also the first psychiatrist to be awarded the Nobel Prize in 1928. Cf. Ellenberger, *Discovery of the Unconscious* p. 837; Büttner, *Freud und der erste Weltkrieg*, pp. 104–6; R. W. Clark, *Freud, the Man and the Cause* (London: Jonathan Cape, 1980), pp. 404–5.

58 1955c, XVII : 211–15.

59 K. R. Eissler, *Freud und Wagner-Jauregg* (Wien: Löcker, 1979), pp. 98–101.

60 Ibid., p. 222. Freud seems to have been aware of this, cf. 1955c, XVII : 214.

61 1955c, XVII : 213.

62 Eissler, *Freud und Wagner-Jauregg*, p. 54.

63 1955c, XVII : 212–13.

64 Ibid., p. 214.

65 Eissler, *Freud und Wagner-Jauregg*, p. 53.

66 Showalter, 'Hysteria, feminism and gender', p. 304.

67 Ibid., p. 325. Cf. Showalter, *Female Malady*, pp. 173–5.

Chapter 13

1 1921c, XVIII : 89.

2 Ibid., p. 114.

3 1889a, 1:94; cf. 1890a, VII : 296–8.

4 1916–17, XVI : 460.

5 1890a, VII : 293.

6 1914d, XIV : 49.

7 1913c, XII : 127.

8 1912e, XII : 118.

9 1905e, VII : 22

10 Ibid., p. 26.

11 Ibid., p. 59.

12 Ibid., p. 37.

13 R. de Saussure, 'Sigmund Freud', in W. Ruitenbeek (ed.), *Freud As We Knew Him* (Detroit: Wayne State University, 1973), p. 359.

14 Ibid., p. 109.

15 1912e, XII : 115.
16 1916–17, XVI : 288; 1940a, XXIII : 174.
17 1923a, XVIII : 238.
18 1909d, X : 166; cf. 1905a, VII : 267; 1926e, XX : 224.
19 1916–17, XVI : 288; cf. 1913c, XII : 135 n. 1.
20 Cf. E. Gellner, *The Psychoanalytic Movement: Or the Cunning of Unreason* (London: Granada, 1985), p. 57.
21 M. Foucault, *Madness and Civilization: A History of Insanity in the Age of Reason* (London: Tavistock, 1971), pp. 277–8; cf. S. Frosh, *The Politics of Psychoanalysis* (Houndmills: Macmillan, 1987), pp. 79–80; 259–60.
22 Cf. S. Viderman, 'The analytic space: meaning and problems', *Psychoanalytic Quarterly* 48 (1979): 278–9.
23 Ibid., p. 440; cf. 1926e, XX : 221; 1937c, XXIII : 239.
24 1895d, II : 294–5.
25 1910k, XI : 225.
26 1916–17, XVI : 451.
27 1909d, X : 166.
28 1914g, XII : 151.
29 1926e, XX : 224; cf. 1912b, XII : 103–4; 1916–17, XVI : 456; 1920a, XVIII : 163.
30 1916–17, XVI : 433.
31 1937c, XXIII : 235.
32 Ibid., p. 238; cf. 1920g, XVIII : 19; J. Laplanche and J.-B. Pontalis, *The Language of Psycho-Analysis* (London: Hogarth Press, 1980), pp. 395–6.
33 1895d, II : 305.
34 1916–17, XVI : 433.
35 Ibid., p. 434.
36 1919a, XVII : 165.
37 1916–17, XVI : 454.
38 1912b, XII : 108.
39 1895d, II : 302–3.
40 1905e, VII : 116.
41 1916–17, XVI : 445.
42 1914g, XII : 152.
43 1912b, XII : 101; cf. 1916–17, XVI : 453.
44 1940a, XXIII : 177.
45 1913c, XII : 139.
46 1914g, XII : 150; cf. 1912b, XII : 108; 1940a, XXIII : 177 (original emphasis).
47 1914g, XII : 154.
48 1916–17, XVI : 443.
49 Ibid., pp. 443–4.
50 Cf. Frosh, *Politics of Psychoanalysis*, p. 237; J. B. Abramson, *Liberation and Its Limits* (New York: Free Press, 1984), p. 112.
51 1926e, XX : 224–5.
52 T. E. Wartenberg, *The Forms of Power: From Domination to Transformation* (Philadelphia: Temple University Press, 1990), pp. 61–2, 183–213.

53 Ibid., p. 184.
54 1940a, XXIII : 175.

Chapter 14

1 Cf. E. Gellner, *The Psychoanalytic Movement* (London: Granada, 1985), p. 112.
2 1910k, XI : 225 (original emphasis).
3 E. V. Wolfenstein, 'A man knows not where to have it: Habermas, Grünbaum and the epistemological status of psychoanalysis', *International Review of Psychoanalysis* 17 (1990): 38.
4 1890a, VII : 292.
5 1893h, III : 36; cf. 1926e, XX : 187.
6 1926e, XX : 187–8; cf. 1890a, VII : 283; 1916–17, XV : 17.
7 1905a, VII : 260–1 (emphasis added).
8 J. B. Abramson, *Liberation and Its Limits* (New York: Free Press, 1984), pp. 119–20; J. Habermas, *Knowledge and Human Interests* (London: Heinemann, 1978), p. 228; Wolfenstein, 'A man knows not where to have it', p. 39.
9 1909b, X : 104.
10 1937d, XXIII : 262; cf. 1905e, VII : 57; 1925h, XIX : 235, 239.
11 1937d, XXIII : 265.
12 1916–17, XVI : 452–3. Grünbaum has made much – in my view, too much – of this passage, from which he derives what he calls the 'tally argument'; cf. A. Grünbaum, *The Foundations of Psychoanalysis: A Philosophical Critique* (Berkeley: University of California Press, 1984).
13 1926e, XX : 220.
14 1914g, XII : 151.
15 1912b, XII : 108.
16 Ibid., p. 108.
17 e.g. 1914g, XII : 151, 154.
18 1912e, XII : 117.
19 Ibid., p. 119.
20 Cf. T. E. Wartenberg, *Forms of Power* (Philadelphia: Temple University Press, 1990), pp. 209–13.
21 Gellner, *Psychoanalytic Movement*, p. 54.
22 Ibid., p. 49.
23 Ibid., p. 55.
24 Cf. A. Clare, 'Freud's cases: The clinical basis of psychoanalysis', in Bynum, Porter, and Shepherd (eds.), *Anatomy of Madness*, vol. 1; J. Cremerius, 'Die Bedeutung der Dissidenten für die Psychoanalyse', *Psyche* 36 (1982): 496–503; L. Edmunds, 'His master's choice', *Johns Hopkins Magazine* 40 (April 1988): 40–9; K. Obholzer, *The Wolf-Man Sixty Years Later: Conversations with Freud's Controversial Patient*, trans. M. Shaw (London: Routledge and Kegan Paul, 1982); F. J. Sulloway, 'Reassessing Freud's case histories: The social construction of psychoanalysis', *Isis* 82 (1991): 245–75.

25 e.g. F. Crews, 'The unknown Freud', *New York Review of Books*, 18 November 1993, pp. 55–66.

Part IV

Chapter 15

1 1905d, VII : 198.
2 Ibid., p. 182.
3 1914c, XIV : 91.
4 Ibid., pp. 74–5.
5 1923b, XIX : 27.
6 1930a, XXI : 67.
7 1926d, XX : 155.
8 1914c, XIV : 90.
9 1905d, VII : 150.
10 1900a, IV : 258; cf. 1914c, XIV : 98; J. Sandler, 'The background of safety', *International Journal of Psychoanalysis* 41 (1960): 352–6.
11 1915c, XIV : 138.
12 1921c, XVIII : 105.
13 1933a, XXII : 62; cf. 1926d, XX : 146.
14 1917c, XVII : 130.
15 1905d, VII : 186.
16 1916–17, XV : 206; cf. 1900a, IV : 257.
17 1924d, XIX : 176.
18 1905d, VII : 199 n.
19 1923e, XIX : 145 (original emphasis).
20 1924d, XIX : 176.
21 Ibid., p. 177.
22 1933a, XXII : 129.
23 1940a, XXIII : 194.
24 1918a, XI : 205; cf. 1920a, XVIII : 169.
25 1909c, IX : 237.
26 1916–17, XVI : 337.
27 1930a, XXI : 129; cf. J. Sandler, 'On the concept of the superego', *Psychoanalytic Study of the Child* 15 (1960): 128–62; J. Sandler, A. Holder and D. Meers, 'The ego ideal and the ideal self', *Psychoanalytic Study of the Child* 18 (1963): 139–58.
28 1931b, XXI : 229.
29 1905d, VII : 207 (translation modified); cf. 1930a, XXI : 103.
30 1910a, XI : 45.
31 1905d, VII : 242.
32 1927c, XXI : 104.
33 Ibid., p. 105.
34 1925e, XIX : 219 (translation modified); cf. 1930a, XXI : 103–4.

35 1930a, XXI : 109.
36 Ibid., p. 109 (translation modified).

Chapter 16

1 D. Caroll, 'Freud and the myth of origin', *New Literary History* 6 (1975):
   513–28; Y. Gabriel, *Freud and Society* (London: Routledge, 1983), p. 41;
   P. Ricoeur, *Freud and Philosophy* (New Haven: Yale University Press, 1970),
   p. 208; E. V. Wolfenstein, *Psychoanalytic- Marxism* (London: Free Association Books, 1993), p. 36.
2 1912–13, XIII : 141.
3 Ibid., p. 103n.
4 1921c, XVIII : 122.
5 Ibid., p. 140.
6 1939a, XXIII : 84.
7 14 May 1912, S. Freud and C. G. Jung, *The Freud/Jung Letters: The Correspondence between Sigmund Freud and C. G. Jung*, ed. W. McGuire (London:
   Routledge and Kegan Paul, 1974), p. 504.
8 1939a, XXIII : 81; cf. 1912–13, XIII : 141.
9 1912–13, XIII : 143.
10 1939a, XXIII : 81.
11 1912–13, XIII : 144.
12 Ibid., p. 142.
13 Ibid., p. 144.
14 1939a, XXIII : 82.
15 Cf. M. O'Brien, *The Politics of Reproduction* (London: Routledge and Kegan
   Paul, 1981).
16 1912–13, XIII : 148.
17 1939a, XXIII : 82 (original emphasis; translation modified); cf. P. Rieff,
   Freud: The Mind of the Moralist (London: Methuen, 1965), p. 197.
18 1930a, XXI : 95; cf. P. Roazen, *Freud: Political and Social Thought* (New York:
   Random House, 1970), p. 270.
19 1912–13, XIII : 148.
20 Ibid., p. 145.
21 Ibid., p. 144.
22 Ibid., p. 143.
23 Ibid., p. 145.
24 E. Jones, *Life and Work of Sigmund Freud*, vol. 3 (New York: Basic Books,
   1953–7), p. 313; cf. Sulloway, *Freud: Biologist of the Mind* (London: Bur-
   nett/André Deutsch, 1979), pp. 274–5.
25 S. Freud, *A Phylogenetic Fantasy: Overview of the Transference Neuroses*, ed.
   I. Grubrich-Simitis (Cambridge, Mass.: Belknap Press, 1987).
26 1905d, VII : 225 n. 3.
27 Cf. J. Forrester, *Language and the Origins of Psychoanalysis* (London: Macmillan, 1980), pp. 63–130.
28 1916–17, XV : 199.

29 Ibid., p. 371.

30 1918b, XVII : 120 (original emphasis).

31 1939a, XXIII : 100; cf. 98–102, 133.

32 1912–13, XIII : 157.

33 1915f, XIV : 269.

34 1940a, XXIII : 190n.

35 1939a, XXIII : 101.

36 Ibid., p. 100 (translation modified).

37 S. J. Gould, *Ontogeny and Phylogeny* (London: Belknapp Press, 1977), p. 126.

38 1937c, XXIII : 252; cf. 1939a, XXIII : 99; 1918b, XVII : 119–20; 1925d, XX : 37; 1930a, XXI : 131.

39 1927c, XXI : 53. Three years later Freud's comments were much more pessimistic, cf. 1930a, XXI : 74.

40 1927c, XXI : 54–5; cf. 1910d, XI : 147–8.

41 1933a, XXII : 171.

42 1927c, XXI : 53.

43 Ibid., p. 43.

44 1930a, XXI : 74.

45 1939a, XXIII : 54–5. Freud's earlier comments on the Soviet Union were less negative; cf. 1927c, XXI : 9; 1933a, XXII : 180–1.

Chapter 17

1 29 August 1883, Freud, *Letters of Sigmund Freud*, ed. E. L. Freud (New York: Basic Books, 1975), pp. 50–1 (translation modified).

2 1927c, XXI : 7–8 (translation modified).

3 Ibid., p. 8 (translation modified); cf. 1930a, XXI : 115–16; 1933b, XXII : 212.

4 1939a, XXIII : 108.

5 Ibid., p. 89.

6 Ibid., p. 18. On Freud's fascination with Moses cf. P. Roazen, *Freud: Political and Social Thought* (New York: Random House, 1970), pp. 167–92.

7 S. Freud and W. C. Bullitt, *Thomas Woodrow Wilson: Twenty-eighth President of the United States: A Psychological Study* (London: Weidenfeld and Nicolson, 1967).

8 Cf. Roazen, *Freud: Political and Social Thought*, p. 310. On the problems of authorship and authenticity in the study of Woodrow Wilson, cf. pp. 301–7; S. L. Warner, 'Fourteen Wilsonian points for Freud and Bullitt', *Journal of the American Academy of Psychoanalysis* 16 (1988): 479–89.

9 P. Rieff, *The Feeling Intellect: Selected Writings*, ed. J. B. Imber (Chicago: University of Chicago Press, 1990), p. 46.

10 Freud and Bullitt, *Thomas Woodrow Wilson*, p. xii.

11 Cited in Warner, 'Fourteen Wilsonian Points', p. 487. Cf. E. Jones, *Life and Work of Sigmund Freud*, vol. 3 (New York: Basic Books, 1953–7), p. 17.

12 1939a, XXIII : 109.

13 Ibid., p. 47.

14 P. Roazen, 'Psychoanalytic ethics: Edoardo Weiss, Freud, and Mussolini', *Journal of the History of the Behavioral Sciences* 27 (1991): 370.

15 1930a, XXI : 115–16 (translation modified).

16 J. van Ginneken, 'The killing of the father: The background of Freud's group psychology', *Political Psychology* 5 (1984): 392. Cf. J. S. McClelland, *The Crowd and the Mob: From Plato to Canetti* (London: Unwin, 1989), pp. 155–236; S. Moscovici, *The Age of the Crowd: A Historical Treatise on Mass Psychology* (Cambridge: Cambridge University Press, 1985); R. A. Nye, *The Origins of Crowd Psychology: Gustave Le Bon and the Crisis of Mass Democracy in the Third Republic* (London: Sage, 1973).

17 Nye, *Origins of Crowd Psychology*, p. 67; J. van Ginneken, '1895 debate on the origins of crowd psychology', *Journal of the History of the Behavioral Sciences* 21 (1985): 375–82.

18 Nye, *Origins of Crowd Psychology*, pp. 60–2.

19 McClelland, *Crowd and the Mob*, pp. 169–70, 183–4.

20 1921c, XVIII : 81 (translation modified).

21 Ibid., pp. 88–9.

22 Ibid., p. 95 (translation modified).

23 M. Borch-Jacobsen, *The Freudian Subject* (Stanford: Stanford University Press, 1988), pp. 135–7.

24 G. Le Bon, *The Crowd: A Study of the Popular Mind* (London: Ernest Benn, 1952), pp. 166–207.

25 1921c, XVIII : 70.

26 T. E. Wartenberg, 'Social movements and individual identity: A critique of Freud and the psychology of groups', *The Philosophical Forum* 22 (1991): 364.

27 1930a, XXI : 112.

28 Ibid., p. 122.

29 Ibid., p. 111 (translation modified).

30 1921c, XVIII : 91 (translation modified).

31 Ibid., p. 92 (translation modified).

32 Ibid., p. 102.

33 Ibid., p. 116.

34 Ibid., p. 121 (translation modified).

35 1930a, XXI : 115.

36 1921c, XVIII : 98; cf. 1927c, XXI : 13; 1930a, XXI : 115.

37 1921c, XVIII : 99.

38 1939a, XXIII : 109–10.

39 1921c, XVIII : 93–4 (translation modified).

40 Ibid., pp. 123–4 (translation modified).

41 Ibid., p. 127 (translation modified).

42 1939a, XXIII : 109.

43 1921c, XVIII : 113.

44 Wartenberg, 'Social movements and individual identity', p. 371.

45 1921c, XVIII : 115 (translation modified).

46 1910a, XI : 54.

47 1933a, XXII : 179.

48 M. Foucault, *The History of Sexuality* (Harmondsworth: Penguin, 1981), p. 152. On Foucault's complex relationship with psychoanalysis, cf. J. Forrester, *The Seductions of Psychoanalysis: Freud, Lacan and Derrida* (Cambridge: Cambridge University Press, 1990), pp. 286–316; P. H. Hutton, 'Foucault, Freud and the technologies of the Self', in L. H. Martin, H. Gutman and P. H. Hutton (eds), *Technologies of the Self: A Seminar with Michel Foucault* (London: Tavistock, 1988), pp. 121–44.

Conclusions

1 Cf. Q. Skinner, 'A reply to my critics', in J. Tully (ed.) *Meaning and Context* (Princeton: Princeton University Press, 1988), p. 269.

2 F. Kermode, *The Classic: Literary Images of Permanence and Change* (Cambridge, Mass.: Harvard University Press, 1983), p. 80.

3 In relation to Freud's work this term has also been used by Patricia Kitcher, albeit in a different context and with a different meaning. Cf. P. Kitcher, *Freud's Dream: A Complete Interdisciplinary Science of Mind* (Cambridge, Mass.: MIT Press, 1992).

4 C. Rycroft, *The Innocence of Dreams* (Oxford: Oxford University Press, 1981), p. 4. For similar arguments cf. W. I. Grossman and B. Simon, 'Anthropomorphism: Motives, meaning and causality in Psychoanalytic Theory', *Psychoanalytic Study of the Child* 24 (1969): 78–114; G. Klein, 'Freud's two theories of sexuality', in L. Berger (ed.), *Clinical Cognitive Psychology: Models and Integrations* (New York: Prentice Hall, 1969); R. R. Holt, 'Freud's mechanistic and humanistic images of man', in R. R. Holt and E. Peterfreund (eds), *Psychoanalysis and Contemporary Science*, vol. 1 (New York: Macmillan, 1972); A. MacIntyre, *The Unconscious* (London: Routledge and Kegan Paul, 1958), p. 60.

5 1914d, XIV : 44.

6 1927a, XX : 252.

7 Ibid., p. 257.

8 F. J. Sulloway, *Freud, Biologist of the Mind* (London: Burnett/Andre Deutsch, 1979), p. 421; cf. P. Amacher, *Freud's Neurological Education and Its Influence on Psychoanalytic Theory* (New York: International Universities Press, 1965; *Psychological Issues*, vol. IV); R. R. Holt, 'A review of some of Freud's biological assumptions and their influence on his Theories', in N. S. Greenfield and W. C. Lewis (eds), *Psychoanalysis and Current Biological Thought* (Madison: University of Wisconsin Press, 1965), pp. 93–124.

9 Later Sulloway admitted that his book 'did not devote sufficient attention to [Freud's] application of his methods within a clinical context'. F. J. Sulloway, 'Reassessing Freud's case histories: The social construction of psychoanalysis', *Isis* 82 (1991): 245.

10 1916–17, XV : 158–9.

11 J. Forrester, *Language and the Origins of Psychoanalysis* (London: Macmillan, 1980), pp. 167–8.

12 M. Foucault, *The Order of Things: An Archeology of the Human Sciences* (New York: Vintage, 1970), p. 361.

13 J. Lacan, *Écrits: A Selection* (New York: W. W. Norton, 1977), p. 160; J. Lacan, *The Four Fundamental Concepts of Psychoanalysis* (New York: W. W. Norton, 1978), p. 280.

14 P. Ricoeur, *Freud and Philosophy* (New Haven: Yale University Press, 1970), p. 65.

15 Ibid., p. 363; cf. pp. 394–5.

16 Ibid., p. 374.

17 J. Habermas, *Knowledge and Human Interests* (London: Heinemann, 1978), p. 214.

18 Ibid., p. 254.

19 For comprehensive reviews of this debate and the philosophical and methodological questions involved, cf. C. Hanly, 'The concept of truth in psychoanalysis', *International Journal of Psycho-analysis* 71 (1990): 375–83; C. Nussbaum, 'Habermas and Grünbaum on the logic of psychoanalytic explanations', *Philosophy and Social Criticism* 17 (1991): 193–216; R. S. Steele, 'Psychoanalysis and hermeneutics', *International Review of Psycho-analysis* 6 (1979): 389–409; C. Strenger, *Between Hermeneutics and Science: An Essay on the Epistemology of Psychoanalysis* (New York: International Universities Press, 1991; *Psychological Issues*, Monograph 59); E. V. Wolfenstein, 'A man knows not where to have it: Habermas, Grünbaum and the epistemological status of psychoanalysis', *International Review of Psycho-Analysis* 17 (1990), pp. 23–45.

References

A. References to the Standard Edition

1888b   Hysteria, 1:41–59.
1889a   Review of August Forel's *Hypnotism*, I : 91–100.
1890a   Psychical (or mental) treatment, VII : 283–302.
1892–3   A case of successful treatment by hypnotism, I : 117–28.
1892–4   Preface and footnotes to the translation of Charcot's *Tuesday Lectures*, I : 123–43.
1893a   On the psychical mechanism of hysterical phenomena: Preliminary communication, II : 3–17.
1893c   Some points for the comparative study of organic and hysterical and motor paralyses, I : 160–72.
1893h   On the psychical mechanism of hysterical phenomena, III : 27–39.
1894a   The neuro-psychoses of defence, III : 45–61.
1895c   Obsessions and phobias, III : 74–82.
1895d   *Studies on Hysteria*, II : 21–305.
1895f   A reply to criticisms of my paper on anxiety neurosis, III : 123–39.
1896a   Heredity and the aetiology of the neuroses, III : 143–56.
1896b   Further remarks on the neuro-psychoses of defence, III : 162–85.
1896c   The aetiology of hysteria, III : 191–221.
1898a   Sexuality in the aetiology of the neuroses, III : 263–85.
1900a   *The Interpretation of Dreams*, IV : 1–338, V : 339–621.
1905a   On psychotherapy, VII : 257–68.
1905c   *Jokes and their Relation to the Unconscious*, VIII : 9–236.
1905d   *Three Essays on the Theory of Sexuality*, VII : 130–243.
1905e   Fragment of an analysis of a case of hysteria, VII : 7–122.
1907b   Obsessive actions and religious practices, IX : 117–27.
1908b   Character and anal erotism, IX : 169–75.
1908c   On the sexual theories of children, IX : 209–26.
1908d   "Civilized" sexual morality and modern nervous illness, IX : 181–204.
1908e   Creative writers and day-dreaming, IX : 143–53.
1909b   Analysis of a phobia in a five-year-old boy, X : 5–147.

1909c   Family romances, IX : 237–41.

1909d   Notes upon a case of obsessional neurosis, X : 155–249.

1910a   Five lectures on psycho-analysis, XI : 9–55.

1910c   *Leonardo da Vinci and a Memory of his Childhood*, XI : 63–137.

1910d   The future prospects of psycho-analytic therapy, XI : 141–51.

1910i   The psycho-analytic view of psychogenic disturbance of vision, XI : 211–18.

1910k   "Wild" psycho-analysis, XI : 221–7.

1911b   Formulations on the two principles of mental functioning, XII : 218–26.

1912b   The dynamics of transference, XII : 99–108.

1912c   Types of onset of neurosis, XII : 231–8.

1912e   Recommendations to physicians practicing psycho-analysis, XII : 111–20.

1912–13   *Totem and Taboo*, XIII : 1–161.

1913c   On beginning the treatment, XII : 123–44.

1913f   The theme of the three caskets, XII : 291–301.

1913j   The claims of psycho-analysis to scientific interest, XIII : 165–90.

1914b   The Moses of Michelangelo, XIII : 211–36.

1914c   On narcissism: An introduction, XIV : 73–102.

1914d   On the history of the psycho-analytic movement, XIV : 7–66.

1914g   Remembering, repeating and working-through, XII : 147–56.

1915b   Thoughts for the times of war and death, XIV : 275–300.

1915c   Instincts and their vicissitudes, XIV : 117–40.

1915d   Repression, XIV : 146–58.

1915e   The unconscious, XIV : 166–204.

1915f   A case of paranoia running counter to the psycho-analytic theory of the disease, XIV : 263–72.

1916a   On transience, XIV : 305–7.

1916–17   *Introductory Lectures on Psycho-Analysis*, XV : 15–239, XVI : 243–463.

1917a   A difficulty in the path of psycho-analysis, XVII : 137–44.

1917c   On transformations of instinct as exemplified in anal eroticism, XVII : 127–33.

1917d   A metapsychological supplement to the theory of dreams, XIV : 222–35.

1918a   The taboo of virginity, XI : 193–208.

1918b   From the history of an infantile neurosis, XVII : 7–121.

1919a   Lines of advance in psycho-analytic therapy, XVII : 159–68.

1919f   Victor Tausk, XVII : 273–5.

1920a   The psychogenesis of a case of female homosexuality, XVIII : 147–72.

1920g   *Beyond the Pleasure Principle*, XVIII : 7–64.

1921c   *Group Psychology and the Analysis of the Ego*, XVIII : 69–143.

1923a   Two encyclopaedia articles, XVIII : 235–59.

1923b   *The Ego and the Id*, XIX : 12–59.

1923e   The infantile genital organization, XIX : 141–5.

1924c   The economic problem of masochism, XIX : 159–70.

1924d   The dissolution of the Oedipus complex, XIX : 173–9.

1924e The loss of reality in neurosis and psychosis, XIX : 183–7.
1925d *An Autobiographical Study*, XX : 7–70.
1925e The resistances to psycho-analysis, XIX : 213–22.
1925h Negation, XIX : 235–9.
1925i Some additional notes on dream-interpretation as a whole, XIX : 127–38.
1926d *Inhibitions, Symptoms and Anxiety*, XX : 87–172.
1926e *The Question of Lay Analysis*, XX : 83–250.
1926f Psycho-analysis, XX : 263–70.
1927a Postscript to *The Question of Lay Analysis*, XX : 251–8.
1927c *The Future of an Illusion*, XXI : 5–56.
1928a A religious experience, XXI : 169–72.
1929a Dr Ernest Jones (on his 50th birthday), XXI : 49–50.
1930a *Civilization and Its Discontents*, XXI : 64–145.
1931b, Female sexuality, XXI : 225–43.
1932c My contact with Josef Popper-Lynkeus, XXII : 219–24.
1933a *New Introductory Lectures on Psycho-Analysis*, XXII : 5–182.
1933b *Why War?*, XXII : 197–215.
1937c Analysis terminable and interminable, XXIII : 216–53.
1937d Constructions in analysis, XXIII : 257–69.
1939a *Moses and Monotheism*, XXIII : 7–137.
1940a *An Outline of Psycho-Analysis*, XXIII : 144–207.
1940e Splitting of the ego in the process of defence, XXIII : 275–8.
1950a *The Origins of Psycho-Analysis*, including 'A project for a scientific psychology' (1895), I : 177–392.
1955c Memorandum on the electrical treatment of war neurotics (1920), XVII : 211–15.

B. Other References

Abraham, K., 'Erstes Korreferat', in S. Freud et al., *Zur Psychoanalyse der Kriegsneurosen*.

Abramson, J. B., *Liberation and Its Limits: The Moral and Political Thought of Freud* (New York: Free Press, 1984).

Adler, M. J., *The Idea of Freedom: A Dialectical Examination of Conceptions of and the Controversies about Freedom*, 2 vols (Garden City: Doubleday, 1958–61).

Alexander, F., S. Eisenstein and M. Grotjahn (eds) *Psychoanalytic Pioneers* (New York: Basic Books, 1966).

Alford, C. F., *The Self in Social Theory: A Psychoanalytic Account of Its Construction in Plato, Hobbes, Locke, Rawls, and Rousseau* (New Haven: Yale University Press, 1991).

Amacher, P., *Freud's Neurological Education and Its Influence on Psychoanalytic Theory* (New York: International Universities Press, 1965; *Psychological Issues*, vol. IV).

Bakan, D., *Sigmund Freud and the Jewish Mystical Tradition* (Princeton: Princeton University Press, 1958).

Ball, T., 'Power, causation and explanation', *Polity* (1975): 189–214.

Ball, T., *Transforming Political Discourse: Political Theory and Critical Conceptual History* (Oxford: Basil Blackwell, 1988).

Bauman, Z., *Hermeneutics and Social Science: Approaches to Understanding* (London: Hutchinson, 1978).

Becker, R., *Die Nervosität bei den Juden: Ein Beitrag zur Rassenpsychiatrie* (Zürich: Orell Füssli, 1919).

Benjamin, J., *The Bonds of Love: Psychoanalysis, Feminism, and the Problem of Domination* (New York: Pantheon, 1988).

Berlin, I., *Four Essays on Liberty* (London: Oxford University Press, 1969).

Berger, L. (ed.), *Clinical Cognitive Psychology: Models and Integrations* (New York: Prentice Hall, 1969).

Bergman, M., 'Moses and the evolution of Freud's Jewish identity', *Israel Annals of Psychiatry and Related Disciplines* 14 (1976): 3–26.

Bernheimer, C., and C. Kahane (eds), *In Dora's Case: Freud–Hysteria–Feminism* (New York: Columbia University Press, 1985).

Black, M., *Models and Metaphors* (Ithaca: Cornell University Press, 1962).

Blatt, D. S., 'The development of the hero: Sigmund Freud and the reformation of the Jewish tradition', *Psychoanalysis and Contemporary Thought* 11 (1988): 639–703.

Borch-Jacobsen, M., *The Freudian Subject*, trans. C. Porter (Stanford: Stanford University Press, 1988).

Boyers, R. (ed.), *Psychological Man* (New York: Harper and Row, 1975).

Brennan, T., *The Interpretation of the Flesh: Freud and Femininity* (London: Routledge, 1992).

Brown, R. H., *A Poetic for Sociology: Toward a Logic of Discovery for the Human Sciences* (London: Cambridge University Press, 1977).

Burnham, J. C., 'The medical origins and cultural uses of Freud's instinctual drive theory', *The Psychoanalytic Quarterly* 43 (1974): 193–217.

Büttner, P., *Freud und der erste Weltkrieg* (D. Phil. thesis, unpubl., Heidelberg, 1975).

Bynum, W. F., R. Porter and M. Shepherd (eds), *The Anatomy of Madness: Essays in the History of Psychiatry*, 2 vols (London: Tavistock, 1985).

Carlston, D. E., 'Turning psychology on itself: The rhetoric of psychology and the psychology of rhetoric', in Nelson, Megill and McCloskey (eds), *Rhetoric of the Human Sciences*.

Carotenuto, A., *Kant's Dove: The History of Transference in Psychoanalysis* (Wilmette, Ill.: Chiron Publications, 1991).

Carroll, D., 'Freud and the myth of origin', *New Literary History* 6 (1975): 513–28.

Chamberlin, J. E. and S. L. Gilman (eds), *Degeneration: The Dark Side of Progress* (New York: Columbia University Press, 1985).

Chodorow, N., *The Reproduction of Mothering: Psychoanalysis and the Sociology of Gender* (Berkeley: University of California Press, 1982).

Chodorow, N., *Feminism and Psychoanalytic Theory* (New Haven: Yale University Press, 1989).

Clare, A., 'Freud's cases: The clinical basis of psychoanalysis', in Bynum, Porter and Shepherd (eds), *The Anatomy of Madness*, vol. 1.

Clark, R. W., *Freud: The Man and the Cause* (London: Jonathan Cape, 1980).

Cohen, E., M. Lissak and U. Almagor (eds) *Comparative Social Dynamics: Essays in Honor of S. N. Eisenstadt* (Boulder, Co.: Westview Press, 1985).

Cohen, I. H., *Ideology and Unconsciousness: Reich, Freud, and Marx* (New York: New York University Press, 1982).

Connolly, W. E., *The Terms of Political Discourse* (Oxford: Robertson, 1983).

Craib, I., *Psychoanalysis and Social Theory: The Limits of Sociology* (Amherst: The University of Massachusetts Press, 1990).

Cremerius, J., 'Die Bedeutung der Dissidenten für die Psychoanalyse', *Psyche* 36 (1982): 496–503.

Crews, F., 'The unknown Freud', *New York Review of Books*, 18 November 1993, pp. 55–66.

Cuddihy, J. M., *The Ordeal of Civility: Freud, Marx, Lévi-Strauss, and the Jewish Struggle with Modernity* (New York: Basic Books, 1974).

Dahl, R. A., *Modern Political Analysis* (New Jersey: Prentice-Hall, 1963).

Davidson, A., 'Assault on Freud', *London Review of Books*, 5–19 July 1984, pp. 9–11.

Decker, H. S., *Freud in Germany: Revolution and Reaction in Science 1893–1907* (New York: International Universities Press, 1977; *Psychological Issues*, vol. XI).

Decker, H. S., 'Freud and Dora: Constraints on medical progress', *Journal of Social History* 14 (1980–1): 445–64

Deutscher, I., *The Non-Jewish Jew and Other Essays*, ed. T. Deutscher (London: Oxford University Press, 1968).

Didi-Huberman, G., *Invention de l'hystérie: Charcot et l'iconographie photographique de la Salpêtrière* (Paris: Macula, 1982).

Dowbiggin, I., 'Degeneration and hereditarianism in French mental medicine 1840–90: Psychiatric theory as ideological adaptation', in Bynum, Porter and Shepherd (eds), *Anatomy of Madness*, vol. 1.

Drescher, S., S. Sabean and A. Sharlin (eds), *Political Symbolism in Modern Europe: Essays in Honor of G. L. Mosse* (New Brunswick: Transaction, 1982).

Drinka, G. F., *The Birth of Neurosis: Myth, Malady and the Victorians* (New York: Simon and Schuster, 1984).

Drucker, H. M., 'Just analogies?: The place of analogies in political thinking', *Political Studies* 18 (1970): 448–60.

Drumont, É., *La France Juive*, 2 vols (Paris: Marpon & Flammarion, 1886).

Duffy, J., 'Masturbation and clitoridectomy', *Journal of the American Medical Association* 186 (1963): 246–8.

Eagle, M. N., *Recent Developments in Psychoanalysis: A Critical Evaluation* (Cambridge, Mass.: Harvard University Press, 1984).

Edelson, J. T., 'Freud's use of metaphor', *The Psychoanalytic Study of the Child* 38 (1983): 17–60

Edmunds, L., 'His master's choice', *Johns Hopkins Magazine* 40 (April 1988): 40–9.

Eissler, K. R., *Freud und Wagner-Jauregg vor der Kommission zur Erhebung militärischer Pflichtverletzungen* (Wien: Löcker, 1979).

Elkana, Y., 'Borrowing the concept of energy in Freudian psychoanalysis', in Cohen, Lissak and Almagor (eds) *Comparative Social Dynamics*.

Ellenberger, H. F., *The Discovery of the Unconscious: The History and Evolution of Dynamic Psychiatry* (London: Allen Lane, 1970).

Ellenberger, H. F., 'The story of "Anna O.": A critical review with new data', *Journal of the History of the Behavioral Sciences* 8 (1972): 267–79.

Ferenczi, S., 'Die Psychoanalyse der Kriegsneurosen', in S. Freud et al., *Zur Psychoanalyse der Kriegsneurosen*.

Ferenczi, S., *Further Contributions to the Theory and Technique of Psycho-Analysis* (London: Hogarth Press, 1950).

Fischer-Homberger, E., *Die traumatische Neurose: Vom somatischen zum sozialen Leiden* (Bern: Huber, 1975).

Fisher, S. and R. P. Greenberg, *The Scientific Credibility of Freud's Theories and Therapy*, 2 vols (Brighton: Harvester Press, 1977).

Flechsig, P., 'On the gynecological treatment of hysteria', in Masson (ed.), *A Dark Science*.

Forrester, J., *Language and the Origins of Psychoanalysis* (London: Macmillan, 1980).

Forrester, J., 'Contracting the disease of love: Authority and freedom in the origins of psychoanalysis', in Bynum, Porter and Shepherd (eds), *Anatomy of Madness*, vol. 2.

Forrester, J., 'Rape, seduction and psychoanalysis', in Tomaselli and Porter (eds), *Rape*.

Forrester, J., *The Seductions of Psychoanalysis: Freud, Lacan and Derrida* (Cambridge: Cambridge University Press, 1990).

Foucault, M., *The Order of Things: An Archeology of the Human Sciences* (New York: Vintage, 1970).

Foucault, M., *Madness and Civilization: A History of Insanity in the Age of Reason* (London: Tavistock, 1971).

Foucault, M., *Mental Illness and Psychology* (New York: Harper and Row, 1976).

Foucault, M., *Power/Knowledge: Selected Interviews and Other Writings 1972–77*, ed. C. Gordon (New York: Pantheon, 1980).

Foucault, M., *The History of Sexuality, Volume One: An Introduction* (Harmondsworth: Penguin, 1981).

Freud, S., *The Standard Edition of the Complete Psychological Works of Sigmund Freud*, 24 vols, ed. J. Strachey (London: Hogarth Press, 1953–74).

Freud, S., *The Letters of Sigmund Freud*, ed. E. L. Freud (New York: Basic Books, 1975).

Freud, S., *The Complete Letters of Sigmund Freud to Wilhelm Fliess, 1887–1904* (*Freud/Fliess*), ed. and trans. J. M. Masson (Cambridge, Mass.: Harvard University Press, 1985).

Freud, S., *A Phylogenetic Fantasy: Overview of the Transference Neuroses*, ed. I. Grubrich-Simitis (Cambridge, Mass.: Belknap Press, 1987).

Freud, S., S. Ferenczi, K. Abraham, E. Simmel, and E. Jones, *Zur Psychoanalyse der Kriegneurosen* (Leipzig and Vienna: Internationaler psychoanalytischer Verlag, 1919).

Freud, S. and W. C. Bullitt, *Thomas Woodrow Wilson: Twenty- eighth President of the United States: A Psychological Study* (London: Weidenfeld and Nicolson, 1967).

Freud, S. and O. Pfister, *Psycho-Analysis and Faith: The Letters of Sigmund Freud and Oskar Pfister*, eds E. L. Freud and H. Meng (London: Hogarth Press, 1963).

Freud, S. and K. Abraham, *A Psycho-Analytic Dialogue: The Letters of Sigmund Freud and Karl Abraham 1907–1926 (Freud/Abraham)*, eds H. C. Abraham and E. L. Freud (London: Hogarth Press, 1965).

Freud, S. and C. G. Jung, *The Freud/Jung Letters: The Correspondence between Sigmund Freud and C. G. Jung*, ed. W. McGuire (London: Routledge and Kegan Paul, 1974).

Fromm, E., *The Crisis of Psychoanalysis: Essays on Freud, Marx and Social Psychology* (Harmondsworth: Penguin, 1978).

Fromm, E., *The Anatomy of Human Destructiveness* (Harmondsworth: Penguin, 1977).

Frosh, S., *The Politics of Psychoanalysis: An Introduction to Freudian and Post-Freudian Theory* (Houndmills: Macmillan, 1987).

Gabriel, Y., *Freud and Society* (London: Routledge and Kegan Paul, 1983).

Gaupp, R., 'Schreckneurose und Neurasthenie', in Schjerning (ed.) *Handbuch der ärztlichen Erfahrungen*.

Gay, P., *Freud, Jews and Other Germans: Masters and Victims in Modernist Culture* (New York: Oxford University Press, 1978).

Gay, P., 'Freud and freedom: On a fox in a hedgehog's clothing', in Ryan (ed.), *Idea of Freedom*.

Gay, P., *A Godless Jew: Freud, Atheism, and the Making of Psychoanalysis* (New Haven: Yale University Press, 1987).

Gelfand, T., 'Charcot's response to Freud's rebellion', *Journal of the History of Ideas* 50 (1989): 293–307.

Gellner, E., *The Psychoanalytic Movement: Or the Cunning of Unreason* (London: Granada, 1985).

Gill, M. M., 'Metapsychology is not psychology', in Gill and Holzman (eds), *Psychology Versus Metapsychology*.

Gill, M. M. and P. S. Holzman (eds), *Psychology Versus Metapsychology* (New York: International Universities Press, 1976; *Psychological Issues*, vol. IX).

Gilman, S. L., 'Jewish jokes: Sigmund Freud and the hidden language of the Jews', *Psychoanalysis and Contemporary Thought* 7 (1984): 591–614.

Gilman, S. L., 'Jews and mental illness: Medical metaphors, anti-Semitism and the Jewish response', *Journal of the History of the Behavioral Sciences* 20 (1984): 150–9.

Gilman, S. L., *Difference and Pathology: Stereotypes of Sexuality, Race, and Madness* (Ithaca: Cornell University Press, 1985).

Gilman, S. L., 'Sexology, psychoanalysis, and degeneration: From a theory of race to a race of theory', in Chamberlin and Gilman (eds) *Degeneration*.

Gilman, S. L., *Freud, Race, and Gender* (Princeton: Princeton University Press, 1993).

Gilman, S. L., H. King, R. Porter, G. S. Rousseau, and E. Showalter *Hysteria Beyond Freud* (Berkeley: University of California Press, 1993).

Gilman, S. L., 'The image of the hysteric', in Gilman et. al. (eds), *Hysteria Beyond Freud*.

Ginneken, J. van, 'The killing of the father: The background of Freud's group psychology', *Political Psychology* 5 (1984): 391–414.

Ginneken, J. van, 'The 1895 debate on the origins of crowd psychology', *Journal of the History of the Behavioral Sciences* 21 (1985): 375–82.

Glass, J. M., 'Hobbes and narcissism: Pathology in the state of nature', *Political Theory* 8 (1980): 335–63.

Glass, J. M., 'Notes on the paranoid factor in political philosophy: Fear, anxiety, and domination', *Political Psychology* 9 (1988): 209–28.

Goetz, C. G., 'Commentary', in J. M. Charcot, *Charcot, the Clinician: The Tuesday Lessons*, trans. C. G. Goetz (New York: Raven Press, 1987).

Goldstein, J., 'The hysteria diagnosis and the politics of anticlericalism in late nineteenth-century France', *Journal of Modern History*, 54 (1982): 209–39.

Goldstein, J., 'The Wandering Jew and the problem of psychiatric anti-Semitism in fin-de-siècle France', *Journal of Contemporary History*, 20 (1985): 521–51.

Goldstein, J., *Console and Classify: The French Psychiatric Profession in the Nineteenth Century* (Cambridge: Cambridge University Press, 1987).

Gould, S. J., *Ontogeny and Phylogeny* (London: Belknap Press, 1977).

Graf, M., 'Reminiscences of Professor Sigmund Freud', *The Psychoanalytic Quarterly* 11 (1942): 465–76.

Greenfield, W. S. and W. C. Lewis (eds), *Psychoanalysis and Current Biological Thought* (Madison: University of Wisconsin Press, 1965).

Grossman, W. I. and B. Simon, 'Anthropomorphism: Motives, meaning and causality in Psychoanalytic Theory', *Psychoanalytic Study of the Child* 24 (1969): 78–114.

Grotjahn, M., 'Karl Abraham', in Alexander, Eisenstein and Grotjahn (eds) *Psychoanalytic Pioneers*.

Grünbaum, A., *The Foundations of Psychoanalysis: A Philosophical Critique* (Berkeley: University of California Press, 1984).

Habermas, J., *Knowledge and Human Interests* (London: Heinemann, 1978).

Hale, N. G. (ed.), *Freud and the Americans* (New York: Oxford University Press, 1971).

Hanly, C., 'The concept of truth in psychoanalysis', *International Journal of Psycho-Analysis* 71 (1990): 375–83.

Hegar, A., 'On the sham castration performed by Dr. Israel', in Masson (ed.), *A Dark Science*.

Hoffman, L. E., 'War, revolution, and psychoanalysis: Freudian thought begins to grapple with social reality', *Journal of the History of the Behavioral Sciences* 17 (1981): 251–69.

Holt, R. R., 'A review of some of Freud's biological assumptions and their influence on his theories', in Greenfield and Lewis (eds), *Psychoanalysis and Current Biological Thought*.

Holt, R. R., 'Freud's mechanistic and humanistic images of man', in Holt and Peterfreund (eds), *Psychoanalysis and Contemporary Science*, vol. 1.

Hoppe, H., *Krankheiten und Sterblichkeit bei Juden und Nichtjuden: Mit besonderer Berücksichtigung der Alkoholfrage* (Berlin: Calvary, 1903).

Horowitz, G., *Basic and Surplus Repression in Psychoanalytic Theory: Freud, Reich and Marcuse* (Toronto: University of Toronto Press, 1977).

Hutton, P. H., 'Foucault, Freud and the technologies of the self', in Martin, Gutman and Hutton (eds), *Technologies of the Self: A Seminar with Michel Foucault*.

Isaac, J. C., *Power and Marxist Theory: A Realist View* (Ithaca: Cornell University Press, 1987).

Israels, H. and M. Schatzman, 'The seduction theory', *History of Psychiatry* 4 (1991): 23–59.

Jacoby, R., *Social Amnesia: A Critique of Conformist Psychology from Adler to Laing* (Hussocks: Harvester Press, 1975).

Jacoby, R., *The Repression of Psychoanalysis: Otto Fenichel and the Political Freudians* (New York: Basic Books, 1983).

James, W., 'Degeneration. Max Nordau', *The Psychological Review* 2 (1895): 289–90.

Jones, E., *Life and Work of Sigmund Freud*, 3 vols. (New York: Basic Books, 1953–57).

Keegan, J., *The Face of Battle: A Study of Agincourt, Waterloo and the Somme* (Harmondsworth: Penguin, 1978).

Kermode, F., *The Classic: Literary Images of Permanence and Change* (Cambridge, Mass.: Harvard University Press, 1983).

Kitcher, P., *Freud's Dream: A Complete Interdisciplinary Science of Mind* (Cambridge, Mass.: MIT Press, 1992).

Klein, D. B., 'Assimilation and dissimilation', *New German Critique* 19 (Winter 1980): 151–65.

Klein, D. B., *Jewish Origins of the Psychoanalytic Movement* (New York: Praeger, 1981).

Klein, G., 'Freud's two theories of sexuality', in Berger (ed.), *Clinical Cognitive Psychology*.

Klein, M. H., 'Throwing out the baby with the bathwater: A historical analysis of the antimetapsychology movement, *Psychoanalysis and Contemporary Thought* 12 (1989): 565–98.

Kline, P., *Fact and Fantasy in Freudian Theory* (London: Methuen, 1972).

Kovel, J., *The Radical Spirit: Essays on Psychoanalysis and Society* (London: Free Association Books, 1988).

Krafft-Ebing, R., *Nervosität und neurasthenische Zustände* (Vienna: Hödler, 1895).

Krafft-Ebing, R., *Psychopathia Sexualis: Mit Besonderer Berücksichtigung der konträren Sexualempfindungen. Eine medizinisch-gerichtliche Studie for Ärzte und Juristen* (Stuttgart: Enke, 1918; 15th edition).

Krafft-Ebing, R., *Psychopathia Sexualis: A Medico-Forensic Study*, tr. H. E. Wedeck (New York: Putnam, 1965).

Lacan, J., *Écrits: A Selection* (New York: W. W. Norton, 1977).

Lacan, J., *The Four Fundamental Concepts of Psychoanalysis* (New York: W. W. Norton, 1978).

Lakoff, G. and M. Johnson, *Metaphors We Live By* (Chicago: Chicago University Press, 1980).

Laplanche, J. and J.-B. Pontalis, *The Language of Psycho-Analysis* (London: Hogarth Press, 1980).

Laslett, P., 'The face to face society', in Laslett (ed.), *Philosophy, Politics and Society*.

Laslett, P. (ed.), *Philosophy, Politics and Society* (Oxford: Basil Blackwell, 1963).

Leary, D. E. (ed.), *Metaphors in the History of Psychology* (Cambridge: Cambridge University Press, 1990);

Le Bon, G., *The Crowd: A Study of the Popular Mind* (London: Ernest Benn, 1952).

Levin, K., *Freud's Early Psychology of the Neuroses* (Hussocks: Harvester Press, 1978)

Levine, M. G., 'Censorship's self-administration', *Psychoanalysis and Contemporary Thought* 9 (1986): 605–40.

Lewin, B. D., 'Metaphor, mind and manikin', *The Psychoanalytic Quarterly* 40 (1971): 6–39.

Lichtman, R., *The Production of Desire: The Integration of Psychoanalysis into Marxist Theory* (New York: The Free Press, 1982).

Lombroso, C., *Genie und Irrsinn in ihren Beziehungen zum Gesetz, zur Kritik und zur Geschichte* (Leipzig: Reclam, 1887).

Lombroso, C., *The Man of Genius* (London: Scott, 1891).

Lombroso, C., *Der Antisemitismus und die Juden im Lichte der modernen Wissenschaft* (Leipzig: Wigand, 1894).

Lorand, S., 'Sandor Ferenczi', in Alexander, Eisenstein and Grotjahn (eds) *Psychoanalytic Pioneers*.

Löwenfeld, L., *Die nervösen Störungen sexuellen Ursprungs* (Wiesbaden: n.p., 1891).

Lukes, S., *Power: A Radical View* (London: Macmillan, 1974).

Lutz, T., *American Nervousness, 1903: An Anecdotal History* (Ithaca: Cornell University Press, 1991).

McClelland, J. S., *The Crowd and the Mob: From Plato to Canetti* (London: Unwin, 1989).

McGrath, W. J. M., 'Freud as Hannibal: The politics of the brother band', *Central European History* 7 (1974): 31–57.

McGrath, W. J. M., *Freud's Discovery of Psychoanalysis: The Politics of Hysteria* (Ithaca: Cornell University Press, 1986).

McGrath, W. J. M., 'Oedipus at Berggasse 19', *New York Review of Books*, 18 August 1988, pp. 25–9.

MacIntyre, A., *The Unconscious* (London: Routledge and Kegan Paul, 1958).

Macpherson, C. B., *The Political Theory of Possessive Individualism* (Oxford: Clarendon Press, 1962).

Mahony, P., *Freud as a Writer* (New York: International Universities Press, 1982).

Maik, L. L., 'Nordau's *Degeneration*: The American controversy', *Journal of the History of Ideas* 50 (1989): 607–23.

Marcuse, H., *Eros and Civilization: A Philosophical Inquiry into Freud* (Boston: Beacon Press, 1966).

Marcuse, H., *Five Lectures: Psychoanalysis, Politics, and Utopia* (Boston, Beacon Press, 1970).

Martin, L. H., H. Gutman and P. H. Hutton (eds), *Technologies of the Self: A Seminar with Michel Foucault* (London: Tavistock, 1988).

Masson, J. M., *Freud: The Assault on Truth: Freud's Suppression of the Seduction Theory* (London: Faber, 1984).

Masson, J. M. (ed.), *A Dark Science: Women, Sexuality and Psychiatry in the Nineteenth Century* (New York: Farrar, Straus and Giroux, 1986).

Micale, M. S., 'Hysteria and its historiography: A review of past and present writings (II)', *History of Science* 27 (1989): 319–51.

Micale, M. S., 'Charcot and the idea of hysteria in the male: A study of gender, mental science and medical diagnostics in late nineteenth century France', *Medical History* 34 (1990): 363–411.

Miller, A., *Thou Shalt not Be Aware: Society's Betrayal of the Child* (London: Pluto Press, 1984).

Miller, E. F., 'Metaphor and political knowledge', *American Political Science Review* 73 (1979): 155–70.

Miller, J. 'Interpretations of Freud's Jewishness, 1924–1974', *Journal of the History of the Behavioral Sciences* 17 (1981): 357–74.

Mitchell, J., *Psychoanalysis and Feminism* (Harmondsworth: Penguin, 1974).

Mitchell, S. W., *Fat and Blood: An Essay on the Treatment of Certain Forms of Neurasthenia and Hysteria*, 3rd edn (Philadelphia: J. B. Lippincott, 1884).

Moi, T., 'Representation of patriarchy: Sexuality and epistemology in Freud's *Dora*', in Bernheimer and Kahane (eds), *In Dora's Case*.

Morel, B. A., *Traité des dégénérences physiques, intéllectuelles et morales de l'espèce humaine et des causes qui produisent ces variétés maladives* (Paris: Ballière, 1857).

Moscovici, S., *The Age of the Crowd: A Historical Treatise on Mass Psychology* (Cambridge: Cambridge University Press, 1985).

Mosse, G. L., 'Nationalism and respectability: Normal and abnormal sexuality in the nineteenth century', *Journal of Contemporary History* 17 (1982): 221–46.

Müller, F. C., *Handbuch der Neurasthenie* (Leipzig: Vogel, 1893).

Nelson, J. S., A. Megill and D. N. McCloskey (eds), *The Rhetoric of the Human Sciences: Language and Argument in Scholarship and Public Affairs* (Madison: University of Wisconsin Press, 1987).

Niederland, W. G., *The Schreber Case: Psychoanalytic Profile of a Paranoid Personality* (New York: Quadrangle, 1974).

Nonne, M., 'Therapeutische Erfahrungen an den Kriegsneurosen in den Jahren 1914–1918', in Schjerning (ed.), *Handbuch der Ärztlichen Erfahrungen*.

Nordau, M., *Degeneration* (London: Heinemann, 1920).

Nunberg, H. and E. Federn (eds), *Minutes of the Vienna Psychoanalytic Society*, 3 vols (New York: International Universities Press, 1962–74).

Nussbaum, C., 'Habermas and Grünbaum on the logic of psychoanalytic explanations', *Philosophy and Social Criticism* 17 (1991): 193–216.

Nye, R. A., *The Origins of Crowd Psychology: Gustave LeBon and the Crisis of Mass Democracy in the Third Republic* (London: Sage, 1975).

Nye, R. A., 'Degeneration and the medical model of cultural crisis in the French *Belle Epoque*', in Drescher et. al. (eds), *Political Symbolism in Modern Europe*.

Nye, R. A., *Crime, Madness and Politics In Modern France: The Medical Concept of National Decline* (Princeton: Princeton University Press, 1984).

Oakeshott, M., *Hobbes on Civil Association* (Oxford: Clarendon Press, 1975).

Obholzer, K., *The Wolf-Man Sixty Years Later: Conversations with Freud's Controversial Patient*, trans. M. Shaw (London: Routledge and Kegan Paul, 1982).

O'Brien, M., *The Politics of Reproduction* (London: Routledge and Kegan Paul, 1981).

Ornston, D., 'Strachey's influence: A preliminary report', *International Journal of Psycho-Analysis* 63 (1982): 409–26.

Oxaal, I., 'The Jewish origins of psychoanalysis reconsidered', in Timms and Segal (eds), *Freud in Exile*.

Panel Report, 'The concept of psychic energy', *Journal of the American Psychoanalytic Association* 11 (1963): 605–18.

Panel Report, 'Psychic energy reconsidered', *Journal of the American Psychoanalytic Association* 24 (1976): 647–57.

Paul, R. A., 'Freud and the seduction theory: A critical examination of Masson's *Freud: The Assault On Truth*', *Journal of Psychoanalytic Anthropology* 8 (1985): 161–87.

Peck, J. S. 'Ernst Simmel', in Alexander, Eisenstein and Grotjahn (eds), *Psychoanalytic Pioneers*.

Pick, D., 'The faces of anarchy: Lombroso and the politics of criminal science in post-unification Italy', *History Workshop Journal* 21 (1986): 60–86.

Pick, D., *Faces of Degeneration: A European Disorder, c. 1848–c. 1918* (Cambridge: Cambridge University Press, 1989).

Pilcz, A., *Beitrag zur vergleichenden Rassenpsychiatrie* (Leipzig und Wien: Deuticke, 1906).

Pinsker, L., *Autoemanzipation!* (Berlin: Jüdischer Verlag, 1936).

Pitkin, H. F., *The Concept of Representation* (Berkeley: University of California Press, 1967).

Poirier, S., 'The Weir Mitchell rest cure: Doctor and patients', *Women's Studies* 10 (1983): 15–40.

Pönitz, K., *Die klinische Neuorientierung zum Hysterieproblem unter dem Einflusse der Kriegserfahrungen* (Berlin: J. Springer, 1921).

Porter, R., 'The body and the mind, the doctor and the patient: Negotiating hysteria', in S. L. Gilman et al. (eds), *Hysteria Beyond Freud* (Berkeley: University of California Press, 1993).

Rabinbach, A., *Human Motor: Energy, Fatigue and the Origins of Modernity* (Berkeley: University of California Press, 1992).

Reich, W., *Sex-Pol, Essays 1929–1934*, ed. L. Baxandall (New York: Random House, 1972).

Reich, W., *The Mass Psychology of Fascism* (Harmondsworth: Penguin, 1975).

Rice, E., *Freud and Moses: The Long Journey Home* (New York: State University of New York Press, 1990).

Richards, B., *Images of Freud: Cultural Responses to Psychoanalysis* (London: J. M. Dent, 1989).

Ricoeur, P., *Freud and Philosophy: An Essay on Interpretation* (New Haven: Yale University Press, 1970).

Rieff, P., *Freud: The Mind of the Moralist* (London: Methuen, 1965).

Rieff, P., *The Triumph of the Therapeutic* (Harmondsworth: Penguin, 1966).

Rieff, P., *The Feeling Intellect: Selected Writings*, ed. J. B. Imber (Chicago: University of Chicago Press, 1990).

Roazen, P., *Brother Animal: The Story of Freud and Tausk* (New York: A. A. Knopf, 1969).

Rieff, P., *Freud: Political and Social Thought* (New York: Random House, 1970).

Rieff, P., *Freud and His Followers* (Harmondsworth: Penguin, 1979).

Rieff, P., 'Psychoanalytic ethics: Edoardo Weiss, Freud and Mussolini', *Journal of the History of the Behavioral Sciences* 27 (1991): 366–74.

Robert, M., *From Oedipus to Moses: Freud's Jewish Identity* (Garden City: Anchor/Doubleday, 1976).

Robinson, P., *Freud and His Critics* (Berkeley: University of California Press, 1993).

Roith, E., *The Riddle of Freud: Jewish Influences on his Theory of Female Sexuality* (London: Tavistock, 1987).

Rorty, R., *Essays on Heidegger and Others, Philosophical Papers*, vol. 2 (Cambridge: Cambridge University Press, 1991).

Rothman, S. and P. Isenberg, 'Sigmund Freud and the politics of marginality', *Central European History* 7 (1974): 58–78.

Roustang, F., *Dire Mastery: Discipleship from Freud to Lacan* (Baltimore: Johns Hopkins University Press, 1982)

Ruitenbeek, W. (ed.), *Freud As We Knew Him* (Detroit: Wayne State University Press, 1973).

Rustin, M., 'The social organization of secrets: Towards a sociology of psychoanalysis', *International Review of Psycho-Analysis* 12 (1985): 143–59.

Ryan, A. (ed.), *The Idea of Freedom: Essays in Honour of Isaiah Berlin* (Oxford: Oxford University Press, 1979).

Rycroft, C., *The Innocence of Dreams* (Oxford: Oxford University Press, 1981).

Sandler, J., 'The background of safety', *International Journal of Psychoanalysis* 41 (1960): 352–6.

Sandler, J., 'On the concept of the superego', *Psychoanalytic Study of the Child* 15 (1960): 128–62.

Sandler, J., A. Holder and D. Meers, 'The ego ideal and the ideal self', *Psychoanalytic Study of the Child* 18 (1963): 139–58.

Saussure, R. de, 'Sigmund Freud', in Ruitenbeek (ed.), *Freud As We Knew Him*.

Schatzman, M., *Soul Murder: Persecution in the Family* (New York: Random House, 1973).

Schjerning, O. (ed.), *Handbuch der Ärztlichen Erfahrungen im Weltkriege 1914/18* (Leipzig: Barth, 1922/34; vol. IV of K. Bonhoeffer (ed.), *Geistes und Nervenkrankheiten*).

Schneider, W., 'Toward the improvement of the human race: The history of eugenics in France', *Journal of Modern History* 54 (1982): 268–91.

Schorske, C. E., *Fin-de-Siècle Vienna: Politics and Culture* (Cambridge: Cambridge University Press, 1981).

Shaw, G. B., *The Sanity of Art* (New York: Boni and Liveright, 1918).

Sheleff, L., *Generations Apart: Adult Hostility to Youth* (New York: McGraw-Hill, 1981).

Showalter, E., *The Female Malady: Women, Madness, and English Culture, 1830–1980* (London: Virago, 1987).

E. Showalter, 'Hysteria, feminism, and gender', in S. L. Gilman et al., *Hysteria Beyond Freud* (Berkeley: University of California Press, 1993).

Sichel, M., *Die Geistesstörungen bei den Juden* (Leipzig: Kaufmann, 1909).

Sichel, M., 'Die progressive Paralyse bei den Juden', *Archiv für Psychiatrie* 52 (1913): 1030–42.

Simmel, E., 'Zweites Korreferat', in S. Freud et al., *Zur Psychoanalyse der Kriegneurosen*.

Skinner, Q., *The Foundations of Modern Political Thought*, 2 vols (Cambridge: Cambridge University Press, 1978).

Skinner, Q., 'A reply to my critics', in Tully (ed.) *Meaning and Context*.

Smith-Rosenberg, C., 'The hysterical woman: Sex roles and role conflict in 19th-century America', *Social Research* 39 (1972): 652–78.

Spence, D. P., *The Freudian Metaphor: Toward Paradigm Change in Psychoanalysis* (New York: W. W. Norton, 1987).

Sprengnether, M., *The Spectral Mother: Freud, Feminism and Psychoanalysis* (Ithaca: Cornell University Press, 1990).

Steele, R. S., 'Psychoanalysis and hermeneutics', *International Review of Psychoanalysis* 6 (1979): 389–409.

Stekel, W., *The Autobiography of Wilhelm Stekel: The Life Story of a Pioneer Psychoanalyst*, ed. E. A. Gutheil (New York: Liveright, 1950).

Stepansky, P. E., *A History of Aggression in Freud* (New York: International Universities Press, 1977; *Psychological Issues*, vol. X).

Stepansky, P. E. (ed.), *Freud: Appraisals and Reappraisals, Contributions to Freud Studies*, 3 vols (Hillsdale N. J.: Analytic Press, 1986).

Stewart, L., 'Freud before Oedipus: Race and heredity in the origins of psychoanalysis', *Journal of the History of Biology* 9 (1976): 215–28.

Stone, M., 'Shellshock and the psychologists', in Bynum, Porter and Shepherd (eds), *Anatomy of Madness*, vol. 2.

Strachey, J., 'Editor's introduction', in Freud, *Standard Edition*, vol. II.

Strachey, J., 'Appendix', in Freud, *Standard Edition*, vol. III.

Strachey, J., 'Editor's introduction', in Freud, *Standard Edition*, vol. XIV.

Strenger, C., *Between Hermeneutics and Science: An Essay on the Epistemology of Psychoanalysis* (New York: International Universities Press, 1991; *Psychological Issues*, Monograph 59).

Sulloway, F. J., *Freud, Biologist of the Mind: Beyond the Psychoanalytic Legend* (London: Burnett/André Deutsch, 1979).

Sulloway, F. J., 'Reassessing Freud's case histories: The social construction of psychoanalysis', *Isis* 82 (1991): 245–75.

Swaan, de A., 'Zur Soziogenese des psychoanalytischen "Settings" ', *Psyche* 32 (1978): 793–825.

Swales, P. J., 'Freud, his teacher and the birth of psychoanalysis', in Stepansky (ed.) *Freud: Appraisals and Reappraisals*, vol. 1.

Swanson, D. R., 'A critique of psychic energy as an explanatory concept', *Journal of the American Psychoanalytic Association* 25 (1977): 603–33.

Tausk, V., 'On the psychology of the war deserter', *The Psychoanalytic Quarterly* 38 (1969): 354–81.

Taylor, A. J. P., *Illustrated History of the First World War* (New York, Putnam, 1964).

Taylor, C., 'Interpretation and the sciences of man', *Review of Metaphysics* 25 (1971): 3–51.

Timms, E. and N. Segal (eds), *Freud in Exile: Psychoanalysis and its Vicissitudes* (New Haven: Yale University Press, 1988).

Tomaselli, S. and R. Porter (eds), *Rape* (Oxford: Oxford University Press, 1986).

Tully, J., 'The pen is a mighty sword', in Tully (ed.), *Meaning and Context*.

Tully, J. (ed.), *Meaning and Context: Quentin Skinner and his Critics* (Princeton: Princeton University Press, 1988).

Turkle, S., *Psychoanalytic Politics: Freud's French Revolution* (New York: Basic Books, 1978).

Viderman, S., 'The analytic space: Meaning and problems', *The Psychoanalytic Quarterly* 48 (1979): 257–91.

Vogt, H., 'Die Neurosen im Kriege', in O. Hezel, et al., *Die Kriegsbeschädigungen des Nervensystems* (Wiesbaden: Bergmann, 1917).

Warner, S. L., 'Fourteen Wilsonian points for Freud and Bullitt', *Journal of the American Academy of Psychoanalysis* 16 (1988): 479–89.

Wartenberg, T. E., *The Forms of Power: From Domination to Transformation* (Philadelphia: Temple University Press, 1990).

Wartenberg, T. E., 'Social movements and individual identity: A critique of Freud and the psychology of groups', *The Philosophical Forum* 22 (1991): 362–82.

Wartenberg, T. E., 'Situated social power', in Wartenberg (ed.), *Rethinking Power*.

Wartenberg, T. E., *Rethinking Power* (Albany, N. Y.: New York State University Press, 1992).

Weber, S. *Institution and Interpretation* (Minneapolis: University of Minnesota Press, 1987).

Weinstein, F. and G. M. Platt, *The Wish to be Free: Society, Psyche and Value Change* (Berkeley: University of California Press, 1969).

Weinstein, F. and G. M. Platt, *Psychoanalytic Sociology* (Baltimore: Johns Hopkins University Press, 1973).

Weisz, G., 'Scientists and sectarians: The case of psychoanalysis', *Journal of the History of the Behavioral Sciences* 11 (1975): 350–64.

Wietfeldt, H., *Kriegsneurose als psychisch-soziale Mangelkrankheit* (Leipzig: Thieme, 1936).

Wolfenstein, E. V., 'A man knows not where to have it: Habermas, Grünbaum and the epistemological status of psychoanalysis', *International Review of Psycho-Analysis* 17 (1990): 23–45.

Wolfenstein, E. V., *Psychoanalytic-Marxism: Groundwork* (London: Free Association Books, 1993).

Wurmser, L., 'A defense of the use of metaphor in analytic theory formation' *The Psychoanalytic Quarterly* 46 (1977): 466–98.

Yerushalmi, Y. H., *Freud's Moses: Judaism Terminable and Interminable* (New Haven: Yale University Press, 1991).

Zashin, E. and P. C. Chapman, 'The uses of metaphor and analogy: Toward a renewal of political language', *Journal of Politics* 36 (1974): 290–326.

Zilboorg, G., *History of Medical Psychology* (New York: W. W. Norton, 1941).

Index